# SUCH SPLENDID PRISONS

# Such Splendid Prisons

## Diplomatic Detainment in
## America during World War II

HARVEY SOLOMON

POTOMAC BOOKS
AN IMPRINT OF THE UNIVERSITY OF NEBRASKA PRESS

Library of Congress
Cataloging-in-Publication Data
Names: Solomon, Harvey, author.
Title: Such splendid prisons: diplomatic
detainment in America during
World War II / Harvey Solomon.
Description: [Lincoln]: Potomac Books,
an imprint of the University of Nebraska
Press, [2020] | Includes bibliographical
references and index. | Summary:
"Harvey Solomon tells the vivid story
of the roundup, captivity, and eventual
repatriation of Axis diplomats and
their families who were stranded in the
nation's capital after the bombing of
Pearl Harbor"—Provided by publisher.

Identifiers: LCCN 2019015764
ISBN 9781640120846 (cloth: alk. paper)
ISBN 9781640122871 (epub)
ISBN 9781640122888 (mobi)
ISBN 9781640122895 (pdf)
Subjects: LCSH: World War,
1939–1945—Prisoners and prisons,
American. | Prisoners of war—
United States—Biography. |
Diplomats—Germany—Biography. |
Diplomats—Japan—Biography. |
Diplomatic and consular service,
German—United States—History—20th
century. | Diplomatic and consular service,
Japanese—United States—History—
20th century. | Germans—Government
policy—United States—History—20th
century. | Japanese—Government
policy—United States—History—20th
century. | World War, 1939–1945—
Diplomatic history. | United
States—Foreign relations—20th century.
Classification: LCC D805.U5 S65
2020 | DDC 940.53/1773—dc23
LC record available at https://
lccn.loc.gov/2019015764

Set in New Baskerville ITC by
Mikala R. Kolander.
Designed by N. Putens.

To those unsung Americans—men and women, black and white and brown, old and young, native and foreign born—who pitched in to do the right thing at the right time:

auditors, bakers, bathhouse attendants, bellmen, boiler inspectors, bookkeepers, bootblacks, border patrol agents, busboys, cabinet makers, carpenters, cashiers, casino chefs, cafeteria helpers, checkers, chefs, cleaners, coal truck drivers, cold meat men, cottage cleaners, desk clerks, dishwashers, electricians, elevator mechanics and operators, engineers, exterminators, extractors, FBI agents, firemen, fry cooks, gardeners, golf course managers, house physicians, housekeepers, ice plant operators, icemen, incinerator operators, interior decorators, ironers, janitors, laborers, laundry managers, linen women, lobbymen, locker boys, maids, mail clerks, managers, mangel girls, masons, masseurs and masseuses, mechanics, medical directors, movie operators, musicians, painters, pastry helpers, plasterers, plumbers, porters, press girls, printers, purchasing agents, receiving clerks, salad makers, sauce cooks, seamstresses, secretaries, shakers, starchers, State Department agents, state police, stewards, swimming instructors, taxi drivers, technicians, telephone operators, tennis pros and managers, tinners, tree surgeons, upholsterers, utility men, waiters and waitresses, watchmen, and yardsmen.

This book is for them and their families.

# CONTENTS

# ILLUSTRATIONS

# DRAMATIS PERSONAE

**Else Arnecke** German emigré lured from the Waldorf Astoria Hotel to work at the German embassy

**Robert Bannerman** State Department agent overseeing the detainment, specialized in logistics

**Adolf Berle Jr.** U.S. assistant secretary of state, 1938–44

**Francis Biddle** U.S. attorney general, 1941–45

**Margret Boveri** Freelance German journalist and close friend of journalist Paul Scheffer

**Charles Brousse** French press attaché and Allied intelligence agent who worked with (and later married) undercover agent Betty Pack

**Charles Bruggmann** Swiss ambassador to the United States, 1939–54

**William Bullitt** U.S. ambassador to France, 1936–40

**Prince Ascanio dei Principi Colonna** Italian ambassador to the United States, 1939–42

**Hans Dieckhoff** German ambassador to the United States, 1937–38

**Helen Essary** Writer for the *Washington Times-Herald*

**Thomas Fitch** Washington DC–based State Department agent overseeing the detainment

**Bella Fromm** Jewish freelance writer based in Berlin, later emigrated to the United States

**Evelyn Peyton Gordon** Writer for the *Washington Daily News*

**Don Joaquin Rodríguez de Gortázar** Spanish diplomat and liaison to the Japanese detainees

**Gaston Henry-Haye** Ardent Pétainist and French ambassador to the United States, 1940–43

**Cordell Hull** U.S. secretary of state, 1933–44

**Sadao Iguchi**  First secretary at the Japanese embassy and spokesman for the detainees at the Homestead and Greenbrier

**Takeo Iguchi**  Keen-eyed eleven-year-old son of counselor Sadao Iguchi and classmate of Mariko Terasaki

**Adolfo Infante**  Military attaché at the Italian embassy

**Fay Ingalls**  Owner of the Homestead hotel

**Laura Ingalls**  Pilot, America First speaker, and Nazi sympathizer

**Loren Johnston**  General manager of the Greenbrier hotel

**Masuo Kato**  Washington DC correspondent for Japan's official Domei News Agency

**Clarke Kawakami**  Washington DC junior correspondent for Japan's official Domei News Agency

**Saburo Kurusu**  Veteran Japanese diplomat and special envoy to the United States, 1941–42

**John Lawler**  On-site FBI agent overseeing the detainment

**Helen Lombard**  Author and columnist for the *Washington Evening Star*

**Breckinridge Long**  Assistant secretary of state and overseer of the detainment, 1940–44

**Lord Lothian**  British ambassador to the United States, 1939–40

**Hans Luther**  German ambassador to the United States, 1933–37

**Robert McCormick**  Staunch anti–Franklin D. Roosevelt publisher of the *Chicago Daily Tribune*

**Harlan Miller**  Writer and columnist for the *Washington Post*

**Hope Ridings Miller**  Writer and society editor for the *Washington Post*

**Roy Morgan**  Chief on-site FBI agent overseeing the detainment

**Kichisaburo Nomura**  Japanese ambassador to the United States, 1941–42

**George O'Brien**  Assistant manager of the Greenbrier hotel

**John O'Hanley**  On-site State Department agent overseeing the detainment

**Hiroshi Oshima**  Japanese ambassador to Germany, 1938–39 and 1941–45, detained after the war in the United States

**Constantine Oumansky**  Russian ambassador to the United States, 1939–41

**Betty Pack**  Undercover Allied intelligence agent, code name Cynthia, who worked with and later married French press attaché Charles Brousse

**Eleanor "Cissy" Patterson** Staunch anti–Franklin D. Roosevelt publisher of the *Washington Times-Herald*

**Joseph Patterson** Staunch anti–Franklin D. Roosevelt publisher of the *New York Daily News*

**Raphael Pollio** General manager of the Mayflower Hotel

**Edward Poole** On-site State Department agent overseeing the detainment

**Jerzy Potocki** Polish ambassador to the United States, 1936–40

**Alberto Rossi Longhi** Counselor at the Italian embassy and spokesman for the detainees at the Greenbrier and Grove Park Inn

**Hirosi Saito** Japanese ambassador to the United States, 1934–39

**Paul Scheffer** Controversial German journalist and correspondent

**Carl Sennhenn** German embassy staffer and the only known German detainee to be convicted of war crimes

**Roy Sibold** Chief clerk of the Greenbrier

**George Slosson Jr.** General manager of the Homestead

**Charlie Spruks** Chief State Department official overseeing the detainment

**Frederick Stocker** Swiss liaison to the German and Italian detainees

**George Summerlin** Washington DC–based chief of Protocol division of the State Department and overseer of the detainment

**Wilhelm Tannenberg** German envoy and spokesman for the detainees at the Greenbrier

**Gwen Terasaki** American-born wife of Japanese intelligence agent Hidenari Terasaki

**Hidenari Terasaki** Undercover intelligence agent posing as a diplomat at the Japanese embassy

**Mariko Terasaki** Nine-year-old daughter of Hidenari and Gwen

**Dorothy Thompson** Well-known American journalist, columnist, and radio broadcaster

**Annaliese "Bébé" Thomsen** Wife of acting German ambassador to the United States Hans Thomsen

**Hans Thomsen** German chargé d'affaires and acting ambassador to the United States, 1936–42

**Friedrich von Boetticher** Military attaché at the German embassy

**Hildegard "Hildy" von Boetticher** College-aged daughter of the German military attaché

**Baron Ulrich von Gienanth** Envoy (and Gestapo agent) at the German embassy

**Dietrich** and **George von Knoop** Five- and nine-year-old sons, respectively, of German commercial attaché Theodore von Knoop

**Sumner Welles** U.S. under secretary of state, 1937–43

# AUTHOR'S NOTE

During the 1930s and 1940s, the United States was a far more racist and segregated country than it is today. Politicians, the press, and many everyday Americans routinely used language that now seems coarse and pejorative in describing black people, disabled people, Japanese people, and others. The author has retained much of this language verbatim, not to cause offense but to reflect accurately the tenor of the era.

# SUCH SPLENDID PRISONS

# Prologue

Sunday, December 7, 1941, dawns fair and chilly in the nation's capital. The lead story in the *Sunday Star* thunders, "Roosevelt Sends Note to Hirohito," calling the message "an extraordinary, perhaps last-chance move to put up to Japan the whole burden of the preservation of peace in the Pacific."[1]

But the winds of war have been blowing for years, and most everyone in town—and, indeed, all 132 million Americans—are hoping and praying that President Franklin Delano Roosevelt can stay true to his word and keep the United States out of another world war. "I have said this before, but I shall say it again and again and again," FDR intoned last year during a punishing campaign that won him an unprecedented third term. "Your boys are not going to be sent into any foreign wars."[2]

Throughout the day, clouds and sun vie for supremacy. Yet with no precipitation and temperatures reaching the low forties, it's a glorious pre-Christmas Sunday. Church bells ring throughout the city. Hitting newsstands is the new issue of *The American*, a general interest magazine whose cover, featuring a young girl under the mistletoe, teases but one story: "WE CAN WIN ON BOTH OCEANS, by Frank Knox, Secretary of the Navy." Inside, the introduction reads, "With our fighting ships in the thick of the Battle of the Atlantic, and hell ready to pop in the Pacific, the Secretary of the Navy now lays his cards on the table."[3] (Little did an unnamed magazine editorial staffer know that those words about the Pacific would prove so immediate and prophetic.)

On the last day of the regular season, some twenty-seven thousand football fans—including a young naval ensign named John F. Kennedy—pack aging Griffith Stadium to see the hometown Redskins mount a fourth-quarter comeback and defeat the Philadelphia Eagles, 20–14. Anyone not tempted by outdoor activities can catch Humphrey Bogart's latest, *The Maltese Falcon*, at several local theaters. Anticipating another slow Sunday, only two staffers man the Associated Press office at the National Press Building. Their top priority is trying to track down new Soviet ambassador Maxim Litvinov, arriving this morning at National Airport. Neither thinks he'll talk, but maybe they can get something from his English wife. In any event they order in lunch: peanut butter and bacon sandwiches.

Across the Potomac at Fort Myer, General George C. Marshall saddles up for a brisk morning horseback ride, a welcome break from the troubling war crisis. Upon returning to his office, he discovers that the Japanese ambassador, Admiral Kichisaburo Nomura, and Special Envoy Saburo Kurusu have requested an afternoon audience with Secretary of State Cordell Hull. CBS broadcaster Edward R. Murrow, just back from London, tees off at the exclusive Burning Tree golf course in Bethesda. Tonight he's headed to dinner at the White House to update FDR on how the Brits are bearing up. Yet today the president has a purposefully light schedule, only a 12:30 p.m. meeting with the Chinese ambassador. He wants to spend a leisurely Sunday afternoon enjoying his favorite pastime, his stamp collection. He's eager to tear into the envelope sent by the State Department every Saturday that contains the most interesting stamps culled from its daily 'round-the-world correspondence. Ah, the perks of the presidency.

After the ambassador departs he lunches with his constant confidant, Harry Hopkins, who lives just down the hall in the Lincoln Bedroom. FDR has declined his wife Eleanor's request to join yet another of her luncheons, this one for some thirty guests, featuring White House chef and housekeeper Henrietta Nesbitt's notoriously unappetizing food. As he thumbs through his stamp album, the phone rings. It's 1:47 p.m. Secretary Knox is calling to deliver the devastating news: an attack's underway at Pearl Harbor.

Yes, Pearl Harbor, seen up until today as an impregnable and highly unlikely target, as profiled last year in the *American Foreign Service Journal*, the house organ of the State Department: "By reason of Hawaii's great distance from foreign lands it can be readily understood how these islands, particularly with their present fortifications and fleet base facilities undergoing constant expansion and improvement, are well beyond the limits of any offensive action now foreseeable."[4]

Several miles north of the White House, many Japanese diplomats are gathering for the funeral of an assistant military attaché who died of pneumonia two days ago. The venerable S. H. Hines Co. funeral home, housed in a handsome turreted orange brick building on 14th Street NW, hosts the service. Slim, bespectacled journalist Masuo Kato, forty-three years old, correspondent for Japan's official Domei News Agency, is running late. He'd slept in and enjoyed an unhurried breakfast of pancakes with plenty of butter and maple syrup. Little does he know his griddle-cake days are about to be over. He writes two stories: a profile of the late attaché and an update on the precarious Japanese American relations, which he pegs at still having a one-in-three chance for peace.

Emerging from his apartment building, he hands both dispatches to a Western Union messenger and hails a cab. En route the blaring car radio reports that the Japanese have bombed Manila. "God damn Japan," cries the driver. "We'll lick [the] hell out of those bastards now!"[5] Kato wisely decides to keep his nationality to himself. He enters the funeral home's chapel, where the service has already begun. Sitting between a Japanese army officer and a reporter for a Tokyo daily, he quietly asks the officer if he's heard of the Manila attack. The man nods noncommittally. The reporter hasn't heard any news, so Kato suggests they investigate. As they tiptoe out he notices that neither Ambassador Nomura or Special Envoy Kurusu is present. Both had been expected to attend.

The two newsmen grab a cab for the Japanese embassy, a two-story cream-colored stone mansion that's especially beautiful in springtime with its pink cherry trees abloom but is quite stark now. A silent crowd of Americans has gathered out front but let the men enter the heavy iron gates unmolested. Inside Kato finally realizes that the Manila bombing, the only one he'd heard about, is by far the lesser event. The attack on Pearl Harbor has shocked not only the world but the embassy staff, including Nomura and Kurusu. Kept totally in the dark by their superiors in Tokyo, they had delivered a message to Hull earlier that afternoon announcing Japan's cessation of relations with the United States. Hull replied furiously as the pair sat silent and confused, ripping their "infamous falsehoods and distortions . . . on a scale so huge that I never imagined until today that any Government on this planet was capable of uttering them."

For his part, the shell-shocked Nomura might be thinking about the advice an old navy friend had given him last year before he took the job in America: "Be careful. The gang around today are the kind who won't hesitate to pull the ladder out from under you once they've got you to climb up it."[6] In the embassy faces are wracked with anxiety, voices hushed. The atmosphere, Kato feels, is more akin to the funeral home he'd just left than the embassy of a country that just won a stunning, albeit deceitful, victory. One man somberly references the late attaché, saying, "Colonel Shinjo died at the right time."[7]

DC police surround the building "in which," wrote the *Baltimore Sun*, "when a window shade occasionally was lifted, little yellow men could be seen busily at work in their shirt sleeves."[8] Soon staffers are carrying boxes of documents into the gardens out back and setting them aflame. "One guy with a broom was chasing photographers," recalled Associated Press photographer Max Desfor, who went that day from the football game to the State Department to the embassy. "When they ran, we took pictures. When he chased us, the others took pictures."[9] (Desfor later won a Pulitzer Prize for his coverage of the Korean War.) By the time Kato leaves by a side door, the crowd outside has grown larger. And uglier. And vocal. It includes a contingent of Redskins players itching for some off-the-field payback. "We wanted to square the account," said lineman Clyde Shugart, who turned twenty-five that day, "if they were looking for a fistfight."[10] Amid jeers Kato jostles through hard angry faces. Before he can hail a cab a man approaches, saying, "You are the last son of a bitch we're going to let out."

Earlier on this mild Sunday afternoon, Tennessee native Gwen Harold Terasaki—thirty-five years old and married to Japanese diplomat Hidenari Terasaki—has a hankering for the kind of comfort food she grew up on. So the couple, along with her mother and their nine-year-old daughter, Mariko, drive off in his brand new Buick convertible—perhaps a little too fast for his mother-in-law's taste. For him it's a welcome break from the long, grueling hours spent toiling over the last few weeks as tensions have ratcheted up between Japan and America.

After eating at a favorite restaurant outside the city that serves down-home fried chicken and sweet potatoes, they drive back along the Potomac. He wants to stop by the embassy to catch up on the latest dispatches, which have been landing virtually nonstop from Tokyo for the last several days. So he drops the ladies at the Uptown Theater on Connecticut Avenue, just a few blocks from Woodley Park Towers, their apartment building. Mother, daughter, and granddaughter see an eminently forgettable romantic comedy with a portentous title: *Unfinished Business*.

Afterward, walking home past knots of people talking in hushed tones, Gwen Terasaki senses that something's amiss. Inside the lobby the desk clerk informs her that her husband has phoned several times and wants her to ring him back right away. After she hurries up to their apartment it takes several tries before she's connected, but his secretary says he's too busy to come to the phone. "What's wrong?" Gwen asks. The reply: "Don't you know? Then turn on your radio!"[11] He eventually returns her call, lamenting the day's events and unsure when he'll be able to call again since the telephones are about to be disconnected. Old friends ring her up continually to commiserate through a night she later recalls as one of "horror, grief and tears."

But what she and her friends don't know is that her handsome, able husband isn't actually a diplomat but the head of Japanese intelligence in America and that the FBI has been tailing them for months. "According to information from an outside highly confidential and reliable source," writes FBI Director J. Edgar Hoover to Adolf Berle Jr., assistant secretary of state, two days later, "while contacting his wife on December 7, 1941, [Hidenari] stated he was 'one hundred percent disgusted and terribly disappointed' over the situation. He further asserted that 'they' knew nothing about it, whereupon his wife comments she did not understand how 'they could do it to you three men,' meaning Nomura, Kurusu and her husband."[12] During her subsequent conversations with friends, the well-connected FBI source (e.g., a tapped phone line) reports that Gwen termed the Japanese attack "a bolt out of the blue."

Around the time the Terasaki women are at the movies, Hildegard von Boetticher, youngest daughter of the German military attaché, strolls through the campus of Randolph-Macon Woman's College in Lynchburg, Virginia. The spirited but naïve twenty-one-year-old is still spinning over last night's Christmas dance, for which she had served as committee chair. She and her latest beau, a medical student from North Carolina "with awfully cute dimples and a great smile," had glided across the floor to the strains of a "heavenly" big band. After breakfast at the Band Box, a local hangout, and a sweet kiss goodbye, she ambles toward the library to start a long-overdue sociology assignment, an essay on capital punishment. "It had been such a gloriously perfect week-end," she wrote later. "I didn't want it to end."[13]

Up runs her roommate with a breathless pronouncement: "Pearl Harbor has been bombed by the Japanese!" Annoyed by the roommate's theatrics, Hildy shrugs her shoulders and, after a quick exchange, continues on. But the library's typically quiet atmosphere is off, replaced by students abuzz over the news. Suddenly the import of the situation overwhelms her. She rushes back to her dorm, where beleaguered classmates are clogging the telephones on each landing. Some are tearfully trying to find out if their fathers and brothers serving in the navy are all right. Eventually she reaches her parents, who quietly explain that war between the United States and Germany is now inevitable. They'll undoubtedly soon be going home, so she must pack up and join them immediately. "I didn't want to come home," she wrote later. "I had the lead in the play. This was my last year, my graduation year. I stamped my foot. Damn! How could the Japanese interfere with all the activities so important to me?"[14]

After many years of ricocheting between belligerents in Europe and the Far East, all eyes—and enmity—in the nation's capital turn instantly toward the Japanese. Nary a word comes from adroit German chargé d'affaires and acting ambassador Hans Thomsen, then fifty years old, or his charming, sometimes confounding wife, Annaliese, forty-six. A smooth, unwavering voice for Nazism over the last six years, Thomsen quietly monitors the situation and cables Berlin in the evening, revealing an attitude never glimpsed in public. "The Japanese attack on Hawaii and the Philippines struck the American Government and the American people like a bolt of lightning," he writes, unconsciously echoing the same sentiments as Gwen Terasaki. "Bombastic prophesies that a war against Japan would be a 'promenade' have now been silenced."[15]

Later that night Kato dines at the home of American friends, who insist upon accompanying him back to his apartment building in case he's attacked. Their walk is uneventful, though two plainclothes FBI agents are waiting silently in the lobby. Safely back in his apartment, Kato takes a long hot bath before retiring, reasoning that it might be his last chance for a while. At 5:00 a.m. he's awoken by a sharp rapping at his door. He opens it to find the two well-dressed young agents. "Get dressed right away," says one, "and come with us."[16]

And so begins the relocation, isolation, and eventual repatriation of more than a thousand Axis power diplomats, families, staff, servants, journalists, businessmen, and, mixed in, spies. To posh mountaintop resorts they'll go.

# 1

## On the Diplomatic Front Lines

On the balmy spring day of April 28, 1937, a small group gathers for a farewell dinner at a house one block from Rock Creek Park. It's a leafy neighborhood of stately homes and sizable lawns, at least by the cramped standards of row house-dominated Washington DC. Congresswoman Hattie Caraway, the first woman elected to the Senate, lives next door. Outside there's nothing to distinguish this comfortable two-story yellow brick house in the 5300 block of Colorado Avenue NW from its neighbors. Inside it seems rather ordinary too, save for one conspicuous non-American decoration hanging over the mantelpiece: a large autographed picture of Adolf Hitler.

For its renters are silky-smooth embassy counselor Hans Thomsen and his wife, Annaliese. They're hosting this dinner to honor departing ambassador Hans Luther, Hitler's first envoy to America: an effusive fellow with a seemingly endless store of after-dinner jokes. Chubby and bald, he looks like the burgher on a beer stein. That's actually one of his favorite roles, hosting the embassy's popular annual *Bierabends* where staffers dress in Bavarian costumes, a band plays, and dexterous waiters—some clutching a half dozen mugs in one hand—serve up the suds 'til

3:00 a.m. Last year's beer night, actually a propaganda party in raucous disguise, drew a couple hundred revelers, including congressmen and newsmen. "Luther's roots were in old Germany, his class was the upper bourgeoisie," wrote Helen Lombard, both a member of the diplomatic set and a chronicler of its labyrinth ways. "He could sell the new regime by making it appear not too dangerously unlike the old."[1]

Yet four years after his arrival, peddling the Third Reich in America is becoming an increasingly hard sell—even in a city with so many isolationists and Anglophobes eager to swallow the bait. As Hitler's expansionist agenda is gradually becoming less cloaked, Foreign Minister Joachim von Ribbentrop has determined that the fifty-eight-year-old ex–Weimar Republic official is no longer the most appropriate messenger. No, Berlin wants an equally unthreatening but younger, fresher face to represent the new Germany. And tonight's host (and hostess), among other junior embassy staffers, are auditioning for the starring role.

Born in Hamburg on September 14, 1891, Thomsen was the second of four children; he had older and younger brothers and a younger sister. His mother, Elisabeth, was German, his father, Carlo, a Norwegian banker. "He comes from a wealthy, cultured family and has had a broad education," wrote Bella Fromm, a Jewish Berlin-based reporter. "He speaks seven languages, having been all over the world. He is quiet, reserved, and well liked by the diplomatic set."[2] His fluent English, spoken with an Oxford accent, can be a bit unnerving to people meeting him for the first time; it came courtesy of the family's English governess.

Thomsen graduated from Heidelberg University in 1913 and earned a law degree two years later. During the Great War—a term then used interchangeably with the World War—he served in the kaiser's army and forever thereafter, like many fellow soldiers, carried an engraved metal cigarette case as a reminder. Afterward he entered the diplomatic service and spent time in Albania, Italy, Norway, Switzerland, and Yugoslavia before serving Hitler directly as a minister in the Reich Chancellery in Berlin. At a party in 1933, Bella Fromm found that his "suave elegance" contrasted sharply with the plain-looking führer, who kissed her hand and engaged her in some stilted conversation. After he'd moved on, she asked Thomsen if Hitler had a cold. "Why?" he asked. She replied, "He's supposed to be able to smell a Jew ten miles away, isn't he? Apparently his sense of smell isn't working tonight."[3] Thomsen laughed, but not before casting a quick look around to see if anyone had heard.

An international journalist, well-traveled Venezuelan T. R. Ybarra, interviewed Mussolini once and Hitler twice during the early thirties. The second interview was arranged by Thomsen, whom Ybarra astutely measured as the chancellery brimmed with armed, strutting storm troopers. "These toughs contrasted ludicrously not only with their Fuehrer," wrote Ybarra, "but with the officials left over from the pre-Nazi era who were going about in regular, tradition-hallowed toggery as if ashamed of being in such company, looking—and doubtless feeling—like fish out of water. (When I showed the foregoing words, just after I had first typed them, to Hans Thomsen, he fixed wide open eyes on me and asked: 'Do you mean *me?*')"[4]

Thomsen's wife is called Bébé, which is French (the preferred language of diplomacy) for "baby." Her parents, Emil Oskar de Niem, a soldier in the kaiser's army, and Anna Barth, married in 1885. Annaliese was born on February 26, 1892, in Torgau, and her brother, Hans Dietrich, who like his father became a soldier, in December of 1893. With six uncles and two aunts, the de Niem children had many cousins and playmates growing up. She attended a private girl's school in Switzerland and learned English, French, and Italian. Serving as vice consul in Naples after the war, Thomsen commissioned an artist to make a bust of his head. Intrigued by the portrait of a young woman the artist was painting, Thomsen asked to meet her. The artist arranged a small party, the two hit it off, and a year later they married.

In the papers Bébé's usually referred to as Hungarian, though her "auburn locks and black eyes often cause her to be mistaken for a Spaniard or an Italian."[5] Similarly, her blond husband is invariably described as Norwegian, an inaccuracy he never corrects. In the coming years, as the American press continually refers to their nationalities as something other than German, the Thomsens don't mind; the reporters' sloppiness subtly reinforces the benign, friendly image that their bosses in Berlin are so eager for their emissaries to convey.

Conversation tonight might touch upon one of Luther's most recent

**Fig. 1.** Well-hatted ambassadors Hirosi Saito (Japan) and Hans Luther (Germany) share a word. Courtesy of DC Public Library, Washingtoniana Division.

difficulties. Last month, when discussing the upcoming 1939 World's Fair, New York Mayor Fiorello La Guardia had slammed Adolf Hitler: "I'd have a chamber of horrors and as a climax I'd have in it a figure of that brown-shirt fanatic who is now menacing the peace of the world."[6] His remarks touched off a firestorm on both sides of the Atlantic, with Thomsen hand-delivering a protest to the State Department and German newspapers viciously attacking La Guardia, whose mother was Jewish but was raised Episcopalian. "Dirty Talmud Jew Becomes Impudent," shouts the headline in *Völkischer Beobachter*, the Nazi Party's official newspaper.

A disagreeable situation most definitely, but nowhere near as ominous as an international event that's most certainly not on the menu for discussion tonight. Two days ago Spain's bloody civil war between its Republican government and the nationalist forces of General Francisco Franco burst into horrific worldwide view. Out of nowhere, planes swept down on the Basque village of Guernica during its busy once-a-week market day.

Bombers dropped high-explosive and incendiary bombs; fighters raked the panicked crowds with machine-gun fire. Sixteen hundred civilians were slaughtered, more than a third of the village's population; thousands more were injured. The town was obliterated. (The attack was immortalized by Pablo Picasso, who immediately created a huge mural-sized oil canvas entitled *Guernica.* Unveiled that summer in Paris, it initially garnered little attention but has since become recognized as a potent representation of war's destruction of innocent lives. When Picasso was living in occupied Paris during World War II, a Nazi officer visiting his apartment saw a photograph of the work and asked, "Did you do that?" To which Picasso replied, "No, you did.")

The reason for targeting a sleepy town with no strategic military value was unknown, but the perpetrators were not. The subhead of today's front-page story in the *Washington Post* reads "Planes Allegedly Piloted by Germans Mow Down Civilians on Clogged Highways."[7] The planes were not just piloted by Germans; they were German planes from the Condor Legion, a specialized division of the Luftwaffe. The raid was a real-life exercise to test and perfect its lethal aerial warfare. Several years later those tactics help power Nazi assaults across Europe, so overwhelming they'll introduce a fearsome new word into international lexicon: *blitzkrieg,* or "lightning war."

Every advance of the Nazi war machine will put another obstacle in the path of its envoys abroad, culminating in a conflagration that will eventually kill an estimated fifty million civilians worldwide. But the war's still several years away. Tonight is simply another chapter in the polished game of diplomatic musical chairs: the departure of one ambassador, the pending arrival of an unknown replacement. Though Hans Thomsen is too junior to be in the running, he and Bébé are prime operatives who personify Nazism's propaganda of sweetness and light. And the unsuspecting American press is lapping it up. "Herr Thomsen and his attractive wife are a great addition to the diplomatic corps," gushes society reporter Beth Blaine, who goes on to lavish especial praise on Bébé Thomsen. "Frau Thomsen is lovely looking, with dark, slanting eyes and masses of black curly hair, and she is a delightful hostess. Seldom have we seen so many delicious things to eat."[8]

Why, tonight alone she's set out a spread of—wait a minute! What's that she's wearing? Could it be . . . moving?

Yes, perched on her shoulder is a squirrel. A red squirrel she reportedly brought over from Europe, "an adorable little creature," continues Blaine breathlessly, "with tufted pointed ears and a great bushy tail!" His name is Bienchien, and not to be confused with Peterkins, their cocker spaniel that Thomsen is showing this weekend at the annual National Capital Kennel Club in nearby tony Chevy Chase. Yesterday the *Post* ran a photograph of Thomsen, in a flowered dress and wearing a single strand of pearls, holding the pooch.

Bébé Thomsen may be new to America, having sailed into New York harbor early last January aboard the SS *Hansa*. But her inordinate love of animals—even at the risk of others—is lifelong. Several years ago, when Thomsen was still stationed in Berlin, the couple befriended reporter Fromm, a courageous act in a country ostracizing Jews decree by decree. "Baby, his wife, is a merry, vivacious brunette with a passion for animals," Fromm wrote. "I remember once when I was visiting the Thomsens, I started to enter her dressing room. Suddenly, Tommy [a nickname for Hans Thomsen] shouted, 'Don't go in there! You'll get bitten!' When I asked what would bite me, he explained that Baby had a monkey that had been biting everyone. 'In fact, he bit me this morning,' said Tommy in a resigned voice."[9]

Stateside, the energetic if somewhat eccentric Bébé immediately plunges into the capital's de rigueur social scene. Though every city covers society, it's invariably a sidelight; here in the nation's capital it's the spotlight that never dims. "Some like it, some don't, but it's a *must*," writes W. M. Kiplinger, who later becomes best known for imparting financial advice in his namesake publications. "Society is a main course. In the city on the Potomac, where government is the biggest business, official position is more important than charm, money or background in winning friends and influencing people."[10]

From the outset Bébé displays *très chic* attire. At a cocktail party given by the counselor of the Swiss legation, Dr. Eduard Feer, and his wife, she's the only woman besides the hostess to merit a sartorial description: "Frau Thomsen, who is tall and attractive, wore a smart costume topped with

**Fig. 2.** Bébé and Hans Thomsen before departing for a White House diplomatic reception. Around his neck he wears a German Red Cross First Class Order; on his jacket are an Iron Cross, a Baden Faithful Service Medal, a Hanseatic Cross (Hamburg), an Honor Cross of the World War, and an Order of the Crown of Italy (information courtesy of George Borden). Library of Congress, Prints and Photographs Division, Harris and Ewing Collection.

a fox-trimmed dark velvet coat."[11] Four and half years later, immediately after Pearl Harbor, Feer will again host the Thomsens—and, indeed, the entire German delegation—but under far less happy circumstances.

Tonight, while the Thomsens are hosting and toasting the departing ambassador at their home, another old-school German envoy is pursuing a far less social but equally vital Nazi mission. A few miles south, Lieutenant General Friedrich von Boetticher, fifty-five, is lecturing at the Munitions Building, steps from the Lincoln Memorial. Hitler's first military attaché, a respected veteran of the Great War, is a pompous extrovert who hides in plain sight. He's a sanctioned observer of the American military whose stiff appearance is ripe for caricature. "A short, plump man of porcine features, with horizontal creases across the back of his neck, his reddish hair kept in a brush cut, he was often seen strolling the streets in full uniform with riding breeches, boots, monocle, his thick chest heavily ornamented with Nazi medals and insignia," wrote cub reporter David Brinkley, years before moving from print to broadcast and attaining fame for his fifty-year career as a television newsman.[12]

Actually von Boetticher never wore his hair in a brush cut or affected a monocle, but he did grandly strut a two-way street: supplying details of the German military to U.S. War Department officials in exchange for similar information about American armed forces. An officer (the highest-ranking foreign military official in America), scholar (with a keen knowledge of U.S. history), and gentleman, von Boetticher kept his fourth vocation—spy—as well as his virulent anti-Semitism—well hidden. Speaking perfect English thanks to his American-born mother, he ingratiates himself with many senior U.S. military officials who feel Germany had been treated unfairly after the Great War and are quietly more sympathetic to their former enemy than to England or France. He was "an evangelist who proclaimed an identity between the United States and Germany with himself as the bridge," wrote biographer Alfred M. Beck, "as indefatigable in his technical study of the American army as he was in courting its favor."[13]

On this late April evening, the staid von Boetticher is in his element: addressing an audience of U.S. Army reserve officers, rich with potential contacts for obtaining further military information. He waxes eloquent about the Battle of Tannenberg, a Great War encounter in the East Prussian marshes in August 1914 in which the outnumbered Germans outmaneuvered and crushed their Russian opponents. His job entails considerable travel; he receives VIP tours of U.S. military bases, research installations, and plants producing aircraft and weaponry and dutifully sends reports back home. He also visits battlegrounds near the nation's capital, often accompanied by a fellow Civil War buff, Colonel George S. Patton.

Von Boetticher entertains lavishly at his turreted brick and stone mansion in the 3200 block of R Street NW on the upper edges of Georgetown, a home some liken to a nineteenth-century German castle. Next summer,

**Fig. 3.** Hildegard von Boetticher flanked by her proud father, German military attaché Friedrich, and mother, Olga. Courtesy of Alfred M. Beck.

for example, he hosts a garden party for the son of Henry "Hap" Arnold, chief of the U.S. Army Air Corps, to celebrate the boy's acceptance to the U.S. Naval Academy. Von Boetticher lives with his traditional wife, Olga, and their three children. The eldest, Adelheid, will move out in June after marrying a fellow medical student. Their middle child, troubled son Friedrich Heinrich, recently arrived from Germany. He was diagnosed with schizophrenia in his adolescence, and he and his friends had gotten into trouble by criticizing the National Socialist government. Ordered to report for compulsory sterilization, he finally got approval to emigrate thanks largely to his father's influence. But his first years in the United States prove rocky, and his unbalanced mental state could lead to draconian punishment if he ever returns to Germany.

Their youngest, Americanized daughter Hildegard, is the family's pride and joy. When she sailed into New York harbor aboard the *Deutschland* from Hamburg in 1933, the thirteen-year-old marveled at the skyscrapers. She quickly realized that the world of cowboys and Indians—one former classmate had asked her to send him a skin after she shot her first buffalo—was a thing of the past, but the present was mesmerizing. Especially a trip to an amusement park that introduced her to hot dogs ("the expression 'hot dog!' seemed extremely funny to me") and popcorn. "Everything seemed so much bigger here: the automobiles, the trains, the newspapers," she wrote. "Even the people grow taller."[14]

Von Boetticher attends the prestigious Sidwell Friends School, then as now a magnet for the children of Washington's elite. Her father's status not only gets her name into the *Washington Social Register* but into many newspapers simply for attending everyday events like a friend's birthday party, where a magician entertains, or a special matinee of the circus, along with other offspring of the diplomatic set. At school assemblies von Boetticher is often asked to sing the national anthem along with a native Washingtonian classmate and Louis Castillo de Najera, son of the Mexican ambassador. "With patriotic fervour and a dash of Latin flavour, we would belt out 'Oh say, can you see by the dawn's early light,'" she recalled.[15]

This coming Christmas a dance at the Navy Yard will attract some 1,500 attendees, but only a handful merit their names in the news: "Among the many young people who danced at the Sail Loft until the small hours of the morning were Miss Hildegarde von Boetticher . . . Oleg Troyanovsky, son of the Soviet Ambassador[, and] Najera."[16] Next year, as a senior, she serves as president of the Girls' Athletic Association and representative to the student council. The yearbook lauds her sense of humor, loud, hearty laugh, and robust school spirit. Out of a graduating class of nineteen, she's one of four to receive special honors and will enroll in the fall of 1938 at Randolph-Macon Woman's College in Virginia.

But even a privileged life isn't immune to tragedy. Sidwell Friends is a small school where everybody knows each other. The Sunday after her father spoke to the army reserves downtown, senior Robert Hooper went picnicking at Great Falls. Bound for Harvard next fall, he and his friends began playing with the dry ice packed to keep their ice cream cold. At 140 degrees colder than ordinary ice, it can seriously burn the skin if touched. It's even more dangerous if put into a closed container. But boys will be boys, and these boys place dry ice into glass bottles and cap them. As the carbon dioxide builds, they throw the bottles before they blow up.

Only Hooper holds one bottle too long, and the resulting explosion sends chunks of glass tearing into an eye and arm. He's rushed to nearby Georgetown University hospital and undergoes several transfusions but dies. The following month he's honored posthumously at graduation with an award as the school's outstanding student in science.

# 2

# Rivals and Arrivals

On April 29, the day after von Boetticher's speech and the Thomsens' dinner party, Japanese ambassador Hirosi Saito and his wife host that embassy's largest party ever: a gala celebration of the thirty-sixth birthday of Emperor Hirohito. It attracts more than 1,400 guests, a who's who of the city's elite: members of the cabinet, the diplomatic corps, both houses of Congress, military officers, and "cave dwellers," whose families date back generations. Fluent in English, witty, and direct, Saito—so dashing with his fine clothes, slim figure, and pencil-thin mustache—is one of the city's most popular diplomats. He "played a good game of golf, a better game of poker and delighted in American slang."[1]

Today Saito, a sincere proponent of peace who'll fall into increasing disfavor with his country's militaristic government, reigns supreme. "A large punch bowl was refilled frequently as the guests stopped to drink to the health of the Emperor. In the dining room the long tea table had in the center a low mound of red and white carnations, the national colors and one of Japan's most popular flowers. Tall vases and low mounds of roses, gladioluses and carnations in red and white were to be found on almost every table."[2]

Unlike Germany's dreary, dated embassy—a foreboding nineteenth-century eyesore of reddish brown, pigeon-stained brick near Thomas Circle—Japan boasts the city's newest diplomatic jewel. "Designed with exceptional simplicity of arrangement and with restraint of detail, the architects followed the modern trend in neo-classicism. The interior, while designed in the formal spirit of the French Empire, displays artistry of the Far East in ancient wall hangings, in the effectual use of flat surfaces in textures, and in sharp color contrasts," reads the *Washington City and Capital*.[3]

A perfect spring day accentuates its beauty, with the French windows of its back drawing room opened wide so guests can enjoy the warm sunshine and view of Rock Creek Park from its terrace. Outside blossoming cherry trees adorn the lush gardens. The ambassador's two young daughters, Sakiko and Masako, make an especially fine impression by curtseying and greeting guests. They've already become public darlings through the rotogravure sections of the local papers, "two little almond-eyed dolls" dress in kimonos and strolling hand-in-hand with their parents every spring under the cherry trees in Potomac Park—a touching symbol of Japanese American friendship.[4]

But that fraying friendship suffers a serious blow in early July, when Japanese and Chinese troops clash near the Marco Polo Bridge in Peking. Japan exploits the incident to mount a full-scale invasion of China, escalating the campaign it had begun in 1931. Words of warning emanate from Washington but no action. For the Great War ended less than twenty years ago, and powerful isolationist forces stand fiercely opposed to the interventionist policies of the Roosevelt administration. Their diverse grassroots movements will coalesce into the America First Committee, which at its peak numbers 800,000 members in 450 chapters nationwide.

Back in the nation's capital, even free food and drink at continual embassy parties and receptions only go so far. Though most male reporters "never missed a chance to eat a plate of food, sip a glass of punch, and smoke a Havana," writes *New York Times* correspondent Delbert Clark, too many embassies assume their largess will buy favorable press coverage. He recalled one night at the Japanese embassy when staffers plied him and two other reporters with drink after drink. "It was obvious

**Fig. 4.** News correspondent Masuo Kato. Library of Congress, New York World-Telegram and Sun Newspaper Photograph Collection.

what was on the program: a large amount of priming followed by a large amount of pumping. [They] worked hard and faithfully for the Emperor, so faithfully that they got very drunk. One of them, in fact, wound up virtually speechless, thus losing his value as a secret agent."[5]

Into these precarious times a young but seasoned worldwide reporter arrives in Washington, thirty eight-year-old Masuo Kato. Son of a successful store owner and a housewife, he grew up in the city of Nagoya and graduated high school in 1917. After graduating from the Tokyo School of Foreign Languages, he came to America at age twenty-one, in August 1920, to attend the University of Wisconsin. After one year he transferred to the University of Chicago, where he graduated with a BA in sociology with honors in 1923. His keynote graduation speaker, perhaps presaging Kato's subsequent career, was the French ambassador. After returning to Japan, Kato taught English at a college in Tokyo, got married, and began his journalistic career as a correspondent for a news agency that later merged into Domei, Japan's official news agency.

His assignments included a year in Shanghai, and he brought along his wife and infant son. But when the baby needed medical attention, the care was poor, so after transferring back to Japan, his family never traveled with him again. In the early thirties he covered the League of Nations in London and Geneva, traveling to the former via the famed Trans-Siberian Railway from Vladivostok to Moscow and then onto the Continent and Great Britain. In 1933 he returned to the United States as the translator for a Japanese delegation from the League of Nations. Upon returning to Japan he became chief of Domei's branch in Nagoya, his hometown. Less than a year later, his impressive international record and fluent English landed him the job of chief of Domei's Washington bureau: a prestigious posting for a young man who'd only set foot in America as a college freshman sixteen years before.

Kato becomes a member and resident of the swanky University Club, which also serves as home to many members of Congress. He spends leisure hours at the Kenwood Country Club, which stretches more than one hundred acres of countryside in nearby Bethesda. He gets along well with the insular, sometimes prickly Washington press corps: "an affable, ubiquitous" correspondent who "holds that it is well to understand a foreign nation before you discuss its activities, and [he] takes a lot of pretty rough talk with a bland smile. He is popular, and because the news-paper men know he can take it, they sometimes razz him pretty hard."[6]

Foreign writers from governmental news agencies are fully accredited journalists, but all adhere to an unwritten law: none ask any questions at press conferences. So Kato and the representatives of Germany, Italy, and Russia are respected but quiet members of the press corps. They serve indirectly as their embassies' eyes and ears, going places and hearing things the emissaries can't. "In some respects [they] are more effective than their ambassadors," write Drew Pearson and Robert Allen in their prominent syndicated column, "Washington Merry-Go-Round": "They are diplomats without portfolio."[7]

Yet differences among colleagues do flare up. Reporter Sam Tucker files a story in which he calls Kato a Japanese spy, since the press in totalitarian countries is an arm of the government. But the power of the press reverberates, even when it's one small Illinois paper hundreds of miles from the nation's capital. A few days after publication the two meet over a committee room's refreshment table after another tedious hear-ing. Tucker momentarily considers bolting for the door when another reporter offers to introduce them. "With a smile that unveiled a full set of teeth, and a most diplomatic courtesy," he recalled, "Kato bent himself in the middle and said, 'I have heard of the gentleman's paper.'"[8] The two became fast friends.

Just as Kato arrives in DC, noted German journalist Paul Scheffer, fifty-three years old, lands in New York. Born into a family of scholars in Marburg, a city north of Frankfurt, the widely traveled writer worked in the Far East, Italy, Washington, and London before a nine-year stint as correspondent in Moscow for *Berliner Tageblatt*, a well-respected liberal newspaper. After his increasingly anti-Communist coverage earned him the boot from Russia, he returned to Berlin and assumed the paper's editorship with the approval of propaganda czar Joseph Goebbels, who wanted one paper that could be read abroad that wasn't just another party mouthpiece and could convey the (false) impression that a free press existed in Germany. Given this surprising degree of freedom, Scheffer assembled and urged his top-notch staff to write articles that were controversial, or eristic, from the Greek goddess of discord. "The reporting must be different [than the party press]," Scheffer told his staff, according to Margret Boveri, one of his sharp young hires. "Always garlands, laurel wreaths and verses to the Third Reich. We are an anomaly and must remain so."[9]

In the early to mid-thirties such sentiment was dangerous; within a few years it could prove deadly. Scheffer's walking-a-tightrope independence made him many powerful enemies and eventually cost him his job. His Nazi replacement clearly spelled out the new order: "The 'Berliner Tageblatt' intends to be the voice of German interests, not a colorless weakling representative of certain hesitaters who do not know where they should look—forward in the new Germany or backward."[10] With Goebbels's assent Scheffer assumes a new post as correspondent in the United States, where he moves with his wife, Nathalie, and ekes out a living as a freelancer after the Nazis shutter the paper two years later. "He has endeavored perhaps more than any other German writer to make American policies and the American viewpoint clear to the German people," wrote the *New York Times*. "The 'Tageblatt' is the only German newspaper . . . to have covered, as far as the censorship permitted, President Roosevelt's major speeches."[11] In America Scheffer maintains his iconoclastic streak, but his past as a journalist who toiled under the Nazis shadows him and culminates in a desperate bid for freedom after he's interned with the Axis diplomats after Pearl Harbor.

Up until a few years ago the nation's capital was considered an unappealing posting for reporters. New York had all the East Coast glamour and glitter, Hollywood the cinema and celebrities. Overall, Americans preferred to follow movie stars, sports stars, singers, and gangsters—not necessarily in that order—far more than politicians or diplomats. But smooth propagandist FDR and the New Deal made Washington a more popular spot. Two days after his inauguration and three days before his first press conference, First Lady Eleanor Roosevelt hosted one exclusively for women reporters. "Criticized in the male-dominated press of the day as gossipy, 'girlish' sessions of limited news value," wrote Maurine Beasley, "the conferences called attention to American women, thus granting

**Figs. 5 and 6.** Two of the many looks of Bébé Thomsen. Courtesy of DC Public Library, Washingtoniana Division.

them the status of persons with access to the media." Although Eleanor Roosevelt often "baffl[ed] reporters accustomed to waxing eloquent over the dress of prominent women since editors believed this pleased both women and ready-to-wear advertisers."[12]

Mostly male reporters with a sprinkling of women cover "the hill," yet the society pages invariably overlap with a heavy helping of diplomatic dinners, receptions, and goings-on. Here it's women, or "the girls" as they're invariably known, who reign in the four fiercely competitive dailies: the *Daily News*, the *Evening Star*, the *Washington Post*, and the *Washington Times-Herald*. An insider notes that both barbs and honey drip with equal facility from their fingers. Beyond the clothes and cuisine, their reports about who was (or *wasn't*) spotted at an embassy event offer subtle clues as to the latest alliances or fallings-out. "It is said that one can almost trace the course of international politics through the deft manner in which Mrs. Miller reports the social side of the diplomatic circle,"[13] writes *Texas Parade* of Lone Star State native Hope Ridings Miller, society editor of the *Post* and president in 1938–39 of the Women's National Press Club, with more than 150 members. While many cities have localized editions of that society stalwart *The Social Register*, the capital boasts a prominent competitor too: *The Social List of Washington*, a.k.a. The Green Book. Created by blue-blood Helen Ray Hagner, it proudly calls itself "the only social list corrected daily, used by official and social Washington," and famously features an anonymous trio of social arbiters. "The names of the three women are kept secret," writes Sigrid Arne, "in case poisoned arrows fill the air of the drawing rooms after the list is issued."[14]

Newspaper photographs and newsreel footage run invariably in black and white, so in this monochromatic world it's the female reporters who provide local color, literally. At a luncheon at Fort Myer, Bébé Thomsen is "costumed entirely in wine-colored velvet."[15] At a dinner and musicale featuring a star of the German opera, she wears "a gown in a green-gold shade with a cape of green velvet."[16] At the Polish embassy she's "in beige and brown, with a small dark-brown turban trimmed with a cluster of rose flowers in front."[17] Along with her eye-catching outfits, Bébé Thomsen offers over the next few years some subtle shifts in hair color, alternately described by columnists as auburn, black, brunette, red, or titian.

Shadings aside, her hair is always perfectly coiffed. Sitting for portraits at several photo studios, she projects a glamorous look more Hollywood than DC: sitting beside a table with a vase of flowers, dressed in satin or fur, a single strand of pearls around her neck, lipstick, nails, makeup, and hair immaculate. Once she's shot in the garden of her home on Colorado Avenue in a half-sleeved patterned sundress, wearing a wide-brimmed summer hat with an oversized flower atop. And always those pearls. She's a perfect match for her tall, blue-eyed husband with his slicked back hair. He's most often found wearing fine three-piece suits with French-cuffed shirts, silk cravats with tie pins. Sometimes he smokes a pipe. Like many men of the day he tops off his ensembles with a dress hat, often a high-crowned black homburg.

A dapper diplomatic duo. But devious too.

Come summertime diplomats, like many DC residents, flee the heat and humidity for cooler climes. Some, like the Thomsens, prefer Rehoboth on the Delaware shore. Saito opts for the mountains, renting a cottage in Hot Springs, Virginia. His daughters take part in its annual summer water carnival at the pool of the luxurious Homestead Hotel—a site to which Japanese diplomats will be exiled in December 1941 under much less happy conditions. But by then Saito had not only been replaced as ambassador but had died, at fifty-one, a broken man who'd sounded a lonely, increasingly isolated voice for peace. "Turn a deaf ear when men tell you we want war," he once said. "What we want is peace, peace with all the world."[18]

Kato is the last reporter to interview him, though of course neither man knows it at the time. He describes a pale Saito, lying in bed with an ice pack on his chest, talking not about his illness but current events. "I believe," reads Saito's last quote, "in the common sense of the American people."[19] Days later, hundreds attend his Buddhist funeral rites. "If people only would be as kind in life as they are after death," said one attendee. "Half of the people here today wouldn't go near Mr. Saito the last time he attended a White House diplomatic reception."[20] Kato writes a second story that lauds FDR for sending the USS *Astoria* ("nasty asty" to her crew) to deliver the late ambassador's ashes back home. "The offer of President Roosevelt," he wrote optimistically, "might become an important factor in adjusting the relations between the two countries, as nothing is nobler than the friendship remembered in bereavement of a friend."[21]

That fall, despite their personal friendship and Saito's lofty sentiments, FDR addresses head-on the belligerent expansionism of Japan, Germany, and Italy. On October 5, at a bridge opening in Chicago, he delivers an address, which comes to be known as the Quarantine Speech, that reflects his growing desire to shift America away from its traditional policy of nonintervention. "It ought to be inconceivable," thunders Roosevelt, "that in this modern era . . . any nation could be so foolish and ruthless as to run the risk of plunging the whole world into war by invading and violating, in contravention of solemn treaties, the territory of other nations that have done them no real harm and which are too weak to protect themselves adequately. Yet the peace of the world and the welfare and security of every nation is today being threatened by that very thing."[22]

Though he mentions no aggressors by name, everyone knows to whom he's referring. Yet words don't just budge a country still squarely against another military intervention overseas—they trigger a backlash. The Veterans of Foreign Wars unveils a "Keep America out of War" petition that aims to attract twenty-five million signatures. The staunchly isolationist *Chicago Daily Tribune* runs headlines like "Whatever It's Called It's War" and "It's Britain's War," while the *Boston Herald* writes, "It may be true that 'the very foundations of civilization are seriously threatened,' but this time, Mr. President, Americans will not be stampeded into going 3,000 miles across water to save them. Crusade, if you must, but for the sake of several millions of American mothers, confine your crusading to the continental limits of America."[23]

Indeed, less than a week after his Quarantine Speech, FDR's actions belie his own words. Antifascist protestors decry his planned White House meeting with Vittorio Mussolini, twenty-one-year-old son of the Italian dictator. "President Roosevelt—Don't Shake Hands with the Son of an Aggressor!" reads one sign held by protestors outside the Italian embassy on 16th Street NW. Girolamo Valenti, Sicilian-born editor of *La Stampa Libera*, a daily New York newspaper, rails, "He represents the lawlessness of the aggressor nations whom you wish to put in quarantine."[24] Nevertheless, the younger Mussolini and Italian ambassador Fulvio Suvich take tea with the president as scheduled. The ineffectual ambassador, with a poor command of English, returns to Italy next year. He's best remembered, if at all, for inserting a "de" into his name so he became Fulvio de Suvich in the Diplomatic List—though the State Department continued to call him Suvich.

By year's end FDR faces a far more serious crisis when another aerial attack, like the assault on Guernica, claims lives. Only this time it's not done by the Germans but the Japanese—and the lives lost are American. Planes attack the aging gunboat USS *Panay*, on duty in China escorting merchant vessels, and sink it into the muddy Yangtze River. Two sailors and one civilian are killed, and nearly seventy-five people are wounded. Survivors hide in riverbank reeds until nightfall. Front-page headlines worldwide scream the news. Japan immediately apologizes, promises to investigate, and pays a $2 million indemnity. In what the papers call "an extraordinary move," FDR demands that Emperor Hirohito be informed directly that he's "deeply shocked and concerned by the news of the indiscriminate bombing."[25]

Yet once again the president's tough talk is not only fruitless but toothless. While advisors including Admiral William Leahy, chief of naval operations, push for a muscular response like a naval blockade, public and congressional sentiment back a less aggressive approach. A consummate politician, FDR treads lightly while recalling the hostile reaction to his Quarantine Speech. "It's a terrible thing," he told a friend, "to look over your shoulder when you are trying to lead and find no one there."[26]

So FDR demurs, and the deadly incident fades quietly from view. This surprise Japanese raid on an American warship—on December 12, 1937—doesn't trigger war. Four years later a bigger aerial attack by the same country elicits a far different response.

# 3

## Soirees to Spies

Through the first half of 1938, storm clouds continue to gather in Europe. But it's still sunny skies for the German delegation in America and Hans Dieckhoff, Luther's affable though rather physically unimposing successor. With a pleasing smile and manner, he arrived last spring, accompanied by his beautiful wife, Lotte. They immediately headed off to a Virginian mountaintop estate rented for the summer from an ex–Wilson administration official. Apparently not one to get too caught up in work, Dieckhoff and the missus often zipped up to Long Island for the popular Vanderbilt Cup auto race, and last July she sailed back to Germany for the rest of the summer.

"Because of his constant grin, and his singular resemblance to the stone figures you find in rococo gardens, they call him the 'pouting Cupid,'" wrote Fromm. "His hair is kinky. Lucky for him it's blond."[1] He's also related by marriage to German foreign minister Joachim von Ribbentrop, and Berlin has high hopes he'll replicate his previous success in England. There he and Lotte opened doors after the Great War, hosting dinners and balls and laying the foundation for the fascist-friendly Cliveden set. In DC they decide that the aging German embassy isn't suitable for entertaining, so they rent a mansion nearly opposite the British embassy from Countess Széchenyi, the former Gladys Vanderbilt. They embark on an ambitious agenda of courting government officials, society grandees, fellow diplomats, and especially the press. Dieckhoff quickly becomes a favorite, gaining a reputation as a most candid envoy. "The sky's the limit," he tells correspondents. "Any question will be answered. Go to it, boys!"[2]

The Thomsens are also enjoying a charmed life, socializing all about town. They host dinners for the Bulgarian minister and his new bride, for the Austrian and Danish ministers, for the counselor of the Netherlands legation. At an embassy reception for Prince Louis Ferdinand, exiled grandson of Kaiser Wilhelm II, and his Russian duchess bride, Bébé Thomsen introduces them to guest after guest; she's known the couple for years. The Thomsens join not one but two year-round golf and leisure clubs: Burning Tree and the Chevy Chase Club, as well as the exclusive Metropolitan Club blocks from the White House. They book boxes for the President's Cup Regatta on the Potomac, a five-day boating extravaganza that attracts international competitors and a crowd of a hundred thousand.

But Thomsen's true sporting love is horseback riding, though a nasty spill she took after first arriving stateside resulted in several broken bones and a pause in her riding. After recovering she buys a chestnut mare named Kitty-Carr and joins the Potomac Hunt, an esteemed club with hounds leading riders hunting foxes. "Riding all morning," reported the *Washington Post* from a local horse show, "Frau Thomsen turned up looking no end smart in a tiny dark hat trimmed with a huge pink cabbage rose."[3] She joins a small group of women who ride and hunt weekly on the outskirts of Washington, the only diplomatic member who's delighted that their conversation runs typically to horses and sports, not politics. They call themselves the Gandhi Gang, not for the famous bespectacled Indian proponent of nonviolence but for their instructor.

Though the riding and the parties roll on, controversy begins to surround Thomsen—and not because of her penchant for reading guests' tea leaves. She confides her opposition to Hitler to friends, swearing them to secrecy. The wife of a diplomat criticizing her own country's government? *Quelle horreur!* One columnist hears her tale as the two stroll a beach in Rehoboth and fears for Thomsen's safety if such opinions became widely known. But when the columnist hears a French diplomat repeat the same story, she (and others) begin wondering: does she "hate Hitler and all his works, or is she an agent provocateur with the histrionic powers of a Bernhardt [celebrated French actress Sarah Bernhardt] spying on her friends and keeping a black book of those opposed to Hitler?"[4] Society hostess Vera Bloom, daughter of influential Congressman Sol Bloom, calls Thomsen "the enigma of the diplomatic corps. . . . There was simply no avoiding her. She would dash up to you anywhere and buttonhole you with a long hysterical tirade."[5] Thomsen incessantly insists that whatever happens, she'll never go back to Germany. It's still a few years before the mercurial frau will face that choice after the bombs at Pearl Harbor bring war.

Conjecture about Bébé Thomsen aside, the society pages continue to run endless stories about who entertained who and who wore what. But such gushy mentions never reveal, at least on purpose, anything really significant. A story about one of the Thomsens' parties, for example, notes a newly arrived attaché, Baron Ulrich von Gienanth. A former graduate exchange student in the United States at Johns Hopkins University, the handsome Prussian aide is actually a Gestapo agent whose far-reaching propagandistic portfolio includes monitoring politics, movies, books, radio, press, music, and art. Fact is, the press is often played for fools by calculating emissaries whose true agendas remain hidden behind smiles, soft patter, and smorgasbords. "Despite the prevalent Washington attitude of cold scorn for the Hitler regime, the German diplomats in Washington remain personally popular, and quite deservedly so," enthused Harlan Miller. "The Dieckhoffs, Thomsens and Scholzes of the embassy group behave themselves socially with consummate tact and impeccable poise. Frau Thomsen and Frau Scholz are among the most attractive women in Washington."[6]

Attractive, most definitely, but also claws-up bitter rivals. The oblivious columnist doesn't know the half of it; behind the drawing room curtains looms a nest of spies under diplomatic cover whose manners and spoken English are impeccable. The men are handsome, suave blond Nazis—the stuff of debutantes' dreams—any of whom could be a model for the popular Arrow shirt collar adverts and magazine covers by German American

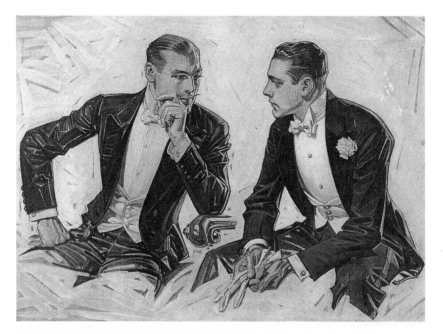

**Fig. 7.** A drawing by popular German-American artist J. C. Leyendecker, suggestive of the chiseled young Nazi diplomats.

artist J. C. Leyendecker. One perfectly chiseled example, Herbert Scholz, occasionally attended diplomatic receptions in his SS uniform instead of the customary white tie and tails. Dieckhoff updated the diplomats' dress, replacing their traditional, ornate uniforms with a fresh white tie look. The tail coat featured eighteen-karat gold buttons, with a matching narrow gold stripe down the side seam of the trousers. "Just enough gold to dazzle," said Dieckhoff, "but not enough to blind."[7]

Dazzling is a perfect description of the Scholzes: droll Herbert and his vivacious blonde wife, Lilo, who entertain frequently at their rambling house near the National Cathedral. She's the daughter of influential German industrialist Georg von Schnitzler, who realized early on that supporting Nazism would be good for business. (His company IG Farben, the world's largest chemical conglomerate, went on to produce Zyklon B gas for the death camps.) Scholz—the archetypal power behind the throne—had shadowed Luther relentlessly, reporting back to his Gestapo bosses in Berlin whenever he felt the ambassador's zeal for Nazism might

**Fig. 8.** Ambassador Hans Dieckhoff addresses a meeting of Nazi colleagues and business-men in New York City. Note the swastika and American flag hanging side by side. U.S. National Archives and Record Administration, Record Group 131.

be flagging. Now the couple ladles out "honeyed propaganda. . . . Neither Herbert nor Lilo desire any publicity; their object is, on the contrary, to avoid it. They flatter and soothe, then wait to see the serum's effect."[8]

With Dieckhoff now in charge, Thomsen firms up his position. As a testament to the high esteem with which he's held in the highest Nazi ranks, he receives an extraordinary offer: an invitation to accompany Hitler as chief translator on an upcoming trip in April to Italy. Thomsen joins an entourage that includes luminaries Rudolf Hess and Heinrich Himmler on a pageant of Roman grandeur. The elaborately choreo-graphed week-long tour is jam-packed with military parades, live displays of naval, ground, and air power and visits to select museums and galler-ies. "A massive display of fascist spectacle," wrote professor Paul Baxa, "designed to appeal to Hitler's political, artistic and militarist sensibil-ities . . . to send a message to the rest of the world about the character and destiny of fascism."[9]

Upon his return, Thomsen sends his own message. Scholz, angling for a promotion, has been lobbying his bosses in Berlin to have Thomsen canned. But he doesn't realize just how high his superior's connections go, though Thomsen's recent Italian trip might have been a tipoff. So Gestapo agent Scholz gets his comeuppance, banished to the consulate in Boston. Meanwhile, Thomsen compiles a scrapbook filled with tour photographs. Society columnist Betty Beale, her sister, and a friend visit the Thomsens' house one night to dine with other embassy staffers. "After supper, we Americans were given a scrapbook to peruse photographs taken during Hitler's triumphal meeting with Mussolini in Italy," wrote Beale. "The others were eagerly and happily listening to the news on the radio about Hitler's latest triumphs. We turned the pages while whispering comments of disgust to each other, then took our leave. The evening was a manifestation of the Nazis' arrogance vis-à-vis the anti-involvement mood that prevailed in the United States."[10]

During a Berlin stopover before returning to Washington DC, Thomsen visited Fromm, who candidly described the increasing indignities being heaped upon Jews in Germany. He listened gravely, then replied, "Don't think we have an easy time of it, over there. Hatreds and rebuffs all the time."[11] Indeed, for State Department appointments he's often left waiting as envoys from other countries whisk by. This fall Thomsen draws headlines and derision during hearings by the newly formed House Committee on Un-American Activities into the German American Bund, a homegrown fascist organization led by outspoken anti-Semite Fritz Kuhn. Often called the Dies Committee for its chairman, Martin Dies Jr., the House Committee on Un-American Activities will make its most (in)famous reputation under Senator Joe McCarthy during the Red Scare of the early fifties. For now, it's investigating twin subversive threats from the left and right: Communism and Nazism.

The Bund shines a most unwelcome spotlight on the covert efforts of the German embassy that have thrived under Thomsen's tutelage. An undercover agent, appearing on the witness stand in his Bund uniform, testifies that "Nazi consuls attended Bund meetings and offered or provided financial aid for radio broadcasts and other Bund propaganda activities." Thomsen refutes the charges, claiming that the embassy prohibits any German nationals from joining the Bund. "It is their duty to refrain from any interference in internal American affairs. The government of

**Fig. 9.** An undercover agent demonstrates the Nazi salute while testifying before the House Committee on Un-American Activities. Library of Congress, Prints and Photographs Division, Harris and Ewing Collection.

the United States is informed about this point of view adopted by the German government."[12] His claims are met at best with raised eyebrows. But talk about clandestine Nazi activities quickly becomes yesterday's news when Germany, the tinderbox of Europe, explodes in November 1938.

For years Germany has been goose-stepping toward confrontation, menacing both natives and neighbors. Last March the world watched anxiously as German troops occupied Austria, an annexation known as the *Anschluss* that Austrians welcomed with waving flags and open arms. In September, when Hitler threatened to similarly seize the Sudetenland in Czechoslovakia, England and France capitulated and signed the Munich Pact, ceding the territory to Germany without a shot and dooming British Prime Minister Neville Chamberlain to everlasting ignominy.

In late October Germany expelled some seventeen thousand Jews of

Polish origin, including the family of Herschel Grynszpan, a seventeen-year-old refugee living in Paris. On November 7 he bought a pistol, entered the German embassy, and killed a junior official. The assassination provided the perfect pretext two days later for the Nazis to launch Kristallnacht, a night of unbridled, unprecedented violence against Jews throughout Germany. SS troops and state-sanctioned thugs torched synagogues, homes, schools, and businesses. They rounded up, beat up, and tortured Jews, murdering nearly a hundred and sending thirty thousand to concentration camps.

"A hurricane is raging here," Dieckhoff cables Berlin about America's reaction.[13] In the midst of the crisis he hosts a famous visitor, filmmaker Leni Riefenstahl. Exceptionally poor timing found her arriving in New York on November 4 on a trip to find a distributor for *Olympia*, her landmark documentary of the 1936 Olympics in Berlin. She spends one night at the Dieckhoffs' mansion, briefly tours the city, and departs the next day for the more hospitable pro-German Midwest. No detailed record of her Washington DC visit remains; she omits any mention of it in her autobiography. But she misses Bébé Thomsen—sailing back from Europe where she'd been visiting family in Halle, near Leipzig—by a day or two. They would have had much to talk about, these slim, dark-haired, childless Aryan women with little interest in family but much in outdoor activities like horseback riding and mountain climbing.

Responding to Kristallnacht, FDR recalls American ambassador Hugh Wilson from Berlin. The Nazi savagery, combined with Congress's revelation of the embassy's domestic propaganda operations, costs Dieckhoff his job. He slinks back to Germany, boarding an ocean liner in New York via its cargo gangplank, but reporters track him down. "What can I say?" he exclaims reluctantly. "I didn't expect to meet any members of the press when I sailed."[14] Dieckhoff remains ambassador in name only, never returning to the United States.

The same fate befalls Alexander Troyanovsky, the only Soviet ambassador to the United States since it first recognized the Communist government in 1933. The rise of the Russian bear has vexed both West and East, with countries alternately fearing or courting the new Marxist colossus that calls for worldwide worker revolution. The embassy announces that Troyanovsky and his wife only want to remain close to their son, Oleg—the former Sidwell Friends classmate and occasional dance partner of Hildy von Boetticher—who recently enrolled at the University of Moscow after his freshman year at Swarthmore College. "Tales that the ambassador is being purged are preposterous," said Alexander Troyanovsky's successor, counselor Constantine Oumansky, whom few believe.[15] For the last two years he has played the same role Scholz did with Luther: shadow the boss and report back to government masters.

Next month Oumansky, a propagandist-cum-henchman turned diplomat, and his wife, Raisa, host a twenty-first anniversary celebration of the Russian Revolution at the embassy, a grand mansion built by the widow of railroad entrepreneur George Pullman. Purchased by Emperor Nicholas II in 1913, this bastion to what unfettered capitalism can buy exuded czarist luxury. But now the huge portraits of Lenin and Stalin and paintings of the revolution seem jarringly incongruous. Gold gilt furniture and plush red velvet draperies give it an overdressed, vulgar look. Just like the banished czars, though, the Bolsheviks offer an abundant spread of Russian delicacies, heaping bowls of caviar, copious salmon and sturgeon: "They imported a sturgeon so big it had to be shipped in two pieces and stitched together again on its arrival."[16]

But the capital's crowning year-end event is the White House's annual diplomatic reception. "International turns and twists, upheavals in Europe, the maelstrom in the Far East" roil the event though guests from unfriendly nations dutifully "proved themselves artful dodgers." Borrowing a hoary showbiz cliché—the show must go on—reporters trumpet fashion over affairs of state: "Rivalry of nations notwithstanding, women are women the world over when it comes to out-feathering the peacock on state occasions, and some of the most exquisite gowns ever to float across the Washington scene came into the picture. In fact, never was 'what they wore' more worthy of note than last evening, when men as well as women appeared in their flossiest finery."[17] Standing boldly apart from the German delegation's white tie and tails, a reminder of the departed Dieckhoff's good taste, Friedrich von Boetticher "look[s] every inch the soldier" in a handsome gray coat with an embroidered

**Fig. 10.** Ambassador Prince Don Ascanio dei Principi Colonna arrives at the White House to present his credentials to President Franklin Roosevelt, accompanied by Stanley Woodward, State Department's assistant chief of protocol. Library of Congress, Prints and Photographs Division, Harris and Ewing Collection.

red collar and matching red stripes down his gray trousers. A few nights later Hildy, on Christmas vacation from college, does up the town too. As part of a debutante group she attends a tea dance at the swank Sulgrave Club, housed in a turn-of-the-century mansion in Dupont Circle near Embassy Row. Her mother, Olga, who accompanied her husband to the White House gala, serves as a chaperone.

Besides Germany and Russia a record seven countries including Japan, China, and Italy replace their ambassadors this year: unprecedented turnover reflective of the mushrooming international unrest. Italy's new royal replacement is Prince Don Ascanio dei Principi Colonna, or Prince Colonna for short, its fourth ambassador in the last eight years. Scion of a noble family with roots dating back to the Middle Ages, he has served in diplomatic posts in Constantinople, London, and Budapest. Charged with "doing what he can to prove that Fascism is not frightful," Colonna is an old-school diplomat—meaning he's far more interested in pomp and parties than policy.[18] Alone among ambassadorial spouses, the elegant Grecian-born Princess Colonna draws a special allowance for entertaining that can cover anything from corsages to furs. The two hold court in Italy's striking Italian Renaissance–style embassy built in 1924 of materials that arrived under a special license from State, making it "certainly the largest item which ever came into Washington duty-free."[19] It was designed by Warren and Wetmore, the architectural firm renowned for New York's Grand Central Terminal and many hotels including several Ritz-Carltons, Biltmores, and Washington's venerable Mayflower Hotel.

When Thomsen first arrived, he stayed at the Mayflower for several months until he secured the house on Colorado Avenue. Now he has a regular table and dines there frequently, like many other influential Washingtonians, none more than FBI Director Hoover, who lunches there every day and orders the same meal: chicken soup, white toast, half a grapefruit, cottage cheese, and Bibb lettuce. And always with the same companion: protégé Clyde Tolson. (Nearly three-quarters of a century later, when the Mayflower undergoes a makeover, it opens a new upscale eatery: Edgar Bar & Kitchen.) "When you step into the lobby of this world-famous hostelry you instantly feel that it is a great hotel," boasts a 1940 magazine advert, "great in the sense that it is the home of international personages and a colorful setting for the great events occurring daily within its corridors."[20]

As New Year 1939 dawns, the Mayflower hosts a low-key envoy who's less an international personage than an international person who'll play a significant but unrecognized role in the lead-up to war. Unrecognized to most, but not to Hoover.

# 4

## Inactive Vigilance

As a young boy Raphael Pollio immigrated from Italy to America with his parents and four siblings. He grew up playing in the neighborhood where the Mayflower later stood. At sixteen he started as a stock boy at the Arlington Hotel and worked his way up in the business at hotels in Chicago, Jacksonville, and New York. Upon returning to his hometown ten years ago he became the Mayflower's resident manager. In January 1939 Pollio hosts two longtime friends: Japanese diplomat Hidenari Terasaki and his wife, Gwen. The couple is just passing through town, as he's been promoted from chargé d'affaires in Cuba to a new posting in Shanghai.

It's a happy return for the Terasakis, who fell in love in Washington in 1931, the year Japan staged an act of sabotage as a pretext for invading Manchuria. That eventually led into a long-term clash preceding World War II, but that worldwide conflict was a still a decade away. For Gwen and Hidenari, 1931 was a time for love. Tennessean Gwen Harold, twenty-three, was wintering with an aunt when she met the dashing thirty-two-year-old diplomat at an embassy reception. "His large eyes were very black and luminous, and I was aware that he kept them on me," she wrote in her best-selling postwar memoir, *Bridge to the Sun.* Fluent in English

**Fig. 11.** Gwen Harold and Hidenari Terasaki upon their wedding announcement. Library of Congress, Chronicling America.

after his studies at Brown University, Terasaki confided his frustration about having to escort middle-aged American matrons and answer their silly questions about his country. The next day he sent her a package of Japanese books and pictures, a fan, green tea, and yellow roses. Later he gave her a daguerreotype of Confederate hero Robert E. Lee which Pollio helped him acquire.

Soon the smitten couple was taking long walks in Rock Creek Park. He proposed but she demurred, fearful of her family's opposition and the sizable gulf between East and West. The ambassador felt taking an American wife would impede his career, calling the union "Terasaki's Folly." Hidenari had stationery engraved that read "Deeper than the Pacific Ocean, higher than Fujiyama," and told Gwen, "We would have much to endure, but we would walk through a few doors and open a few windows together—and that would be our compensation."[1] So interracial love, with a whiff of the unknown (and perhaps danger?) triumphed. They married in a small service at her aunt's house, honeymooned in

New York, boarded a train for San Francisco, and took an ocean liner that arrived in Yokohama on Christmas Eve 1931. Gwen suffered culture shock, first in Tokyo and later in Shanghai. War-torn China was a perilous place, and Hidenari's work brought him into contact with many foreign nationals. He took an especial dislike to arrogant Germans, and when one Nazi diplomat demanded a private car for a train trip, Terasaki suggested he contact a tourist bureau to make arrangements.

As the Terasakis now enjoy their return to DC after nearly eight years, Bébé Thomsen heads to Palm Beach shortly after Christmas to recuperate from an unspecified illness. Since arriving in America she's made many out-of-town trips: up to New York to show the city's sights to visitors from Germany; summertime vacations to Rehoboth Beach; and to a nearby Loudon, Virginia, mountain town called Bluemont, changed from its previous name of Snicker's Gap or Snickersville to better appeal to prospective wealthy vacationers. The capital's papers that so avidly chronicle the comings and goings of the diplomatic set lose her scent but the *Palm Beach Post* picks up the slack. Her activities seem far less about convalescing than carousing: cocktail parties, luncheons, teas, dinners, and dances at clubs and friends' houses; a concert of the popular local Romany Chorus and Orchestra at the Paramount Theatre; a YWCA charity luncheon at gilded Whitehall, the storied mansion of railroad magnate Henry Flagler; dinner at another posh estate, La Claridad; and activities at the popular Everglades Club and Bath & Tennis Club.

Thomsen enjoys escaping the hothouse atmosphere of Washington and the ever-present suspicions that hover over Axis representatives. While she blends seamlessly into the crème de la crème of Palm Beach society, Masuo Kato heads off on his own solo springtime southern sojourn. Traveling from the Carolinas to Georgia to Florida, he arrives in New Orleans in May and shows off his familiarity with American slang perfected in his many years stateside. "So far," he tells the *New Orleans States*, "everything looks swell, jake and kosher to me." His snappy language skills are matched by his snazzy appearance, with "sartorial inclinations towards ice-cream trousers and bichrome shoes."

Yet his commentary on world affairs is strictly a repetition of official talking points. No need to worry about his country's rampant expansionism; it's simply a reflection of Japan's desire to find new trading partners. "China?" he asks. "So many people have got us wrong. We don't want to conquer China, we want China to cooperate with us. . . . We want to increase the buying power of the Chinese, because that will enable us to sell more goods." He similarly dissembles about plans for the Philippines: "We want to buy and sell with the Philippines, but as to political ambitions—nothing doing!" In reality, Japan invaded China in 1931—and will invade the Philippines hours after it attacks Pearl Harbor. But now, two and a half years before December 7, 1941, Kato claims that "the friendship between your country and mine is traditional. I don't believe any circumstance that would disturb this pleasant harmony is probable." Then he reverts to a smooth, aw-shucks finish: "From here I expect to go to Vicksburg, then Memphis, and so trickle through the high spots of Dixie. That is, if one can trickle in high spots—English still has some bunkers for me."[2]

A handsome, benign face delivering soothing words in colloquial English: even Hans Thomsen couldn't have done it better. Back in Washington, the spotlight still shines brightly on the growing turmoil overseas. Yet some employ gallows humor to deflect tensions. One night at the Polish embassy, where dinner is served on plates decorated with the country's eagle-crested coat of arms, Ambassador Jerzy Potocki hosts several Axis couples, including the Thomsens. When Bébé Thomsen compliments the plates' beauty, a smiling Italian envoy quips, "Never mind. They'll be yours soon."[3]

Clairvoyance: such a useful diplomatic skill, and in short supply.

Far unkinder remarks appear regularly in the Jewish press, with one columnist delighting in lampooning Bébé Thomsen. "Frau Thomsen gets little opportunity to exhibit her pulchritude nowadays. The Capital's social whirl passes her by, nothing German being popular," writes leftist Zionist writer Joseph Brainin under the pseudonym Phineas J. Biron.[4]

Such a taunt has little effect on the Thomsens, who are used to being ostracized and soon have a new reason to celebrate. Hans Thomsen is elevated to chargé d'affaires: the de facto head of the German delegation in lieu of an ambassador, a position he'll maintain until the embassy closes down immediately after Pearl Harbor. But for now Thomsen's power, just like anti-Nazi sentiment in America, is growing. Just before Christmas a speech by Secretary of the Interior Harold Ickes compares Germany's persecution of Jews as harkening back to "a period of history when man was unlettered, benighted and bestial." Thomsen immediately meets with Under Secretary of State Sumner Welles to lodge an official protest over such "coarse and insulting" remarks. Welles replies that 99.5 percent of Americans agree with Ickes's position and that such a protest "came with singularly ill grace" given the Nazi government–sanctioned violence of Kristallnacht.[5] He refuses to accept the protest and lectures Thomsen about the ramifications of such reckless action.

His words fall on deaf ears. On March 14, 1939, Hitler browbeats the elderly, ailing new president of Czechoslovakia into submission. The next day, amid a late winter snowstorm, Wehrmacht troops pour into the country unopposed. That night Hitler makes a triumphant entrance into Prague, demonstrating the abject failure of the Munich Pact and the sham of appeasement. The advances of the Nazi war machine make Thomsen's job immeasurably harder as FDR continues to use the bully pulpit to hammer Germany. Privately, Thomsen vents to his Berlin bosses. "President Roosevelt's bid for leadership in matters of world politics is aimed at annihilating National Socialist Germany with all means available, and hence at nullifying the New Order in Europe," he writes in a diplomatic cable unearthed after the war that reveal sentiments he never showed in public. "The credulous and easily led majority of the mentally dull American people has completely succumbed to the insidious propaganda that Germany is America's 'Enemy No. 1.'"[6]

Meanwhile, Germany's embassy personnel can only sit back and seethe as Washington turns upside down over the most anticipated arrival anyone can remember: King George VI and Queen Elizabeth. The town's sent a-tizzy by the first-ever visit by a reigning monarch to this former colony, though tongues, especially those of the isolationists, wag about the trip's possible ulterior motive to heighten Britain's standing among Americans as the country remains split between interventionalists and isolationists. When some advance coverage proves less than flattering, the British Foreign Office sends an urgent cable to its ambassador: "For God's sake, *do* something about the American Press!"[7]

**Fig. 12.** Handsome devil Charlie Spruks of the Protocol Division, Department of State. Courtesy of Jean Spruks Russell.

Arrangements are handled by affable, able Charlie Spruks, ceremonial officer of State's Division of Protocol. The Scranton, Pennsylvania, native attended Syracuse and George Washington universities before joining the army and serving in France during World War I. Returning home he worked in his family's lumber business before joining the Foreign Service in 1927. He held posts in Havana and Warsaw before jumping to State's protocol division, which deals with all matters diplomatic. "Slim, gracious, handsome," writes one reporter, "he is the one who decides who sits where, what the band plays when, who rides in what auto, who is introduced and how."[8] "He was a diplomat himself," said his daughter Jean Spruks Russell, who along with her older brother, Henry, often met visiting dignitaries whom her father brought home for dinners after he transferred to Miami.[9] She recalls Marines lining the walk to their small house for a visit by princes Faisal and Khalid, who later became successive kings of Saudi Arabia. She particularly remembers their elaborate garb and headdress and their bodyguard's huge sword. Above all she prizes the signed photographs given by the king and queen to her dad—who rose from humble roots to rub shoulders with international royalty.

And what a visit it is! Crown, clothing, coiffure, ceremony . . . the town's regal fever hits fever pitch, and her royal highness receives especially rave reviews. "The queen was beautiful and gracious and queenly, with a special humanity of her own that could not be concealed by the royal trappings," wrote reporter Marquis Childs.[10] In official circles anyone who's anyone waits breathlessly for an invitation to one of the intricately plotted parties and receptions. Rarer still are dinner invitations. The Thomsens finagle an invitation to a gargantuan garden party at the British embassy. The society pages shift into overdrive to describe in (s)lavish detail the outfits of select guests among the 1,400-plus attendees, especially women who've long agonized over what to wear and how to address the royal couple. Bébé Thomsen wears a beige dress with a lace waist, plaited silk skirt, and dark brown straw hat. Thomsen wears a conventional cutaway jacket with striped trousers, "a swastika in his lapel."[11]

While the regal visit's like the circus—the biggest show in town—it also spawns a tawdry sideshow involving ambitious twenty-four-year-old Count Igor "Ghighi" Cassini, grandson of a former White Russian ambassador to

**Fig. 13.** Adoring crowds welcome Queen Elizabeth II during her royal visit with King George VI. Library of Congress, Prints and Photographs Division, Harris and Ewing Collection.

the United States and younger brother of future famous fashion designer Oleg. In his gossip column for the *Times-Herald* he dishes about a woman in the horse-riding set in Virginia's tony Fauquier County who nabbed a coveted party invitation thanks to her brother, a tutor for the royal family. But her husband was miffed because he wasn't invited too. While squiring their twenty-year-old daughter, Austine, better known as Bootsie, to a country club dance, he's kidnapped by a trio including Bootsie's two older brothers. Angry at his unflattering portrayal of their prominent family, they drive him to a remote spot and tar—later clarified in court as "road oil"—and feather him. Their lawyers argue his column is a "regular cesspool of scandal that creates a stench in the nostrils of decent people," while his attorneys counter that "they subjected Cassini to indignities that to say the least were picturesque in their vulgarity."[12]

The threesome is convicted of assault and fined five hundred dollars. Eight months later the previously "oiled and feathered" Ghighi elopes with Bootsie McDonnell, the first of his five marriages. The notoriety from this odd affair catapults his career. His new column "These Charming People" quickly becomes a name-dropping must-read. Next year in his self-styled Cassini Awards, quite pretentious puffery, he names Bébé Thomsen as the capital's "greatest animal lover." During the war he'll serve in Army Intelligence in Europe. Later in life he coins the term "jet set," writes an autobiography (*I'd Do It All Over Again*) and observes, "The world is full of people who love to be told what to do."[13]

Soon after the king and queen depart in July, tensions escalate in the Pacific. Japan's bloody conquest of Chinese territory, the endangering of American lives during its frequent attacks, and the futility of "moral" but unenforceable embargoes prompts FDR to terminate Japan's annual trade agreement in effect since 1911. "Government's Course Unique in Our History since Time of French Revolution," thunders the *New York Times*, noting that the move "meet[s] Japan with the only language that the military-dominated government seems to understand."[14] Kato reports that this abrogation of the treaty is primarily a political move "intended to popularize the administration in the eyes of the American public." He coins a new term that aptly and somewhat derogatorily sums up FDR's watching and waiting: "inactive vigilance," a policy that continues for the next two and a half years until dawn breaks in Pearl Harbor on December 7, 1941.[15]

Inactive vigilance could also describe the reaction of Great Britain and France to Germany's naked European expansion, where threatening developments lead to more finger-wagging and official expressions of displeasure. In May, to no great surprise, Germany and Italy announce their Pact of Steel alliance. But on August 23 Hitler and Stalin deliver a thunderbolt: a nonaggression pact of their own that "has decisively altered the balance of power, not only in Europe but throughout the world, in favour of the Axis Powers with all that that implies," crows Thomsen in a private telegram to the Foreign Ministry in Berlin: "a masterly piece of diplomacy by the Führer and Reich Chancellor, and the severest defeat for Britain and France since Munich."[16]

Within days the drumbeats of war reach a crescendo as German troops mass at the Polish border. For ten days straight the front page of the *Evening Star* runs above-the-fold, margin-to-margin headlines; on August 31 it screams "PEACE NEGOTIATIONS AT 'PAUSE,' SAY NAZIS." Relegated to page 2 is news of yesterday's meeting between the president and new British envoy Lord Lothian, a genial noncareer diplomat whose tenure is hoped might usher in a new era at an embassy "long regarded as a citadel of rigid correctness." When Lothian emerges from his hour-and-a-half talk with FDR—the lengthiest presidential meeting with a new ambassador in memory—he picks up a passing black cat while giving an impromptu press conference on the White House steps. Reminded of the famed black cat that frequents 10 Downing Street, a reporter asks, "How about black cats being bad luck? Will it bring peace or war?" Lothian replies, "Peace, undoubtedly."[17] In England black cats signify good luck, not bad. Later on newsmen name the cat Crisis; a local policeman adopts and presents it to his young granddaughter, who promptly, though not particularly presciently, renames it Peace.

Missing all the hoopla is First Lady Eleanor Roosevelt, who has traveled to New York harbor to welcome home her mother-in-law. Returning from a visit with her sister in Paris, Sara Delano Roosevelt cut short her vacation on the advice of William Bullitt, U.S. ambassador to France, who "thought it would be a good thing if [she] came back at once."[18] Also on board the liner are actor Edward G. Robinson and his wife and young son. Robinson's latest feature, *Confessions of a Nazi Spy*, was the first American movie to depict Nazism as a threat to the United States. It prompted a complaint earlier this summer by Thomsen to State that the film will provoke resentment between his country and America.

Tomorrow's blitzkrieg does that and more.

# 5

## Reverberations of War

"These are today's main events," begins noted BBC announcer Alvar Lidell on his broadcast of September 1, 1939. "Germany has invaded Poland and has bombed many towns. General mobilization has been ordered in Britain and France."

This year Americans are buying a record-setting eight million radios, including 850,000 newfangled portables. So today most U.S. households own at least one radio so night owls can hear the startling news in the wee hours. FDR is awoken by a 2:50 a.m. call from Ambassador Bullitt in Paris. Most Americans awaken to the news via newspapers rushed out at dawn. Street corners ring with newsboys' cries of "Extra! Extra!" Papers offer headlines but scant details, so radio becomes the go-to medium. "As soon as it warmed up—I think the future historian would like to have this detail—the radio . . . brought the war," wrote reporter Mark Sullivan. "Hardly had a bomb fallen on a Polish town before the news of it was detonating in ten million American homes."[1]

Backed by more than 2,000 tanks and 1,000 planes, 1.5 million Wehrmacht troops sweep across the border from Prussia and Slovakia. The blitzkrieg decimates the Polish military, including an army that still maintains cavalry units. Luftwaffe bombers not only destroy army and air force bases but rail junctions and towns and villages, murdering tens of thousands and triggering a mass civilian evacuation that jams roads and impedes military traffic. Secure behind its Maginot Line, the French army does nothing. Poland's other key ally, England, sends a few bombers to drop payloads over several German cities of tons of . . . propaganda leaflets decrying the attack.

Back in Washington, government staffers and foreign emissaries race to work. Diplomats from belligerent and neutral nations alike sift through masses of fragmentary radio and cable reports, trying to stay abreast of events halfway around the world. Polish Ambassador Potocki is flooded with telegrams, letters, and calls of support. The German embassy issues a terse "no comment," though activity remains brisk with hearty "Heil Hitlers" echoing through its reception room decorated with photographs of the Führer and former president Paul von Hindenburg. The next day Thomsen hand-delivers a short note to Hull that claims Germany did everything in its power to resolve the dispute peacefully, but privately he tells his bosses in Berlin that America isn't buying it: "The German standpoint that our military actions were first and foremost precipitated by Polish general mobilization is not accepted by public opinion. Responsibility is placed exclusively on the German leadership."[2]

Ever mindful of strong isolationist sentiment, the administration refuses to panic. Hull, just back from vacation at the posh Greenbrier Hotel in West Virginia, strikes a casual tone with restless reporters by holding forth on one of his favorite pastimes: croquet. When one newsman broaches the subject of war, Hull announces he hasn't read his dispatches yet but should know more tomorrow. When FDR addresses the American public, he reiterates the country's continued neutrality. "Let no man or woman thoughtlessly or falsely talk of America sending its armies to European fields."[3] But that's exactly what the Soviet Union does on September 17, invading Poland from the east less than a month after Stalin and Hitler signed their nonaggression pact. By the end of the month a battered Poland surrenders, and the joint victors carve up their prey.

Speaking by radio on the Mutual Broadcasting System, Thomsen smartly cites a legal principle: *audiatur et altera pars,* "hear the other side

**Fig. 14.** Hans Thomsen. Courtesy of DC Public Library, Washingtoniana Division.

too." He praises the United States for not getting entangled in European affairs and heaps blame upon England and France for unjustly accusing Germany of striving for world domination. Privately he cables Berlin that "since the outbreak of the war we have been completely boycotted by so-called good society here and the greater part of the Diplomatic Corps that is neutral. It is the same phenomenon as in 1914 and something that can be borne with equanimity."[4] At a joint session of Congress the only touch of color among the dark-suited representatives comes from the Thomsens' next-door neighbor, Senator Hattie Caraway. The diplomatic galleries are packed with the notable absence of Germany, Italy, and Japan; both Thomsen and Colonna cite previous (and undoubtedly separate) luncheon engagements. A solemn FDR presses Congress to repeal the Neutrality Act so the United States can sell arms on a cash-and-carry basis to England and France. Two weeks later, despite stiff isolationist opposition, the repeal passes and ends the embargo on sales of implements of war.

War talk so dominates the capital that a society lady reports that when she attended a recent prenuptial party, the bride and groom were discussing armed neutrality. Still, the political scene soldiers on. "Diplomats are a gloomy lot these days," writes a well-known participant hiding behind a pen name. "They still kiss your hands, but not as if they meant it."[5] The society page editors take what they can find. "Talk of giving parties seems somewhat like attending a large ball the night after your mother has died," writes one columnist. "Still, life must go on and as this country is not at war, the current gloom is expected to be enlivened from time to time by entertaining."[6] Not just entertaining but entertainment: the National Symphony Orchestra opens its winter season in late October with a concert featuring works by a Polish refugee. Season box holders include both Thomsen and Potocki, invader and invaded, as well as the British and Soviet ambassadors. If only music could soothe the savage beast.

Next month's annual celebration of the Russian Revolution at the Soviet embassy is a decidedly downbeat affair: nary a Supreme Court justice, cabinet member, senator, or top State Department official in sight. The wife of isolationist senator William Borah, a Republican from Idaho, attacks the snubbing. "I think it is terrible the way people in this town are acting toward diplomats who individually can't help what their countries do," says Little Borah, the diminutive woman who detractors call the guardian angel of morals and manners of the Senate.[7] (The Borahs had no children, though he fathered one with his mistress, Alice Roosevelt Longworth, eldest daughter of President Teddy Roosevelt.) Her naïvety inadvertently but succinctly sums up a long-held misconception that ambassadors are mere functionaries with no real idea what their governments are plotting. It's a role that false-front diplomats like Thomsen perform masterfully. The poor turnout isn't only due to Russia's alliance with Germany but near-universal disdain for its ambassador. He "belonged to the new school of offensive Soviet diplomats," recalled State official Dean Acheson. "Oumansky had no redeeming qualities. To frustrate him with icy politeness had given me considerable pleasure."[8]

In addition to attendance, culinary downsizing is evident too. Instead of the usual centerpiece, a massive sturgeon reposing in solitary splendor, small cut pieces are arranged in side dishes. Vodka is dispensed only upon request from a small bottle. And caviar, traditionally offered in brimming bowls, is served on modest canapés. Many embassy chiefs attend, including Hans and Bébé, who arrive early and stay late. He sports a short white morning coat with a white-piped vest; she wears a short mink jacket, a stylish green velvet frock, and a rounded hat with a snood.

Well-liked minister of Finland Hjalmar Procopé is the first diplomat to arrive. And leave, within fifteen minutes.

Three weeks later the Soviet Union invades Finland. Expecting a cakewalk as in Poland, the Red Army is initially rebuffed by the outgunned, outmanned Finns. Finn-mania engulfs Washington as relief groups pop up; women engage in knitting marathons to make clothing to help warm winter warriors; Jean Sibelius's "Finlandia" tops many musical programs. Even tempestuous Tallulah Bankhead, daughter of the Speaker of the House, voices her support for gallant Finland. She's here appearing at the National Theater in *The Little Foxes*, a stage performance that Bette Davis admits emulating in next year's movie version. Just before Christmas several Supreme Court justices, senators, and envoys of twenty-three nations cosponsor a benefit concert at Carnegie Hall. One surprising patron: Ambassador Colonna, a thumb in the eye to Italy's ally Germany, which has also aligned with Russia. Even Japan voices support for Finland, another confounding stance by a totalitarian state. "Nippon is thoroughly democratic," said Kato disingenuously. "Naturally we're sorry to see an unfortunate little democracy overrun by a big despotism."[9]

While diplomats and other government staffers may be masters of double-talk, there's no more straight-shooting reporter than Dorothy Thompson. Kicked out of Germany in 1934, she broadcasts on the radio and pens a syndicated column read by millions every week. Last summer she graced the cover of *Time* and once got into a public spat with Hans that generated a tailor-made headline: "Thompson Versus Thomsen." Later she'll champion the cause of old friend Paul Scheffer, the German journalist whose story is one of the strangest to emerge during the forthcoming Axis detainment. But for now she unloads on Communist and fascist aggression in her inimitable, in-your-face style. "Gangsterism is contagious," she writes. "The Russians have exactly as good a case in Finland as the Germans had in Poland, Czechoslovakia or Austria . . . as an excuse for gobbling them up, preferably by blackmail, and if necessary by unprovoked and undeclared war."[10]

A few days after the invasion, Thomsen offers a unique defense of expansionism in an interview with columnist Helen Essary in the *Washington Times-Herald*. "I read somewhere recently that an Indian tribe wants the United States and Canada to give back Niagara Falls—Niagara originally belonged to the Indians, didn't it?" he asks before jumping forward, somewhat inaccurately, in American history. "When your government wanted the land that is now Texas in 1848 it merely moved in and took it from Mexico. . . . To some of us in Europe, it seems both necessary and simple procedure to rearrange the map of Europe in the same way."[11]

His linking of the invasion of Finland—and by inference, Nazi takeovers of Austria, Czechoslovakia, and Poland—to the expansionist history of America sparks international scrutiny. Ambassador Lothian cables London, noting Thomsen's prediction that Russia will move down the continent through Romania and aim at full control of the Bosporus. He adds a gratuitous slap at Essary, "a local journalist who generally devotes her daily column to less serious subjects and has no special reputation for trustworthiness as a reporter."[12] Actually, she was a veteran correspondent married to the head of the Washington bureau of the *Baltimore Sun* and acknowledged dean of the Washington press corps. Essary wrote extensively about world affairs when her husband was stationed in London in the twenties. She is a complicated woman: elected next year as president of the Women's National Press Club, she's a Democrat writing for one of America's most stridently isolationist papers. An English-language daily in Jerusalem, the *Palestine Post*, calls the interview "a particularly subtle piece of diplomacy. . . . As a piece of hardboiled commentary on world affairs, we prefer the interview to Moscow's shams and pretenses."[13]

As the holidays near, the normally bustling winter season curtails as many hostesses balance entertaining with volunteering—for relief work, that is. With increasing numbers of refugees and the Red Cross ministering to the wounded and sick, many society ladies take up knitting and sewing at home. Rolling surgical dressings can only be done at Red Cross headquarters. It's a joint effort, with the wives of envoys from Poland, France, England, and more banding together. On the other, far smaller side, Bébé Thomsen organizes a group that includes Olga von Boetticher, just back from an ill-timed trip back to Germany, her first in four years. Tongues wag that this kind of social service is 90 percent social, 10 percent service.

Those tongues have something far more momentous to whisper about when Bébé Thomsen spouts off at a winter dinner party. In front of a group that includes Sumner Welles, she announces, "Germany will not be happy until Hitler is killed."[14] So much for her private tirades: this very public outburst brings renewed scrutiny. The camp that's always considered her merely indiscreet now takes a backseat to those who've always doubted that the Nazis would ever tolerate a high-ranking diplomat's spouse speaking so intemperately. Opinion shifts that her show of disarming frankness is just that: an act.

Once again, *the* year-end gathering arrives: the White House's annual diplomatic reception. The tenseness of last year's affair elevates to off-the-charts anxiety. Envoys of nations at war, and many perilously close to being at war, exchange icy stares and stiff bows. But decorum prevails as emissaries pointedly ignore counterparts from unfriendly nations, even when they're but steps away. Unlike at most diplomatic gatherings, the ladies' clothing, as beguiling as ever, pales before the men's resplendent uniforms and decorations. Promptly at 9:00 p.m. the scarlet-coated U.S. Marine Corps Orchestra strikes up "Hail to the Chief." Since each chief of mission's length of service in Washington dictates the order of precedence to meet the president and first lady, first up is the ambassador of Peru. Under this traditional rule Potocki, the ambassador without a country, precedes the representatives of the two countries that have "absorbed" Poland—an event not recognized by the United States. Of the envoys from fifty-three countries in attendance, Thomsen winds up third from last (only ahead of Iran and Estonia) since he's only a chargé d'affaires, ranking behind all ambassadors and ministers. "Careful spacing by aides ke[e]p[s] the groups from rubbing shoulders in the reception line," writes the *Evening Star*. "After it br[eaks] up, little knots form . . . in the state dining room as distinct as if they [a]re miles instead of feet apart."[15]

While attendance may be down from last year, papers still devote multiple pages to the evening and its elaborate costuming: "Gold Braid, Plumed Hair, Diamond Bracelets and Tiaras Abound at Party for Envoys" and "Warfare Fails to Curtail Splendor as Diplomats Gather at White

House for Reception" read subheads in the *Post*.[16] Bébé Thomsen wears a full-fitted pale pink organza gown with a tight rhinestone-embroidered bodice. A double string of pearls and diamond pendant earrings complete the outfit. Despite once again being singled out for her stunning look, Thomsen had confoundingly confided recently to a friend: "I did not buy any clothes in Europe before I came, thinking I would buy them here. But now since the war started it looks as if . . . there is no occasion to wear them."[17] Accompanying her parents, Hildy von Boetticher wears a white tulle robe de style, a throwback design popular with young ladies of the Jazz Age. Eleanor Roosevelt wears a cream brocade gown with an heirloom ivory lace mantilla, offset with a corsage of pink orchids, at this, the last large diplomatic reception the Roosevelts will ever host.

Shortly before year's end, reporters note that Hans Thomsen now spends much of his time reading press dispatches and listening to shortwave news broadcasts on a small radio on his desk. Also prominent on that desk is a photo of Hitler that avid photographer Thomsen took himself. He mystifies visitors during an off-the-record chat with a comment they aren't sure is real or jest: "When we win the war, Germany will deem it a fitting gesture to give Bermuda to the United States."[18] In Bermuda, Great Britain maintains a massive underground apparatus that inspects, opens, and censors mail entering and exiting the United States.

At a year-end diplomatic reception, a Dutch attaché approaches Thomsen, and they cordially shake hands. An onlooker describes this overture as a textbook example of sliding gracefully between Scylla and Charybdis. When an aghast French envoy's wife corners the Dutchman afterwards and asks if he enjoyed that exchange, the young man replies that he much prefers kissing the hand of a beautiful lady—and does just that.

War news fades from the headlines, replaced by the Phoney War, the term coined to describe the European wintertime lull in fighting. New Year 1940 dawns, not especially chilly in DC but downright frigid in Berlin: the coldest winter in more than a century. "People said that the new friends of Germany, the Russians, threw this cold in, gratis, along with the friendship pact," writes William Russell, an American embassy staffer. "Coal was hard to get, and food harder."[19]

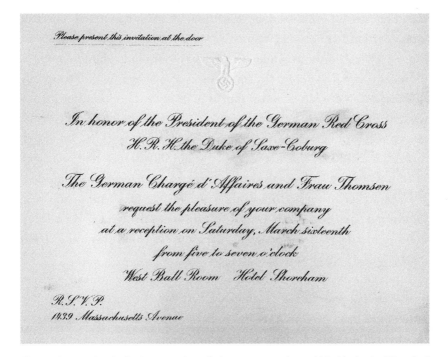

Please present this invitation at the door

In honor of the President of the German Red Cross
H. R. H. the Duke of Saxe-Coburg

The German Chargé d'Affaires and Frau Thomsen
request the pleasure of your company
at a reception on Saturday, March sixteenth
from five to seven o'clock
West Ball Room    Hotel Shoreham

R. S. V. P.
1439 Massachusetts Avenue

**Fig. 15.** A reception invitation prominently features an embossed Nazi insignia. Historical Society of Washington DC, Clarence Hewes Collection.

Stateside there are no such shortages, and the Thomsens—perhaps knowing something others don't—kick off the spring season with their largest-scale (and last) entertaining ever. It's a multi-event celebration for the president of the German Red Cross, the Duke of Saxe-Coburg. This grandson of Queen Victoria, educated at Eton, and his entourage are met at Union Station by the German delegation and Red Cross officials. His presence offers the Thomsens the added benefit of pissing off the Brits. A rare crossover guest on an errand of mercy, he allows many Washingtonians to temporarily ignore Germany's recent transgressions. Hundreds attend the opening reception at the Mayflower, including Scholz, now plying his undercover espionage in Boston. Scholz "announced to some of his old friends," writes Lombard, "that it was quite comical that 'an insignificant little man with a title,' as he described the duke, could induce Washington to swallow the swastika with its champagne."[20]

Indeed, engraved invitations for tomorrow's reception at the Shoreham

Hotel feature an embossed eagle with its wings outstretched, perched atop a garland containing a swastika. Later there's a private black tie dinner at the Thomsens' home. In the narrow two-hour window between events the social couple even squeezes in a stop at a birthday celebration for the shah at the Iranian embassy; perhaps Thomsen was invited when the delegates stood together in the back of the line at the White House reception at Christmas. Before the Duke departs he, Thomsen, and American Red Cross Chairman Norman Davies get a half hour with FDR in the White House—the only personal audience with the president Thomsen ever receives. In a cable to Berlin he gloats about the visit: "Roosevelt's parting words [were] 'I am sure your trip will do a lot of good.' . . . The Washington press reported extensively and objectively on the Duke's entire stay."[21]

Afterward the Thomsens slip back into lower profile: joining a distinguished list of patrons for a visiting circus to benefit Children's Hospital; attending a local performance by the Philadelphia Orchestra; going to a luncheon at the Mayflower hosted by an American colonel and his wife, alongside military attaché Friedrich von Boetticher and his wife, Olga. The list of Americans willing to socialize with Nazis shrinks every day. One of von Boetticher's oldest friends, fellow World War I vet General Charles Burnett, now a U.S. Army liaison officer, recently passed away, shortly after von Boetticher visited him at Walter Reed medical center. Afterward Olga von Boetticher told their son, Friedrich, "We have no American friends anymore."

Meanwhile, Hildy von Boetticher has friends galore, as her collegiate life goes along swimmingly. Nobody takes any notice of her German heritage, except for classmates who need help with their German language assignments, for which she charges fifty cents an hour. For spring break she accompanies a classmate, daughter of a prominent judge, back to her home in Atlanta. The girls attend a weeklong whirl of parties and dances. Back at school this fall, Hildy remains active in its theater group. She appears in *Springtime for Susie*, a sprightly three-act farce, and plays an angel in a Christmas production. In another skit, she recalls, "I strode onto the stage dressed like a Wagnerian Brunhilde to do a grotesque imitation of a German prima donna singing, 'Ohhh I vish I vere in ze land of cotton.'"[22]

Privately, the von Boettichers face an agonizing family problem. Their son, Friedrich, institutionalized at an asylum near Baltimore, is variously described in subsequent government memos by people who've never met him as an "idiot" or an "imbecile" or "insane." In hindsight such pejorative terms sound shocking, but at the time such descriptions of people with mental disorders were commonplace. Nevertheless, his schizophrenia, which turns out to be nowhere near as awful as described, is still an unmentionable shame to his rigid military father. To make matters worse, the boy's uncertain future could turn immeasurably darker if the family returns to Germany after von Boetticher's assignment ends. Under the Nazis' draconian policy toward the disabled, Friedrich could be executed. After Pearl Harbor shutters the German embassy, von Boetticher frantically mines his government connections to plead that his son be allowed to stay in the United States.

As spring arrives in the nation's capital two opposite sentiments collide: anticipation over the pending cherry blossom season, which always has a rejuvenating effect, and apprehension about potential renewed hostilities and an end to the Phoney War. On a drizzly Wednesday in early April, Ulrich von Gienanth addresses the International Relations Club at the University of Maryland in nearby College Park. The Gestapo agent posing as embassy secretary sounds a familiar refrain, blaming "the oppression of German minorities" for the current conflict. Great Britain meddled "because Germany was becoming too powerful," and France is but "a hitchhiker on the English truck."[23] It's the last time he'll ever peddle this particular party line, for this spring proves to be the proverbial calm before the storm. And that storm is closer than anyone imagines.

In the early morning hours of April 9, 1940, the Nazi blitzkrieg strikes again by land, air, and sea. This time its ill-fated targets are Denmark and Norway, and any remaining doubts as to Hitler's true intentions are silenced forever.

Official Washington is caught completely unaware as consternation and confusion reign. FDR is in Hyde Park; Hull in Atlantic City; the Swedish and Finnish ministers at a banquet in Philadelphia; and the

Danish minister vacationing in Charleston, South Carolina. Only Norway's minister is in town, and State Department brass panics when it learns both he and Thomsen are in their building for separate meetings. Fortunately the two never cross paths. Poor international communications and conflicting reports force embassies, especially those of invaded countries, to seek information from State or news outlets. That night a Norwegian counselor skips his previously scheduled dinner at the Thomsens' house, an evening that seemed perfectly acceptable only twenty-four hours before. Others cancel too, and in the end the only attendees are an American couple, a Hungarian couple, and various German embassy staffers drafted to fill the empty seats.

When envoys begin arriving at State the next day, a crow perches above the diplomatic entrance. Reminding some of Edgar Allan Poe's ominous raven, the black bird caws loudly as each diplomat enters: first Lord Lothian, later Thomsen, then the Danish minister. At first reporters are amused. "At least he's not taking sides," one says.[24] As the long day wears on, and its noisy cries greet the Swedish minister, the crowd goes silent. Neutrals like Sweden try scrupulously not to take sides; Switzerland's longevity in maintaining its independence amid belligerents has earned it the moniker "professional neutral." One observer likens the task of an envoy laboring to uphold his country's status as a neutral to a debutante's mother seeking to preserve her daughter's reputation for virtue. It's tricky business.

Meanwhile, Germany can't match its territorial gains in Europe with similar success in Washington. After the *Anschluss* the Austrian minister, Edgar Prochnik, dutifully handed over the embassy's keys to Ambassador Dieckhoff. The two even stood on the embassy's little wrought-iron balcony and drank a toast. Soon thereafter Prochnik retired and became a lecturer at Georgetown University. But when Thomsen demanded title to the Czech embassy its ambassador refused, so he didn't bother to ask the Poles for theirs. The Austrian embassy sat empty for months, as many considered it unlucky, but the new Danish ambassador apparently wasn't superstitious. Last fall he leased it for a single year instead of the customary three; he paid that year in advance, and now his country's gobbled up ten months later. An inside joke is that the German embassy will soon add

**Fig. 16.** The Nazi and Austrian flags fly from the Austrian embassy in Washington DC following the *Anschluss*. Library of Congress, Prints and Photographs Division, Harris and Ewing Collection.

a new member to handle its burgeoning real estate holdings. Though the Nazi shadow extends intermittently across Embassy Row, Germany abandons its long-standing plans to build a grand new embassy when its overseas invasions trigger the resignation of its American architect, Harry Cunningham.

"The Germans pick up so many embassies for nothing," Cunningham writes in a letter published by the Associated Press. "Why do they need to build any?"[25] He receives more than two hundred congratulatory letters and telegrams from people worldwide, but asking for payment for services rendered to date produces a curt rebuttal. Strangely enough, next spring, when an embassy is beset by termites, it's not the dilapidated German one but the grand new British one. When queried by reporters, Thomsen offers a diplomatic "no comment."

Many nations are unsurprisingly unhappy and critical of Germany's expansionist march. But an unexpected critic weighs in too, or perhaps not so unexpected given her erratic history. Bébé Thomsen writes a ten-page letter to Secretary of State Hull's wife, Frances, whose father was a Jewish immigrant from Austria—an inconvenient fact and political liability Hull sought to keep secret. The letter expounds upon Thomsen's familiar criticism, denouncing Hitler and his evil ways.

In a "city of strange contradictions [where] nothing is what it seems to be," writes a columnist, "Mrs. Hull said it's about the most extraordinary thing that has happened to her."[26]

# 6

## Isolation versus Intervention

On May 10, 1940, one month after Germany's invasion of Denmark and Norway, Winston Churchill replaces Neville Chamberlain as prime minister. Three days later the new prime minister declares in his legendary speech before the House of Commons that he has "nothing to offer but blood, toil, tears, and sweat."

Yet his ascension is but a footnote to the day's biggest story. Germany's long-feared offensive tears into Belgium, Holland, and Luxembourg, advancing through the supposedly impenetrable Ardennes forest and bypassing France's vaunted Maginot Line. German troops cross into France, and all four countries are soon crushed and surrender. In France, the last to fall a scant six weeks after the invasion, as many as eighty-five thousand of its troops perish. Uncertainty grips both the American public and government. "Events in Europe have taken place with such rapidity in the last few months that it is difficult to grasp the ramifications of each startling change on the continent from day to day," writes the editor of the *American Foreign Service Journal.*[1] A follow-up article on the Nazis' shattering military victories concludes with an eerily prescient final sentence: "*As long as the country's possible enemies continue to hold the initiative, they, rather than the United States, will choose the location of the battlefield, as well as the time of the battle.*"[2]

Little does anyone know that eighteen months from now the attack that plunges the United States into World War II will come not from Hitler's army but Japan's navy.

Daily life on the capital's social scene is upended as the glamour and glitter that has always categorized the diplomatic corps recedes. "The thought," writes columnist Dudley Harmon, "of an envoy having to sit through an entire meal next to his enemy would freeze any hostess."[3] Yet as distinct camps emerge, an oddly bifurcated view surfaces of Nazism's chief representative. "Thin-lipped Herr Hans Thomson of the Nazi Embassy has approximately the same respectable standing here as a Capone lawyer used to have in Chicago," writes Harlan Miller, summing him up as a "devil's advocate."[4]

But Helen Essary, the reporter whose interview with Thomsen about European expansionism shocked so many last winter, presents a polar opposite view that epitomizes the age-old expression, "everybody loves a winner"—especially businessmen eager to do business in Europe. It's a brand new day, she claims, now that "Germany has been devouring the Low Countries and there is fear that she may conquer even greater slices of Europe. The German diplomats have become desirable dinner guests at the tables of Washingtonians anxious to know the Right People. Hitler's envoys are suddenly charming to have about again."[5]

Charming or repulsive: it's all in the eyes of the beholder, and those beholden to the isolationist cause ignore the Nazi onslaught and press on. Especially powerful voices emanate from Essary's boss, Eleanor "Cissy" Patterson, publisher of the *Washington Times-Herald*; her older brother, Joseph Patterson (*New York Daily News*); and her cousin Robert McCormick (*Chicago Daily Tribune*). Dubbed "The Three Furies of Isolation" by rival publisher Henry Luce, they use their multimillion-circulation papers to continually bludgeon the president and his interventionist policies. Their scathing editorials find considerable support, but ubiquitous news coverage of the war subliminally undercuts their message. For while most Americans know little about the other conquered countries, France is another story. Photographs and newsreel footage of Nazi troops goose-stepping past the

Arc de Triomphe and a trench-coated Hitler and minions inspecting the Eiffel Tower bring a chill. When Germany begins bombing England next month, images of devastated British cities—plus the riveting radio broadcasts of Edward R. Murrow from London—will arouse sympathy among millions of Americans for the victims of Nazi aggression.

But the isolationists send a strong message too. Their strongest messenger is famed aviator Charles Lindbergh, whose nonstop solo flight across the Atlantic in 1927 made him an instant American icon. Lanky, fair-haired, and blue-eyed, he cuts a dashing figure. But he also became a tragic figure after his namesake infant son, Charles, was kidnapped and murdered five years later. Wherever he goes on behalf of the America First Committee, which enemies dub the "Nazi transmission belt," he attracts headlines and huge crowds—and the private appreciation of the German embassy. "The greatly gifted Lindbergh, whose connections reach very far, is much the most important of them all. The Jewish element and Roosevelt fear the spiritual and, particularly, the moral superiority and purity of this man," reads a Nazi cable to Berlin cosigned by Thomsen and von Boetticher.[6] (Cables coming from only Thomsen invariably contain far less overt anti-Semitism.) Lindbergh's prewar tours and praise of Germany and his acceptance of a medal from Field Marshall Hermann Göring in 1938 have dented his once-pristine reputation. Mindful of the public relations disaster of the Bund's overt Nazism, Thomsen presses his masters to reign in German newspapers' effusive praise of Lindy.

Nazi propaganda efforts have one goal: keep America out of the war, or at least delay its entry as long as possible. Lindbergh makes for a perfect mouthpiece, but he isn't the only famous pilot attracting standing-room-only crowds on the America First lecture circuit. An enthusiastic if somewhat eccentric aviatrix who draws adoring audiences also gained worldwide attention for an audacious aerial stunt.

On September 26, 1939, a silver monoplane swoops low over a jittery Washington DC and drops a load of "peace" pamphlets espousing favorite Nazi talking points. In the cockpit sits diminutive Laura Ingalls (no relation to Laura Ingalls Wilder, author of the Little House on the Prairie series), a one-time rival to Amelia Earhart until the latter's mysterious disappearance after taking off from New Guinea during an attempted world flight in 1937. In the thirties Ingalls set several world records herself: the first coast-to-coast flight, Brooklyn to Los Angeles, in just under sixteen hours, and the first solo woman's flight over the Andes and around South America, a twenty-two-thousand-mile jaunt. A child of privilege, she'd followed a circuitous path to airborne fame. After attending finishing schools in Paris and Vienna, Ingalls attempted disparate careers as a concert pianist and nurse before careening to ballet dancing. She even toured as a dancer and actor with a vaudeville troupe. Nothing clicked until she discovered flying.

She's also a true though closeted believer in Nazism. "American women do not intend to have their men again sent to die on foreign soil!" cry the crude red, white, and blue pamphlets she drops.[7] They were written by fellow fascist Catherine Curtis, an ex-actress and radio host who bankrolled Ingalls's isolationist exploits. Curtis channeled her rabid anti-Semitism and hatred of Communism into several women's organizations including the National Legion of Mothers of America, though neither she nor Ingalls were married or had children. Many Fascist-inspired antiwar groups used the word *mother* in their titles, a ploy to tug on heartstrings.

Some fliers land on the White House lawn, and Ingalls' pilot's license is suspended for flying over restricted airspace and dropping materials without permission. The feisty flyer's subsequent claims of ignorance of the regulations fall flat. "The respondent showed disturbing deficiencies in her knowledge of the current provision of the civil air regulations," writes the Civil Aeronautics Authority.[8] It won't be the last time Ingalls's antics land her in court, but next time the charge—working as a paid, unregistered agent of the German government—will have far more serious ramifications. And the charge will be true, because she's been secretly pocketing cash from embassy spymaster von Gienanth. This relentless peddler of Nazi propaganda, masquerading as messenger of peace, fancies herself a Mata Hari. "Without America [the British] are beaten," she writes privately to Thomsen. "Heil Hitler!"[9]

But Ingalls's conspicuous public behavior pales before the work of oddball George Sylvester Viereck, who was born in Munich in 1884 and emigrated to America as a boy. During World War I he propagandized on behalf of Germany and later achieved notoriety as the author of several erotic novels. His zealous support of National Socialism prompts Thomsen to hire him to spearhead anonymous efforts to influence members of Congress and opinion makers in articles disseminated through libraries and news and travel agencies. Much of the embassy money is funneled through First Secretary Heribert von Strempel, another Gestapo agent and von Gienanth's superior. But Viereck's boldface proselytizing makes him few friends. "A man with two loves—American dollars and German ideologies," writes the *New York Post*, "he is the leading exponent of Hitlerism in this country."[10]

The Overseas Press Club of America clearly spells out its reasons for demanding Viereck's resignation. "We didn't like him or the men he brought to our meetings," said Bernet Hershey, its executive secretary, "all kinds of Gestapos and bundists [who'd] create disturbances while our speakers were talking." But the silver-tongued ex-poet and author returns fire, calling their demand "merely another phase of the same mass hysteria which blinds men's eyes at a lynching bee and makes them do things for which they are ashamed after it is all over."[11]

But it's Viereck's ghostwriting that Thomsen uses to best effect. The Germanophile's speeches and articles are printed in the *Congressional Record* and mailed out for free by the millions through the franking privileges of twenty-four isolationist congressmen unaware of the Nazi backing, a practice of which Thomsen's tightfisted overseers in Berlin undoubtedly approve. Over and over the propaganda hammers home the risk to American soldiers' lives and massive potential U.S. military spending, all to help Great Britain maintain its empire. "'England expects every American to do his duty' might be particularly effective," cables Thomsen, recommending a phrase that could easily have come from Viereck's pen.[12]

But Thomsen sets his sights even higher, aiming surreptitious fire at FDR to defeat him or at least damage his reelection bid. Spreading around fifty thousand dollars from Berlin, he has delegates invited to the Republican convention who add isolationist language to its platform. Yet the resulting plank is so ambiguous that even caustic journalist H. L. Mencken writes it could "approve both sending arms to England or sending only flowers."[13] Thomsen bankrolls a full-page ad that runs in papers nationwide under the authorship of the National Committee to Keep

# PROGRAMM

zu der vom Deutschen Generalkonsulat veranstalteten
Gedenkstunde anlaesslich des

# Deutschen Nationalfeiertages

am Mittwoch, den 1. Mai 1940, abends 8 Uhr 30

in der Schwabenhalle

ECKE MYRTLE UND KNICKERBOCKER AVENUE
BROOKLYN, N. Y.

---

STAR SPANGLED BANNER

1) Festmarsch aus der Oper "DIE FOLKUNGER" ........ *Kretschmer*

2) „SCHAFFENDES VOLK - DEIN FEIERTAG"
 Kantate gesprochen und gesungen von dem
 Sprechchor unter Leitung von Hanns Münz

3) „MIT VEREINTEN KRÄFTEN", Marsch ......... *Egger-Rieser*

4) ANSPRACHE ............. Generalkonsul DR. HANS BORCHERS
 Anschliessend gemeinsamer Gesang des
 DEUTSCHLAND- UND HORST WESSEL-LIEDES

5) „VOM RHEIN ZUR DONAU", Potpourri ............. *Robrecht*

6) VORFÜHRUNG DEUTSCHER FILME
 a) „Die Donau" (Vom Schwarzwald bis Wien)
 b) „Deutsche Arbeit" (Glasherstellung)
 c) „Neueste Bilder aus der deutschen Heimat"
 (*Ufa-Wochenschau*)

7) „WIR FAHREN GEGEN ENGELLAND", Marschlied ...... *Niel*

---

**Fig. 17.** Program and ticket for a pro-Nazi rally in Brooklyn. Courtesy of George Borden.

America out of Foreign Wars, headed by isolationist senator Hamilton Fish: "To the delegates of the Republican national convention and to American mothers, wage earners, farmers and veterans. Stop the march to war. . . . The Democratic party, we believe, is the interventionist and war party and is rushing us headlong into war in efforts to quarantine and police the world with American blood and treasure."[14]

The Nazis' stealth campaign is an utter fiasco. Republicans go on to nominate long-shot Wendell Wilkie, who supports the interventionist position too but is routed in November. As ham-handed as their propaganda is, it's not as inept as the Nazi spies sent by the Abwehr, German intelligence. The FBI infiltrates and monitors its biggest ring, eventually busting and convicting thirty-three spies in front-page blockbuster news. Thomsen registers his disgust to his superiors back home: "Such poorly organized operations by irresponsible and incompetent agents, which most likely have not benefited our conduct of the war, may cost us the last remnants of sympathy which we can still muster here in circles whose political opposition is of interest to us."[15]

The spying also puts the embassy's covert activities squarely in the FBI's crosshairs. Never above ignoring the line between legal and illegal, Hoover oversees a massive operation that taps phones, reads mail, and surveils and photographs people entering and leaving the embassies of not only Germany but Italy, Japan, and neutrals Spain and Portugal. He's not the only spymaster; Canadian businessman Bill Stephenson leads England's massive stateside spying apparatus, which initially operated under the cover of the British Passport Control office in New York before adopting the acronym BSC, for British Security Coordination. It's tasked with the opposite mission of the Nazis: get the United States into the war on the Allied side, the quicker the better. Code-named Intrepid, he's also known informally as Little Bill to Big Bill, that is, Wild Bill Donovan, founder of America's nascent foreign intelligence agency, the Office of Strategic Services (OSS), forerunner to the CIA. "Bill Stephenson," said Donovan, "taught us all we ever knew about foreign intelligence."[16]

At the Italian embassy, a counselor brings in the leaders of several Italian American clubs but claims there's "nothing in particular" he wants to discuss. An FBI investigation reveals he's relaying orders from

Rome instructing the groups to lobby against the Selective Service and Training Act, a bill the Axis wants to see defeated. When papers report that the embassy is promoting fascism in America, Colonna protests to Hull that Italian nationals are "keeping themselves apart not only from the so-called 'un-American activities but from any political activity whatsoever'" and that his envoys "have always strictly limited their activities to their legal consular functions."[17]

Far less adept than their German counterparts, the Italians run a barebones spying operation. Military attaché Adolfo Infante takes a novel approach after discovering that newsreels screened before movies often include footage of U.S. military preparations and plants churning out tanks and planes. He buys and ships a newsreel to Rome, which responds that yes, the information is valuable, but couldn't he save money by simply going to the theater and taking notes? Early next year Mexican customs officials, acting on a tip from the FBI, discover $2 million being smuggled in by an Italian aide—stripping away any pretense that the Italian embassy isn't a facade for subversive activities. But in reality they're only following orders, just as Hitler is increasingly dictating Mussolini's direction and policies. Thomsen's staff begins tailing Italian diplomats, just like the FBI has been doing, and prescribes the Italians' activities by specifying what invitations can be accepted and what guests may be entertained: only Germans, Japanese, Spaniards, and staffers from several South American countries, which prompts Lombard to note that Italy is "wagging the tail of the Axis."[18]

As fall approaches, ongoing war in Europe and increasing investigations of Axis skullduggery at home cut into the Thomsens' social schedule. Yet Bébé remains her effervescent self. The couple surfaces at a party at the Dominican Republic's embassy for strongman Rafael Trujillo: "Frau Thomsen, who defied the arrival of autumn in a white ensemble, went into raptures over her recent vacation in Colorado."[19] One afternoon in the Mayflower's restaurant, dispossessed diplomats gather: at one table the American ambassadors to Belgium, France, and Poland huddle with Welles, while a few feet away Hans Thomsen lunches with staffers. Both parties studiously avoid each other.

Rumors fly that Hans Thomsen may soon be recalled, but at year's end he's promoted to minister of the first class: one grade below that of ambassador. Just a little more than four years after arriving in America, he's outlasted two ambassadors to become acting ambassador, the highest-ranked Reich official. Yet detractors still snipe. "The beautiful wife of Nazi Ambassador Hans Thomsen is a most puzzled woman these days," writes a constant tormenter. "Here's her Fuehrer doing everything he can to improve the world for the Aryans—and an exclusive Aryan hunt club accidentally-on-purpose forgot to invite her to its biggest affair this year."[20] Music, though, knows no boundaries, and the Thomsens join an international array of diplomatic star power at two hot-ticket concerts at Constitution Hall: the incomparable pianist and composer Sergei Rachmaninoff, and Leopold Stokowski leading the Philadelphia Orchestra.

Last September Germany, Italy, and Japan signed the Tripartite Pact in Berlin, formalizing the Axis alliance and issuing a stark warning to the United States. The countries promise to "undertake to assist one another with all political, economic and military means if one of the Contracting Powers is attacked by a Power at present not involved in the European War or in the Japanese-Chinese conflict."[21] The agreement exacerbates the already fraught relations in the nation's capital, where war has triggered upheaval and reset alliances. Many diplomats of conquered countries now represent governments in exile. The Vichy French government replaces its ambassador with Gaston Henry-Haye, sent by eighty-four-year-old Marshal Henri-Philippe Pétain, a World War I hero and hoped-for savior of France. Cloaked in patriotism, his collaborationist regime promulgates a Nazi-ish foundation of *famille, travail, patrie*: family, work, fatherland. He gives his new ambassador a succinct mission: "save American friendship."[22]

Henry-Haye, fifty years old, brings an impressive resume: currently a senator and mayor of Versailles, he not only fought alongside the Allies in World War I and received the Legion of Honor, France's highest distinction, he came to the United States to help train American soldiers. In his introductory letter to Franklin D. Roosevelt he sounds all the right notes, lamenting that "my unhappy country has just suffered the most cruel reverses which it has ever had to record in the course of the vicissitudes of its long and glorious past," and likens his mission to that of Benjamin Franklin in 1776. "I shall certainly not have the presumption to claim to possess the incomparable attributes of that American ambassador extraordinary. But I may doubtless hope, in attempting to solve the difficult problems before me, to have the benefit of your personal good will and the generous understanding of your countrymen."[23]

Indeed, many have high hopes for the new ambassador, whom reporter Kathleen Cannell, living in Paris, describes as an "ideal spokesman and one of the 'new men with new ideas' [whose] courage won eminence."[24] But such lofty words crash upon the arrival of Henry-Haye, a frequent stateside visitor and fluent English speaker who helped train U.S. troops during World War I. Before that he visited the United States and explored the country by foot, bicycle, car, and train, and was reportedly once arrested as a tramp. A little man who wears shoes with abnormally high heels, he sports a Hitlerian mustache Hull once anthropomorphized as "truculent." Upon deplaning he's greeted by picketers denouncing him as a Nazi stooge, a rude welcome that presages his stormy tenure—one that'll end several years later with an internment apart from the Nazi and Italian diplomats with whom he collaborates from day one. In his first official party for the press, Henry-Haye tacitly acknowledges his masters by honoring two newsmen: Germany's press agent Kurt Sell and Masuo Kato, newly returned from an eight-month assignment in Tokyo.

Kato's return coincides with the biggest diplomatic shift of the year: the arrival of a new Japanese ambassador. Kichisaburo Nomura, a well-regarded naval officer, had served in the United States during the Great War. He's blind in one eye, the result of an attack by a Korean independence activist in 1932. In the United States he brings high expectations and carries a lofty title: Ambassador Extraordinary and Plenipotentiary of His Majesty the Son of Heaven. When he arrives at Union Station, the first diplomat to shake his hand as he steps off the train? Hans Thomsen. (Next month Thomsen suffers the loss of his father, Carlo, who dies back in Hamburg at age eighty-one.) Italy sends its second in command, Alberto Rossi Longhi. "Surely here was a man who could bring about in the United States that understanding of Japan's aspiration which was need for an amicable settlement of outstanding issues," wrote Kato optimistically, who feels no issues between the countries "could not be settled by a diplomatic wave of the hand."[25]

Buried in a flurry of personnel changes coinciding with Nomura's arrival is the return of Hidenari Terasaki as second secretary for press relations. He, his American wife, Gwen, and their daughter, Mariko, along with Masuo Kato, sail into San Francisco harbor from Yokohama in late March 1941 on the *Tatsuta Maru*. They arrive too late to attend the funeral of their friend Raphael Pollio, the longtime manager of the Mayflower who recently passed away. His funeral attracts a who's who of influential Washingtonians including an ambassador, a Supreme Court justice, a senator, a governor, several associate justices, commissioners, and J. Edgar Hoover. Delighted to be back on her native soil, Gwen is unaware that her husband is not simply a diplomat but a political intelligence and propaganda agent. Spying is still the purview of military attachés; Terasaki's duties include estimating "the total strength of the United States, focusing on politics, economics, and the military. In addition, the embassy was to research all persons and organizations that openly or secretly opposed participation in the war."[26]

In late March another Japanese ocean liner, the *Nitta Maru*, pulls into a different American port: Pearl Harbor. Onboard is a new consular staffer, twenty-nine-year-old Tadashi Morimura. Within days the unassuming young man, fluent in English, is acting more like a tourist than an employee: touring the island, strolling the piers, snorkeling the harbor, cruising in glass-bottomed boats, and taking tourist flights to get a birds-eye view of Oahu. His colleagues think him a lazy young fellow and heavy drinker who often doesn't even bother to return to the office after lunch. Actually, he's anything but idle: he's the industrious eyes and ears of Admiral Isoroku Yamamoto, architect of the forthcoming surprise attack.

His real name is Takeo Yoshikawa, a former trainee pilot turned spy who takes no notes or photographs but commits everything to memory. He doesn't try to sneak into restricted military bases or pilfer documents. Blending into the large Japanese American population he moves about easily and, as a real estate expert specializes in location, he focuses on one location in particular: the Shunchoro Tea House atop Alewa Heights. Its panoramic view of Pearl Harbor does double duty: providing Yoshikawa with an eagle-eye seascape of ship movements, and attracting lots of customers including American officers. They chat up its beautiful geisha girls—who he also uses for cover on his sight-seeing activities and who unwittingly supply rich eavesdropping opportunities. Upstairs there's even a room with a telescope that the friendly owners let him use to take naps, where he spies even closer on harbor activities. To top it all off he often picks up hitchhiking sailors and casually pumps them for information.

For the next nine months Yoshikawa transmits invaluable information, but there's one thing he doesn't know: his messages can be read by the Americans. The Allies have broken the Japanese diplomatic code, a cryptographic coup termed Magic. But with up to seventy-five transmissions every day and a lack of qualified Japanese translators, the flow—not to mention the interpretation and prioritization—of information to a highly restricted group of recipients is fragmentary. Plus Yoshikawa's transmissions are in a lower-priority naval code so they're never afforded the attention of Magic. Sifting through and disseminating the blizzard of Magic decrypts is an arduous job, but it has revealed one key stateside piece of intelligence: Terasaki's role as a spymaster.

"At the Japanese embassy Terasaki is, for all intents and purposes, head of the Japanese intelligence service," wrote Adolf Berle Jr., a belief echoed in numerous top-secret memos from top government officials.[27] The FBI watches the Terasakis from the moment they arrive, tapping their home phone and monitoring their mail. Within a few months Terasaki is traveling extensively to set up intelligence networks. Upon returning from South America he's met by Gwen and Mariko at the Nashville airport, where an undercover Office of Naval Intelligence (ONI) agent chatting up Gwen discovers that her husband traveled more than twenty thousand miles to Mexico, Peru, and Ecuador. Keeping spies requires considerable cash, and soon he becomes the third highest-paid employee at the embassy, behind only Ambassador Nomura and counselor Sadao Iguchi.

Despite his occupation, Terasaki opposes (and fears) war with America. "It [is] a mistake to think that Japan would give in if it was driven into a tight corner by the United States," he writes in one surveillance

**Figs. 18 and 19.** Hosiery workers and supporters march to the White House to protest a proposed boycott of Japanese silk. Library of Congress, Prints and Photographs Division, Harris and Ewing Collection.

report.[28] Like Thomsen, he secretly hires surrogates—only Westerners, never Japanese—to write and speak publicly on behalf of his country in the United States. And like Thomsen, his activities run afoul of the Dies Committee. One committee member calls Japanese undercover operations "greater than the Germans ever dreamed of having in the Low Countries" and adds it would be a "tremendous force to reckon with in the event of war."[29] Nevertheless, Terasaki's communications with isolationists are more sincere than the cynical machinations of Thomsen, who cultivates contacts only to delay U.S. entry into the war on the Allied side; Terasaki genuinely wants to avoid war.

The signing of the Tripartite Pact, along with America's innate racism against the "yellow peril," contributes to a deepening ostracism of Japanese in the nation's capital. So who better to provide a cover and natural entrée into society for Terasaki than a beautiful American wife? In an extraordinary sign of troubled times, no Japanese—who in previous years have always played high-profile roles—attend the annual Cherry Blossom Festival in April 1941. When reporters spot and approach a group of Orientals and ask where they're from, they get a one-word answer: Thailand.

Kato especially feels the chill of local ill will when denied membership in both the University Club and the Kenwood Country Club, where he'd previously been welcomed. Even at the National Press Club he feels excluded, and a friend reveals that a U.S. intelligence officer has been asking around about him. After the war, in Tokyo, he runs into an old colleague from the Associated Press who's surprised to see Kato in civilian clothes.

"Then you weren't really a commander in the [Japanese] Navy after all!" exclaims the man, revealing that persistent rumors circulated that Kato was a spy.[30] The FBI bugged his Dupont Circle apartment and compiled a thick dossier.

# 7

## War Wary

The Nazis' espionage operations in Washington are far more entrenched and effective than anything the Japanese or Italians ever muster. Yet hampered by the public's increasing distrust of Germany, Thomsen must devise creative ways to stealthily advance its agenda. One of his strangest finds is a Quaker and peace activist named Malcolm Lovell.

At Thomsen's urging Lovell met Lord Lothian at the British embassy in July 1940, offering to work as a go-between to broker a secret pie-in-the-sky peace plan. A year later Thomsen shifts hemispheres by arranging a meeting between Lovell and counselor Iguchi for another quixotic peace initiative; his preposterous schemes distract allies and enemies alike. The Thomsens often socialize with Lovell and his wife, with Thomsen masterfully playing the putative peacemaker by divulging misinformation that seems genuine. Lovell naively passes along Thomsen's words verbatim to spy chief Donovan. In a memo to Donovan, Lovell quotes Thomsen: "Undercover agencies in the U.S. communicate with Germany directly through their own system, and never through the embassy facilities. I would under no circumstances permit it. I have always believed that such undercover methods by either side promote ill will and gain little information of value."[1]

Had Thomson been Pinocchio, his nose would have grown noticeably with such an audacious lie.

A firm believer in unconventional operations, Donovan swallows the bait and has Lovell offer Thomsen a $1 million bribe if he'll defect and denounce the Nazis. Privately Hans and Bébé must have had a good laugh over this extravagant but boneheaded offer that never had a scintilla of being accepted. Far from discouraging undercover operations, Thomsen has developed some deep connections, including one inside a location thought impregnable: the State Department's code room. An isolationist working there discusses the contents of some Magic intercepts with a like-minded friend who asks for copies to show sympathetic legislators on the Hill. But the friend is actually on Thomsen's payroll and passes along information that prompts Thomsen to send a telegram to Berlin marked Top Secret: "As communicated to me by an absolutely reliable source, the State Department is in possession of the key to the Japanese coding system and is therefore also able to decipher information telegrams from Tokyo to Ambassador Nomura here regarding Ambassador Oshima's reports from Berlin."[2]

In a stunning example of what-goes-around-comes-around, the following month U.S. analysts decrypt a message from Oshima that reveals what Thomsen had ascertained. So now the Allies know that the Japanese know but, astonishingly, they don't heed Thomsen's warning. After a cursory investigation the Japanese wrongly conclude their key ciphers remain unbroken. In the arcane world of code-breaking and secrets revealed, it's really not all that surprising because everyone likes to believe their system is impenetrable. For example, last year an official at the U.S. embassy in Berlin made a remarkable discovery: details of Operation Barbarossa, Hitler's secret plan to invade Russia. Seeking to curry favor with the Soviets, Sumner Welles revealed the information to Russian Ambassador Oumansky, who promptly reported to Thomsen that the Americans were trying to foment dissent between their countries by spreading lies.

In truth, this disclosure was but one of many reports about Hitler's impending invasion of its erstwhile ally. Stalin ignored them all. So on the morning of June 22, 1941, he was shocked, shocked!—just like Captain Renault (actor Claude Rains) in the forthcoming wartime saga *Casablanca*—when the Wehrmacht troops he knew had been massing on his border invade. Three million soldiers, backed by thousands of tanks and planes, sweep into their former ally's homeland across a two-thousand-mile front from the Arctic to the Black Sea and inaugurate what will become the bloodiest fighting of the European theater.

The news sends shockwaves across Washington DC, where the German and Italian delegations are still reeling from FDR's recent closure of consular offices nationwide and expulsion of all personnel. Pressure had been building for years, with the attorney general of Massachusetts recently claiming that, diplomatic immunity be damned, he'd haul suspected Nazi agents before a grand jury to "show that the laws which they laugh at have sharp teeth at times."[3] His dubious legal threats notwithstanding, it falls to a torpedo—fired by a German U-boat that sunk an American cargo ship in the South Atlantic—to finally torpedo most of their stateside subversive activity. "We must take the sinking of the 'Robin Moore' as a warning to the United States not to resist the Nazi movement of world conquest," Roosevelt tells Congress. "Were we to yield on this we would inevitably submit to world domination at the hands of the present leaders of the German Reich. We are not yielding and we do not propose to yield."[4]

While most Americans welcome the closings, some see overreach. "This action is fully unjustifiable, dishonest, offensive and unnecessary," one man writes to Secretary of State Hull. "True indeed, the Axis form of government is a definite contradiction to our precious Democratic way of life, but the manner in which our government is acting shall positively not destroy that ideology but shall, I feel, only establish a totalitarian regime on our own soil!"[5] The administration shutters all twenty-four consulates, including the Boston branch that houses Scholz and his wife. "Washington long ago decided that if the cruel, ruthless Nazi policy could be pictorialized in human form by some inspired artist, Dr. Scholz should sit for the portrait," wrote Arthur Krock, the iron-handed chief of the Washington bureau of the *New York Times*.[6] The news reaches Scholz in New York where he's staying at the Waldorf Astoria. When he settles his bill (with the customary 50 percent diplomatic discount), the cashier addresses him in German. When he asks if she's from Germany, she answers affirmatively. "In Washington," he says, "at the embassy, people are wanted. Apply." Young Else Arnecke recalls, "That sounded like an order."[7]

Born in Bremerhaven, Germany, the adventurous thirty-year-old had always dreamed of America. So at age eighteen she'd emigrated, and she loved it from her first day. She worked as an au pair before becoming a waitress at the hotel, took night courses in shorthand and bookkeeping, and moved up to cashier. She's intrigued by the job offer and trains for an interview. "Miss Arnecke, have I ever paid my bill to you?" asks Thomsen politely, and soon the multilingual young woman has a new job: stenographer.[8] The next day the embassy hires twenty-year-old Albert Christian Schweikle, an entry-level clerk, messenger boy, and FBI informant. That same day Franklin D. Roosevelt uncharacteristically lashes out at a German citizen working as a clerk at the German embassy. Married to an American woman, twenty-eight-year-old Dr. Carl Sennhenn once applied for U.S. citizenship and was battling to defer a draft notice received last April. Claiming Sennhenn took out his citizenship papers in bad faith, Roosevelt thunders, "This man is morally unfit to become a member of the Army of the United States."[9] Little does he know how true those words are: Sennhenn, later interned with the German diplomats, will become the only known detainee to be convicted after World War II of war crimes.

The U.S. government also closes the German Library of Information, the German Railway and Tourist Agencies, and the Transocean News Service—longtime hotbeds of subversive activity and propaganda. All Italian consulates and similar organizations are also shuttered. Both countries respond by closing all U.S. consuls in their lands and the countries they occupy. In mid-July 450 staffers sail for Europe, but 45 refuse to leave. Some, away from their countries for years, don't support fascism or Nazism and fear imprisonment upon return. Others have American spouses, are ill, or simply fail to report to the docks as required. Similar recalcitrance will surface when all embassy diplomats, staffers, and families are interned after Pearl Harbor—though this removal of some five hundred will considerably shave the numbers detained at year's end.

In addition to the expulsions, assets are frozen, effectively ending all trade between the United States and the two European Axis powers. This extraordinary series of diplomatic hammer blows signals the worst relations between the United States and Germany since the Great War, but for many it's still not enough. "The Chargé d'Affaires Hans Thomsen, who conducts the business of the Embassy in the absence of the Ambassador, should, in common parlance, be given his walking papers and the Embassy should be closed," writes fiery Brooklyn congressman Emanuel Celler to the president. "Destroy this Nazi nest of sabotage now cloaked in diplomatic immunity. Complete the task so courageously and nobly begun. Public opinion now hardening against the Nazis will be wholeheartedly with you."[10]

Public opinion also hardens against the puppet Vichy regime when a *j'accuse!* attack fills the August 31 front page of the *New York Herald-Tribune.* "VICHY EMBASSY IN U.S. SHOWN AS HEADING CLIQUE OF AGENTS AIDING NAZIS." It's a most unwelcome spotlight upon Henry-Haye, who's labored mightily to advance the illusion that Vichy France is not under the Nazis' thumb. Like a magician's sleight-of-hand misdirection, just last week he'd emphasized the sunny side of French living by proffering tips in the *Washington Post* on how to make the perfect French salad dressing: use vegetable, not olive oil (its "perfume" spoils the dressing), and never use mustard.[11] His nonstop charm offensive has scored some successes, like gracing the cover of *Time* last March. Henry-Haye is quite dapper in a three-piece, double-breasted suit and petting his dalmatian, Pop. But now he's forced to publicly rebuke the newspaper charges as part of "an unjustifiable campaign by certain Americans and Frenchmen to break up diplomatic relations between the French Government and the United States."[12] Rumors swirl about his imminent recall, but Henry-Haye survives the tumult to continue his courtly courting of amicable Franco-American relations.

Meanwhile, German-American relations continue spiraling down, with unknown agitators chalking V's in front of the German embassy at night and threatening mail pouring in. For the first time Hans Thomsen requests and gets round-the-clock police protection at the embassy. But besides public and political pressure, he is also facing a vexing personal problem. He recently took a trip to Chicago, where FBI monitoring revealed that he dined, went to the theater, and stayed in the same hotel as an attractive single young woman from Michigan. "They secured rooms," reads the report, "so that [her] bedroom connected with Mr. Thomsen's parlor."[13]

Whether or not Bébé knows about his infidelity, a very public spat erupted between them this summer at the Waldorf Astoria, apparently a favorite hotel for German envoys. She told him she'll never return to Germany if he's called back, even if it means the end of their marriage. "He remonstrated. She wept—and slammed the door," the story read, adding that the episode "spikes as a canard" her anti-Nazi posturing and "clearly establishes the sincerity of a woman whom some had come to doubt."[14]

Is it all an act? Time will soon tell.

Hans brushes off the brouhaha, denying her proclamation. "The fact is," he says, "Frau Thomsen has an old mother in Germany whom she would like to see."[15] Lunching with friends at the Mayflower several months later, he chats amiably with a Norwegian woman visiting from New York. Bébé nervously complains about being forced to go fox hunting near Fredericksburg since she's unwelcome in several other prominent Virginia hunting communities. She also lashes out at the "lies told by the wives of the members of the British embassy. . . . How preposterous that I have been accused of trying to get naval secrets!"[16]

The following week Thomsen meets with Assistant Secretary of State Breckinridge Long, known to his friends as Breck, which is coincidentally a popular brand of shampoo for women. (Its popular Breck Girls ads made advertising history.) He asks why Germany hasn't yet responded to a joint U.S. proposal to exchange citizens held within the jurisdiction of four countries. England, France, and Italy have already agreed. Thomsen says he'll cable Berlin immediately, unaware that within a month he himself will be in that exact same boat—an alien held in America—and Long will be overseeing that detention.

For several years America's attention has seesawed back and forth between the European and Far Eastern theaters of war. Now the latter leapfrogs back ahead when the Japanese march into French Indochina with the acquiescence of the Vichy regime. "Inactive vigilance," the term coined by Kato two years ago to describe the Roosevelt administration's

**Fig. 20.** Uncle Sam puts a kink in the Japanese oil supply. Library of Congress, Prints and Photographs Division.

all talk, no action policy, finally elicits a response: economic warfare. In late July FDR issues an executive order freezing all Japanese assets in the United States, effectively severing all economic activity between the two nations and, most crucially, depriving Japan of the petroleum products vital to drive its war machine. Besieged by so much international instability, though, happy occasions are still to be celebrated. So when Hull turns seventy in October, reporters surprise him with a birthday cake with twenty-one candles representing the countries of the Americas benefiting from the U.S. "good neighbor" policy he's championed. A photo of him blowing out the candles goes out on the wires worldwide but doesn't show the polyglot reporters—some from warring countries—applauding vigorously off camera. The camaraderie between them and Hull is so strong that when he first saw Kato upon his return from Japan a few months ago, the secretary exclaimed, "Glad to see you back. Come in and see me anytime."[17]

Right after Hull's birthday bash a new book waltzes into town. Actually, it more accurately jitterbugs in, for *Washington Waltz* turns the capital upside down. In recent years several tell-all tomes made splashy debuts but soon faded. In 1936 it was *Let Them Eat Caviar* by columnists George Abell and Evelyn Gordon; the next year came *Capital Kaleidoscope* by old-school hostess Frances Parkinson Keyes. But *Washington Waltz* quickly eclipses them both. It's gossipy and addictive, told by an insider who not only covers the diplomatic scene but is part of it. Washington native Helen Carusi Lombard, married to Colonel Emanuel Lombard, former French military attaché, reveals the inner machinations. Envoys race to see how they're portrayed, tongues wag, reviewers rave. "Capital is thrown in turmoil by book dissecting diplomats," trumpets the *Sunday Star.*

Each chapter profiles a different embassy, with none spared from Lombard's penetrating profiles of envoys past and present: the haughtiness of the Brits, the faux pas of the French, the snarl of the Russians, the guile of . . . just about everybody. The Axis powers come off especially bad. She reduces Bébé Thomsen to a stereotype: "It is becoming known that there have been Frau Thomsens in most German missions abroad." Prince Colonna becomes "The Fifth Colonna," an unflattering take on the term fifth columnist. "The jigsaw picture of the Washington Diplomatic

Corps has been tossed into a heap," Lombard writes, "and the piece representing Italy is somewhere at the bottom of the lot."[18] When queried by a reporter, Colonna shrugs his shoulders and replies, "Circumstance is at fault, not I."[19] Henry-Haye is "the Ersatz Ambassador" from a vassal state that has "no trouble finding diplomats to represent her ambiguity all over the world—which is one of the things Herr Hitler had in mind when he permitted the old Marshal to fondle his dream of Free France."[20] The Japanese ambassador? "Nomura is like one of those soldier-ecclesiastics of the Middle Ages who wore a cassock over the armored suit and had a sword hidden in the folds of a Bishop's cloak."[21] Describing a "hidden sword" a scant month before Pearl Harbor? Masterful work with eerily prescient timing to boot.

Simultaneously, another new book, *Total Espionage*, zeroes in on Axis spying in America. Author Curt Reiss, a German refugee and former journalist in Berlin, delivers a timely exposé that details the manipulations and machinations of Scholz, Henry-Haye, and a host of other lesser-known operatives. He connects the dots between the activities of Axis and collaborationist governments, noting how the closing of German and Italian consulates last July shifted operations to their Far Eastern brethren. "Steady communication went on between Japanese official representatives and the heads of German espionage," writes Reiss. "As early as June 1941 the number of Germans one ran into at the Japanese Consulate General in New York was constantly growing."[22]

Another frequent caller is Hidenari Terasaki, who visits New York in late October to confer with his agents and mine America First contacts. He reaches out to a minor isolationist for a desperate, ultimately unsuccessful attempt to broker a peace accord. The night before Halloween the man attends an America First rally in Madison Square Garden that attracts a standing-room-only crowd of twenty thousand. "President Roosevelt and his administration preach about preserving democracy and freedom abroad, while they practice dictatorship and subterfuge at home," cries keynote speaker Lindbergh to rapturous applause.[23] Little do they or anyone else know that this huge rally will be America First's last hurrah. When Terasaki meets his contact the next morning, the FBI records their every move. Two weeks later it releases a detailed thirteen-page report under Hoover's signature of Terasaki's spying life, with overviews of a dozen frequent contacts that include Kato.

Yet while U.S. intelligence agencies are intimately aware of his clandestine activities, they're disinclined to stop him for fear of revealing the existence of Magic—a price too steep to pay. The Magic intercepts of Nomura's cables give the administration a strong inside look at Japan's strategy but generate a false sense of complacency too. For back in Tokyo the government is amassing a naval and aerial force, something never communicated in any cables. Anticipating huge changes soon to come, Tokyo quietly reassigns Terasaki to leave for Rio de Janeiro in early December to oversee his burgeoning South American surveillance network.

In early November Nomura's among more than three thousand attendees flocking to the Russian embassy to celebrate the gala twenty-fourth anniversary of the great Socialist Revolution. Now that Russia's waging war against Germany, and FDR has okayed a million-dollar lend-lease grant to the Kremlin, it's once again acceptable for Washingtonians to attend—though Thomsen, Colonna, and Finnish minister Hjalmar Procopé are understandably nowhere in sight. Neither is oafish Ambassador Oumansky, who's being replaced by old Moscow hand Maxim Litvinov. Outside, arrivals are greeted by a young North Carolinian dressed stylishly in a long-tailed green coat with silver buttons and a silk top hat. "I think," the lad admits, "this job is just temporary."[24]

Nomura doesn't know it, but that describes his position too—though next week he receives some help when Special Envoy Saburo Kurusu, a fifty-three-year-old career diplomat, arrives to assist in the ongoing negotiations. On the surface he's a reassuring choice who'd previously served in America as a naval attaché during the Wilson administration. He met and married his American wife in Chicago in 1914; two of his three children were born in America, and one daughter even once met child star Shirley Temple. His arrival makes front-page news, though pessimistic U.S. government circles doubt any accord can be reached. "I think I still have a fighting chance of making a success of my mission," says Kurusu. But when a reporter asks the odds of that success, he diplomatically demurs to the assembled press: "You be the bookmakers."[25] In

**Fig. 21.** Ambassador Kichisaburo Nomura (*left*) and Special Envoy Saburo Kurusu (*touching hat*) after meeting with FDR at the White House. U.S. National Archives and Record Administration, Record Group 208.

his memoirs Hull later writes, "Kurusu seemed to me the antithesis of Nomura. Neither his appearance nor his attitude commanded confidence or respect. I felt from the start that he was deceitful."[26]

Despite Kurusu's presence, discussions drag on with little progress. "The conversations were like an endless dance of the seven veils," writes reporter Marquis Childs. "What was behind it or where it was going one could only guess. Washington was full of uneasy surmises."[27] On the war front, *New York Times* bureau chief Arthur Krock quotes an anonymous high government official who opines that "it is conceivable that the Japanese will move aggressively at any time . . . through Indo-China and Thailand, possibly to the Indies and Burma."[28]

Yet that lone story buried deep within the December 4 issue is no match for today's screaming front-page headline in the *Chicago Daily Tribune*: "FDR'S WAR PLANS! GOAL IS 10 MILLION MEN." An isolationist senator leaked the plan to a reporter, describing a strategy for mobilizing an expeditionary force to invade German-occupied Europe by July 1943. The news hits Washington like a gale-force hurricane, with the press pouncing in its wake. The report is genuine but simply a preliminary contingency plan, says Henry Stimson, secretary of the War Department, who trains his ire and fire back at the messenger, rabid anti-FDR publisher Robert McCormick: "What do you think of the patriotism of a man or a newspaper which would take these confidential studies and make them public to the enemies of the country?"[29]

Thomsen cables Berlin not once but twice on December 4. He gleefully describes the *Tribune*'s reporting as "causing a sensation here," noting that it reinforces the contention that in a potential two-front war, the United States will initially focus on opposing Germany. Thomsen denigrates America's allies, emphasizing the imminent collapse of the British Empire and "the elimination of the Soviet Union as a fighting power by the summer of 1942."[30]

Indeed, advance panzer divisions now stand fewer than twelve miles from Moscow, close enough for Wehrmacht officers to glimpse the capital's spiral towers through binoculars. But ferocious winter weather stalls the bone weary Nazi troops. Less than twenty-four hours after Thomsen's confident prediction, fresh Russian troops transferred from Siberia counterattack. "The Soviet armies punched through an enemy more scarecrow than human," wrote author Michael Peck. "German weapons were frozen, German soldiers were frozen, and sometimes the soldiers froze to the weapons. The survivors could only watch helplessly as the attackers, warmly clad in fur-lined jackets and boots, and camouflaged in white snowsuits, emerged like ghosts through the mist and snow."[31]

Thousands of miles from the subzero temperatures of war-torn Moscow, Washington DC welcomes the reverses of the once seemingly invincible Nazi juggernaut. And warily watches as the talks with Japan appear to be going nowhere. On Saturday, December 6, a newsman learns that his request to interview Kurusu has been granted. His name is H. R. Baukhage ("Buck" to his friends), who hearkens back to earlier journalistic times by using only his last name as his byline; the opening of his NBC radio broadcasts, "Baukhage talking," are nearly as familiar to listeners as "My friends," FDR's beginning of his soothing fireside chats. In the Japanese embassy he's ushered into the office of Terasaki, whose talk is noncommittal. "'If United States wants war, it can have war. If it wants peace, it can have peace.' . . . He paused a moment and started at me steadily with brown eyes that looked as solid as bullets," wrote Baukhage. Leaving after a strained interview with Kurusu, he passes many clerks and asks one if they're always so busy on a Saturday afternoon. "Oh, no," the young man answers, "only these days."[32] And so ends the last interview Kurusu ever gives in America.

Later that afternoon Kato takes a break from covering the talks to attend a farewell luncheon at the Mayflower for the soon-departing Terasaki. Afterwards a group returns to the embassy where Kato and another newsman play ping pong in the basement. Elsewhere in the building staffers are furiously decoding a multipart dispatch that Nomura and Kurusu are slated to deliver to Hull the next day—a feint since an armada of battleships, destroyers, submarines, and aircraft carriers with more than four hundred planes has been silently streaming toward Pearl Harbor for the last ten days.

But outwardly all appears calm. Kato dines at a Chinese restaurant near Union Station with his assistant Clarke Kawakami, son of a well-known Japanese socialist and an Irish American mother, and his wife, a Japanese actress, Chieko Takehisa. Afterward, Kato stops by the National Press Club and runs into Eric Friedman, a reporter for the International News Service, the Hearst newswire. Friedman "turned, recognized an acquaintance, small, brown-skinned, black-haired Masuo Kato, jovial little Washington correspondent of Japan's Domei News Agency," wrote *Time* reporter Ed Lockett. "'Hi Kato,' said Eric. 'Did you hear about the President's message to the Emperor of Japan?'" "'Good God, no,' replied Kato. 'I just cabled the office. All quiet here tonight. No news.'"[33]

Even the veteran newsman has no inkling of the impending cataclysm only hours away. Neither does Hans Thomsen. Two days earlier he had cabled Berlin, accurately summarizing the current situation: "Practically the entire press points out in alarmist articles every day that the issue of war or peace between America and Japan is on the knife's edge." But instead of quitting while he was ahead, Thomsen added a coda that couldn't have been more wrong: "It is known that Japan has no intention of attacking the United States."[34]

That attack comes at dawn the next morning. With it the world changes forever. The tightrope that the Axis diplomats had trod so carefully for so many years snaps, and down they tumble. When Bébé Thomsen first arrived five years ago, confident and radiant, she entertained in high style with that pet squirrel "draped around her neck like a lovely fur neckpiece."[35] Alas, only weeks after her party for departing ambassador Luther, the squirrel ran away.

Seems it didn't take too well to captivity—and neither will Bébé.

# 8

## Full Speed Ahead

The temperatures are mild, the mood is calm. Sunday, December 7, dawns as a welcome day of rest and relaxation for most in the nation's capital. Few can go Christmas shopping because virtually all stores are closed on Sundays. Only some gas stations and restaurants are welcoming customers. Downtown streets are largely deserted. In a department store window on 17th Street NW, across from the dowdy State Department building, a tinseled Christmas sign reads "Peace on Earth." Across the street, where not everyone has the day off, Secretary of State Hull huddles with Secretary of War Henry Stimson and Secretary of the Navy Frank Knox. The phone rings. It's the Japanese embassy requesting that Hull meet with Nomura and Kurusu. A time is set: 1:45 p.m.

The building's largely Sabbath still. High-ceilinged corridors are silent, save for the occasional echoing of an unhurried set of footsteps on the black and white checkerboard passageways. The Japanese envoys arrive twenty minutes late. By that time a naval officer has appeared without warning at Knox's door with bombshell news: Pearl Harbor is being attacked. Knox phones FDR at the White House next door, and a quiet Sunday afternoon turns calamitous for all, and all eternity. News flashes interrupt regular radio programming, and the shocking news spreads like wildfire by phone and word-of-mouth through government, diplomatic, and journalistic circles. Chinese ambassador Hu Shih, who certainly gets around—he had lunch yesterday with FDR at the White House—hears the news while dining at the home of publishers Henry and Clare Luce. A disbelieving general public jams newspaper switchboards with frantic inquiries. Some suspect an elaborate hoax, like Orson Welles's live primetime radio drama on Halloween 1938 of a supposed invasion of earth by Martians that triggered mass panic.

By midafternoon the press office at the White House has become ground zero for 150 reporters descending to transmit the latest to millions of listeners and readers. For the first time ever radio reporters are allowed to broadcast from the press room. Whenever a new development breaks, a Secret Service officer calls out "press conference" and reporters stampede into the cramped office of presidential press secretary Steve Early. A half dozen short, impromptu press conferences ensue until a 4:45 p.m. report with the most disconcerting news so far: Rear Admiral C. C. Bloch, commandant of the Fourteenth Naval District, reports "heavy damage" to the Hawaiian islands with "heavy loss of life." As reporters bolt for the door, Early calls out: "Just a minute. I want to ask you before you leave if any of you represent Japanese news agencies. If so, you are going to get no information from me. I am asking the Secret Service men to take up your credentials."[1]

At that moment the group's most familiar Japanese face, Kato, is at the Japanese embassy. After leaving he considers visiting the National Press Club, another chaotic scene of reporters digging into the biggest story of their lives. (There, since it's a Sunday, the club serves only beer and wine and not its popular thirty-five-cent highballs, but a dance orchestra plays at the season's first Sunday afternoon tea dance.) Kato wisely proceeds instead to a friend's house for dinner and an anguished conversation about an uncertain future, for him and the world. Five days ago he'd received a cablegram from his employer, ordering him to return to Tokyo. He wired back that he wanted to work until the end, whatever happened. Even after learning that embassy staff was

**Fig. 22.** Drawing found in a destroyed Japanese plane. Its characters on the left read, "Listen to the voice of doom! Open your eyes, blind fools!" Courtesy of DC Public Library, Washingtoniana Division.

destroying documents in preparation for departure, he still believed it was in anticipation of some kind of diplomatic rupture. Now he realizes he'd completely misjudged his government's true intentions.

By midmorning in Honolulu local police and FBI agents arrest the Japanese consular staff. In contravention of international diplomatic norms they search the offices, break into desks and filing cabinets, and cart away materials. They keep the envoys under house arrest for the next two months, treatment that Japan calls "extremely cruel and inhuman. The Imperial Japanese Government is astonished at such outrageous measures indulged in by the American authorities [that were] unnecessarily strict and severe[ly] contrary to the international usage and utterly incomprehensible."[2] With several thousand American soldiers and civilians lying dead and a thousand more injured, the protests of the perpetrators never even merit a response.

Through the day crowds still unaware of the magnitude of the carnage and destruction at Pearl Harbor gather outside the White House. Suspense reigns: bombings at Pearl Harbor and Manila, and torpedoing of transport and cargo ships in the Pacific are reported with scant details. FDR hosts a steady stream of cabinet officials and congressmen. A State official, "in view of the Japanese situation," requests that an agent be assigned to accompany Hull to the emergency cabinet meeting.[3] The agent meets him at his residence, the Wardman Park Hotel, and Hull acquiesces. On the ride back, an unmarked car follows with two DC police detectives. The next morning the agent again accompanies Hull to his office, marking the beginning of the secretary of State's permanent protective detail that continues to this day.

Out on the links, a CBS messenger approaches a foursome including Edward R. Murrow with the news. Assuming their White House supper invitation is cancelled, the Murrows ring up to discover it's still on. He does an early evening radio broadcast, likening the capital's calmness and resolve to London's reaction when war came there. He and his wife then partake of a gloomy dinner of scrambled eggs, milk, and pudding; food in this Roosevelt's White House is notoriously awful. In a mood of "well-bred outrage," Eleanor Roosevelt receives periodic notes throughout the meal from aides.[4] Afterwards, as Murrow starts to leave, she tells him the president still wants to see him. He waits on a bench outside his study and watches a parade of solemn VIPs pass by. Around 1 a.m. he and Bill Donovan join FDR for beer and sandwiches. Looking weary and frustrated, the president lets loose on the extent of the destruction and loss of life. When he gets to the planes he pounds a fist on his desk, exclaiming, "On the ground, by God. On the ground!"[5]

Murrow leaves, confused as to whether he should reveal what he heard. It's quite a scoop, but in the end he chooses not to breathe a word. But other colleagues in the press are pouring out reports, frantically trying to make sense of the day. "Washington tonight is a city stunned, not afraid, not excited, but like a boxer who, after three rounds of sparring catches a fast hook to the jaw, rocks back, rolls with the punch," writes *Time* reporter Jerry Greene. "Tonight Washington is rolling back from the clout but in the rolling, sets itself grimly, solidly for the counterpunch."[6]

Early the next morning under presidential orders police—supervised by fourteen FBI agents—cordon off the Japanese embassy. Phone lines are cut, mail service is discontinued, and anyone inside remains sequestered. Police, again supported by FBI agents, guard but don't close the Italian and German embassies where the latter buzzes as silent staffers ferry boxes in and out. But there's really only one story today: FDR's address to a joint session of Congress scheduled for 12:30 p.m. Huge solemn crowds encircle the White House and line his route to the Capitol. Throughout America activity grinds to a halt, traffic too, as millions anxiously tune into the radio at work, home, school . . . everywhere.

Soldiers in trench helmets bearing rifles with fixed bayonets surround the Capitol. (Most Washingtonians have never seen uniformed soldiers on duty, let alone troops with guns and bayonets.) Inside the floor's packed with congressmen, Supreme Court justices, a brace of high-ranking military officials in crisp dress uniforms. Diplomats, with the notable exception of any from the Axis countries, jam into too few reserved seats. A guard mistakenly detains the Chinese ambassador until a senator intercedes. Wives fill the galleries. Dressed in black, a somber Eleanor Roosevelt sits next to former first lady Edith Wilson, in a wine-colored suit and hat. Her late husband was the last president to ask for a declaration of war in these very chambers back on April 2, 1917. "Rumors of the damage at Pearl Harbor hovered like a low-hanging gas," wrote Childs, citing wildly disparate stories of numbers of battleships sunk, casualties, even rumors of enemy planes approaching New York and San Francisco.[7] Rousing cheers and applause interrupt the president's succinct six-and-a-half-minute, five-hundred-word address, and within an hour the war resolution he'd requested passes both houses. The speech now enshrined in history had initially read "a date which will live in history" until FDR crossed out that last word and substituted "infamy."

In the late afternoon Thomsen arrives at his embassy, grim-faced and clutching several newspapers. He declines to answer questions shouted by reporters. Later that night he cables his bosses in Berlin: Americans "had thought that they themselves could choose their enemy and the time to begin the war, and in the meantime let other peoples fight for American imperialism. They now see that they have been terribly deceived in this calculation."[8]

Struck by the previous day's earth-shattering events, one reporter over-reaches with an ominous portrait of sights unseen: "Behind the walls of the [German and Italian] embassies, perhaps was hidden a chapter yet untold in world history."[9] Far less momentously, behind closed doors it's not time for reflection but destruction. "Smoke curled from the chimney of the German chancery and bits of paper floated down to the raised drive on the Massachusetts avenue side of the building, indicating documents were being burned within,"[10] reports the *Evening Star.* Tomorrow, when the Italians—the proverbial day late—follow suit, Polish diplomats across the street take pity on reporters huddled outside in the cold and send over a quart of twenty-year-old Scotch.

Kato is enjoying no such luxuries, but he's comfortable. Picked up earlier this morning by the FBI, he asked about packing a bag and was told he wouldn't need one. He's driven to a nondescript government building a few blocks from his apartment and asked some innocuous questions: name, age, occupation. Afterward he gets a roll and coffee and is transferred to the FBI building, where he reads newspapers, eats a sandwich for lunch, and listens to the radio. He also gets a special visitor: presidential bodyguard Tom Qualters, often glimpsed behind FDR in photographs and newsreels. The president has sent him personally to retrieve Kato's invaluable White House Correspondents Association card, which can open doors all over town. Three fellow Japanese reporters, each carrying a packed suitcase, appear in early evening. All four are taken to a restaurant for dinner, where no one pays them any mind. When Kato asks about packing a bag too, he's told there's no time. Off they're whisked to Union Station to board a dusty red railroad car on a train bound north toward an undisclosed destination.

Kato wasn't the only one awoken this morning by the FBI. Gwen Terasaki, answering her door herself because her black maid Clementine had suddenly quit, faces a brisk, efficient G-man who asks the standard questions about name, age, and so on. He informs her that she and her family can only leave the apartment accompanied by an agent, allegedly to ensure their personal safety. An identical warning goes to the Iguchi family living nearby. Sadao Iguchi is an embassy counselor, and his eldest son, eleven-year-old Takeo, is a classmate of Mariko. Indoctrinated by his country's nationalism—back in Japan, elementary school students write letters every year that are included in care packages sent to Japanese troops in China—he fiercely believes Japan cannot be defeated. His older sister, Tatsuko, disagrees. "A small country like Japan hasn't got a chance of winning against a gigantic country like the United States," she says. "Why in the world did they start this war?"[11]

Gwen's mother, Bertha Harold, astonished to learn she's barred from returning to Tennessee, enlists her congressman's help. Republican Tennessee representative Carroll Reece, a World War I veteran and Purple Heart recipient, calls George Atcheson Jr. of State's Far Eastern desk to facilitate her departure. The night before her finally approved trip home, three generations—mother, daughter, and granddaughter—share a bed. The fear that they may never meet again makes for a restless night for the adults. In the morning, Harold departs. "The firm set of her shoulders and the erect way she walked down the hall braced me for things to come with the memory of her graceful strength," wrote Gwen. "When the elevator closed after her it occurred to me that she had never asked me to stay in America."[12]

Unlike Gwen Terasaki and Masuo Kato, Hildy von Boetticher isn't awoken by the FBI. But at this morning's meeting with her college president she learns some disconcerting news: the FBI has been tailing her for years. "Hildegard, they always knew of your whereabouts, your week-end trips, football games," she recalls him saying. "They didn't seem to think that you were a great threat to the nation."[13] In fact the FBI phoned that morning to tell him that, if she wants, she can remain in college and finish her degree. Staying would also mean she'd see her siblings plus her brother-in-law and their two young children. But deep down the twenty-one-year-old knows that her place is with her parents, and she must return to Germany—a country she hasn't seen since she was thirteen.

So that night she begins packing. "You sure are going home early for

Christmas, Miss Gard," says Ernie, the black janitor who brings down her trunk from the attic.[14] She tosses everything in willy-nilly as friends stop by for an impromptu sob session and party. One brings along the contents of a recent care package from home—Virginia ham, biscuits, and strawberry jam—that get quickly devoured. The next day her class-mates host a farewell lunch in the main dining hall. Heaped at her place setting are cards, small gifts, flowers, and a copy of A. A. Milne's classic *Winnie-the-Pooh*, inscribed, "Let this be your bible." It's a bittersweet time for all. The girls break into a song that undoubtedly played only a couple nights ago at their Christmas dance, "We'll Meet Again"—a current hit stateside by Guy Lombardo and His Royal Canadians, and an even bigger hit as performed by one Vera Lynn in England:

We'll meet again
Don't know where
Don't know when
But I know we'll meet again some sunny day.

Everyone joins in and von Boetticher dissolves into tears . . . until waitresses bring boxes of tissues to every table and tears turn to laughter. Outside it's no sunny day but overcast, matching the unsettled moods of Hildy and Olga von Boetticher—her mother arrived that afternoon. They board a train back to DC around the same time Kato's northbound train pulls into Philadelphia, where he's driven to a rundown immigra-tion station in Gloucester City, New Jersey. In the plain, three-story white building erected in 1912, the internees are herded into a large gymnasium with many windows—most of them broken. They spend a cold, miserable night, barely sleeping on flimsy cots with too few blankets.

Upon arriving home the von Boettichers discover a swastika chalked on their driveway. Like all other Axis diplomatic families, they immedi-ately begin packing, selling, or storing their belongings. In a car parked outside, ubiquitous FBI agents keep watch and note the few friends courageous enough to stop by. One includes Robert Lyle, one of Hildy's favorite teachers at Sidwell Friends, who takes her canary, turtles, and plants. Years later she learns the FBI searched his car and kept him under surveillance as a potential enemy sympathizer (an investigation that undoubtedly ended after Lyle enlisted in October 1942 and served six years in Naval Intelligence). "It was as if a large CONDEMNED sign had been posted on our lawn," she wrote. "Had NaziGerman become one word, as DamnYankee had in another war?"[15] That night FDR reassures a shaken nation in another masterly fireside chat heard by ninety million people, the largest audience to date.

The Thomsens are also at home busily packing, with not just FBI agents watching but reporters. A photographer snaps shots of Hans, nattily dressed in a double-breasted suit, checking off a list of belongings on a notepad. He's surrounded by many large barrels, prompting the wire service to label the photo "Roll out the barrel." Bébé appears from shopping with a new suitcase. Dressed in a full-length fur coat and matching fur hat, she covers her face from the photographer as she hurries into their Colorado Avenue yellow brick house without a word.

Back in Kato's makeshift detention shelter, haste produces considerable problems. The several hundred Japanese, German, and Italian inmates are moved into smaller, more comfortable rooms with heat but are plagued by bedbugs. Their unappetizing food is heavy on beans and potatoes, with a handful of exceptions: turkey on Christmas and a spaghetti dinner cooked by an Italian internee. Meals, served on unpainted pine tables, remind Kato of prison scenes from American movies. At least there's a canteen where he buys fresh milk and pie, and conditions gradually improve. Twice a day they can exercise on the roof. Plus it's not prisonlike; there are rarely armed guards and no barbed wire fences or high walls.

Back at the Japanese embassy, it's a much tighter cordon. The FBI severely limits entry and exit, with non-Japanese help caught in limbo. Several part-time American maids plead to leave, with one insisting she must get home because "I have to have hot compresses for my legs."[16] The most heartfelt appeal comes from Spanish-born butler Leonardo Sanchez, who's lived in America for ten years and joined the staff only a few months ago. His handwritten letter to "The Honorable Cordell Hull" asks for his advice and help: "I am faithful and loyal to this country. So I want you please advise me what I have to do, as far as I concern I should not remain in here one moment more, but I tried several times to go out

**Fig. 23.** Secretary of State Cordell Hull and Under Secretary Sumner Welles. Library of Congress, Prints and Photographs Division, Harris and Ewing Collection, LC-DIG-hec-28644.

of this place, but the police the Federal men stopped me. . . . They treat me nicely and I do not have anything to complain against them. . . . I am worried to death due to the risk and harm it can make to me staying in here. Please let me know and put me to work in some other place."[17]

Hull also receives a request that's less heartfelt but still a matter of life and death. W. R. Frank Hines, whose funeral home held the service for the late Colonel Kenkichi Shinjo on December 7, writes in hopes Hull can expedite payment for his bill of $238. With all Japanese funds now frozen, he "appeal[s] to Your Excellency for such assistance as you may be in a position to render me in the collection of the above debt."[18]

On the same day that Sanchez writes, Stanley Woodward of State's Division of Protocol visits the embassy to read the official statement promising protection and "correct and liberal treatment" of their staff pending departure. "The Japanese Diplomatic and Consular staffs will not be subject to any form of internment prior to their departure, provided, naturally, that they do nothing inimical to American interests while awaiting departure."[19] This treatment assumes reciprocity on the part of the Japanese government dealing with American envoys overseas. Iguchi, appointed the embassy's liaison, hands Woodward a typed memo with added handwritten notes covering many topics, including the release of blocked funds and questions about individual cases like Terasaki's: can he and his family still depart for Brazil? The answer comes back: no.

Simultaneously Charlie Spruks visits the German and Italian embassies and delivers a nearly identical message with one caveat, "in the event of a severance of diplomatic relations between the United States" and Germany and Italy, that anticipates a reality only hours away.[20] The wording of these official statements promising no "internment" winds up backing the United States into a corner. All future references to the subsequent relocation of Axis diplomats are described as a "detainment"—a semantic distinction from which the government never varies. Similarly, an emphasis on reciprocity of treatment for U.S. diplomats held abroad becomes the overarching premise of policy.

With so many trapped inside the Japanese embassy, sleeping arrangements consist of an improvised jumble of cots and sleeping bags. Bathroom lines form early every morning. Officials request State's help in expediting an order from department store Woodward & Lothrop for mattresses, cots, sheets, woolen and cotton blankets, pillows and pillowcases, face towels, and soap. Since a protecting power—a neutral country assigned to handle its affairs—hasn't yet been appointed, State arranges for the rush shipment itself.

Isolated in their apartments or houses many Japanese wives, unable to speak English, demand to join or at least see their husbands. At Long's urging Hoover loosens the FBI's iron grip, allowing married and unmarried staffers, accompanied by a policeman, to go home for an overnight stay. Meanwhile, Gwen Terasaki pitches in to smooth the way however she can, helping arrange medical treatment or other special services for wives and children. She again reaches out to George Atcheson, who'd helped obtain permission for her mother to leave. In her autobiography she notes he's unfailingly polite, always closing their phone calls with a solicitous, "And how are you?"[21] However, in a confidential memo to his boss, Atcheson emphasizes their distance and stresses that, despite his previous assignments in China, he's never met her or her husband: "In her telephone conversations with me her attitude has been that of a person in a very difficult situation who wished to be entirely correct in her attitude and actions. She has several times expressed considerable concern for various of our officers in China with whom she and her husband had friendly relations."[22]

There's an additional invisible layer at work here too, since the FBI tapped the Terasakis' phone line months ago. When Akira Yamamoto, a pregnant wife, complains that an FBI agent slept in their apartment when her husband returned for the night, Gwen relates the incident to Atcheson. A transcript reaches the desk of Hoover, who dashes off a letter to Berle: "Agents remained in the hall of the apartment house during the entire period, and at no time entered the Yamamoto apartment."[23] While State has layer upon layer of bureaucracy to handle the minutiae, Hoover isn't a delegator. He's a remarkably hands-on director who often responds personally to seemingly mundane matters, subtly reminding federal officials of his all-encompassing reach and power.

Atcheson's duties extend far beyond advising Gwen. For the first but certainly not last time, a government agency advocates for searching an embassy. In this case it's the Japanese embassy with Atcheson arguing that since Japanese officials recently searched the British embassy in Tokyo and took away shortwave radios, the United States can do the same. "In the interest of national security," he writes, "the importance of preventing the illicit use of radio transmitting sets by enemy aliens needs no emphasis . . . [and] it is not believed that any technicality should stand in the way of removing it."[24] His claim that a proclamation of war nullifies an embassy's protected status is a hairsplitting interpretation to which others stoutly disagree. Another official from State points out that the Federal Communications Commission has the technical facility to jam transmissions without entering the embassy's sacrosanct ground.

Yet perhaps the most surprising point is that the question was even asked since the FBI, British Security Coordination, Office of Naval Intelligence, and Office of Strategic Services precursor Coordinator of Information have routinely been breaking into Axis and neutral country embassies. Cooperation among the parochial intelligence services remains spotty; they are often unwilling to share information and sometimes actively sabotage others' operations.

As one high-ranking British intelligence official notes exasperatedly, "Does J. Edgar think he's fighting on Bunker Hill against us Redcoats or has he really heard of Pearl Harbour?"[25]

# 9

# Executing an Exodus

As more dispiriting news, like the fall of Guam and Hong Kong, emanates from the Pacific, anti-Japanese outrage erupts throughout America. Roundups begin, a precursor of Executive Order 9096 that Roosevelt signs next month, which triggers the incarceration of 120,000 people of Japanese descent and an additional 20,000 with German or Italian roots. In Washington DC vandals chop down four cherry trees at the Tidal Basin, carving "To Hell with the Japanese" on one. Fearing more vandalism, the Freer Gallery of Art removes all Japanese paintings and sculptures. Stores strip Japanese goods from their shelves. Tunes like "You're a Sap, Mr. Jap," "Goodbye, Mama (I'm Off to Yokohama)" and "We Did It Before and We Can Do It Again" fill the charts. A far more well-known Kato than the genial Japanese correspondent, the Japanese butler to masked crimefighter Britt Reid in the popular *Green Hornet* radio serial, undergoes a nationality shift from Japanese to Filipino.

American citizen Clarke Kawakami, who'd served under Masuo Kato at Domei, talks to the press and pens a letter that's reprinted in the Department of State Bulletin, a rare editorial departure for the official agency publication. He laments both the duplicity of the Japanese attack and his inability to properly say goodbye to his colleagues and friends. "How completely the militarists in Tokyo have gone over to the methods of Hitler and the Nazis," writes Kawakami. "Not only I but my father, too, feel that these acts constitute the blackest and most shameful page in Japanese history. . . . For the sake of future Japanese generations as well as for the sake of peoples everywhere, it is necessary that this type of militarist rule which drugs and drags peaceful people into war, be crushed forever."[1]

In a city with four intensely competitive daily newspapers, local reporters feverishly dig for the latest news about the suddenly isolated Axis embassies and their occupants. Imperious publisher Cissy Patterson now has even more reason to dig up anything that might embarrass FDR. A few days after Pearl Harbor her older brother Joe, a World War I veteran and publisher of the *New York Daily News,* landed an audience with the president. He'd hoped to rejoin the army and serve again. Roosevelt kept him waiting for fifteen minutes, then ripped into his previous isolationist editorials. Reduced to tears, the hardheaded Patterson turned to go when FDR announced he had an assignment for him: "Go back home and read your editorials for the past six months—read every one of them and think over what you have done!"[2]

Yet it's not Cissy Patterson's *Times-Herald* that gets the biggest scoop but the *Washington Daily News,* thanks to peppery Evelyn Peyton Gordon. The savvy veteran newswoman does it the old-fashioned way. With gumption. One day she parks her Ford, passes the police, and knocks at the door of the Nazi embassy. An aide answers, and when she asks to see Hans Thomsen he disappears. Several minutes later another aide appears and asks her name. More waiting. Finally she's invited inside. "If I'm not out in fifteen minutes," she deadpans to a cop, "raid the joint." Inside she waits in a small room dominated by a big portrait of Hitler. Young men in shirtsleeves bustle by carrying papers, books, newspapers. It's the first time she's been inside the aging Victorian brownstone since 1936, when she attended a dance overseen by then-ambassador Hans Luther that attracted a crowd of stylish young people. They sipped French champagne and danced under "crystal chandeliers in a ballroom with frescoed walls and rare Beauvais-tapestried furniture."

More time passes until she spies a familiar face: Ernst Ostermann von

Roth, a suave attaché once dubbed "the debutantes' delight." They speak cordially; off he goes. More minutes tick off 'til he returns. "Tommy said he always has time to talk to a beautiful lady—come this way," he whispers in her ear. Off they walk through the ballroom, now faded and forlorn, and the dining room, passing heavyset "apple-cheeked" Friedrich von Boetticher. They enter Hans Thomsen's book-lined office, where sun pours in through high, velvet-draped windows. He's dressed in a well-tailored, grayish brown tweed suit, a white shirt with a striped collar, and brown tie. He strides to greet her, smiling, holding a strip of yellow ticker dispatches; in an adjoining room the message machine clatters away.

"Have you come to say goodbye, Evelyn?" Thomsen asks pleasantly. "Perhaps because of the reported declaration of war by Germany? I believe the report is premature." She says she came to say hello, not goodbye, and inquires about the reports (and smell) of burning paper. He laughs. They chat amiably, with him deftly avoiding voicing any opinions about anything of import. After a few minutes he leads her out, saying wistfully, "You've been a good friend to me through the press. Again, good luck." At the door she says "Au revoir." With a sad smile, he replies, "Maybe auf wiedersehen."[3]

Off she heads into the sunlight, with that faint smell of burning paper still hanging in the air.

Though Gordon is the only reporter to gain access to any embassy's inner sanctum, others aggressively work their sources too. Stories fly about a shortage of food at the Japanese embassy, where funds are scarce since the U.S. government froze its accounts. Employees pool cash and telephone local grocer J. B. Sprund's Market, which delivers a sizable order of rice, bread, eggs, juice, fruit, jams, and more. An American chauffeur, freed after having been caught while visiting a friend, the embassy's official chauffeur, reports a wild scene inside. "Oh baby, are those Japs swilling whiskey," he says. "They must have put away ten cases of the stuff last night. They insisted that I join them." Asked by a reporter if he did, the man replies, "How could I get out of it? I was in enemy territory, wasn't I?"[4] A follow-up story notes additional cash-on-delivery shipments include oysters, chicken, veal, French bread, beer, soda, and five hundred tablets of aspirin, the latter of which "should be needed in view of reports to the amount of whiskey being consumed."[5]

Editorializing aside, the press does break a far more serious report: Nomura, and perhaps Kurusu, may attempt to commit hara-kiri. Long, overseeing all matters related to the detainment, fears that Japan would report they were murdered, imperiling all Americans held there. He sends Swiss minister Charles Bruggmann, married to Vice President Henry Wallace's sister, to the embassy to gently question the discomfited Nomura. An awkward discussion ensues, and Bruggmann eventually emerges unsure as to Nomura's intentions. In his diary Adolf Berle, who reports to Long, reveals that the information of the potential suicides came from Nomura's secretary. "I do not blame them," he writes. "It must be an unhappy fate to go down in history as having been the cover men for one of the greatest acts of international treachery in modern times. . . . After they get back to Japan, they can do as they please."[6] Neither man attempts to kill himself, now or later.

Publicly, Nomura and Kurusu are the two most reviled men in America as pundits openly and profanely deride them. "With treachery in their hearts, lies on their lips," writes financial reporter Robert Vanderpoel.[7] Newspaper cartoons portray grotesque, buck-toothed Japanese. Columnists pile on, all eager to outdo their colleagues. "A desperate, fourth-rate nation, the spoiled little brat of the Orient," fumes James Clapper.[8] Even the esteemed Old Gray Lady weighs in: "Rank perfidy and treachery [has] characterized the methods of the militarists now in the saddle in Tokyo."[9]

Americans who invariably spout racist vitriol would be even more outraged if they knew of Nomura's private musings. In his diary he voices no shame or resentment at having been duped by his own government; instead, he praises his country and denigrates his captors. "They seem to have awakened from their dream of underestimating Japan's real power," writes Nomura. "The competency and boldness of our naval officers and sailors have startled the world."[10]

Forty-eight tense hours after Thomsen told Gordon that reports of a declaration of war by Germany were "premature," one day after Spruks delivered America's policy on potential detainment the other shoe, or rather shoes, drop. On the morning of December 11 Hitler declares war in a long harangue to the Reichstag while Mussolini simultaneously addresses cheering crowds from the balcony of the Palazzo Venezia in Rome. Newswires hum and radios blare the news, so it's anticlimactic when Thomsen and First Secretary von Strempel arrive at State to deliver official notice. Hull keeps them waiting an hour, nothing new for Thomsen, then sloughs them off on a lower official, saying he's "too busy with important matters to see them."[11]

Soon thereafter Prince Colonna arrives without even a declaration of war since he's received no instructions from his government. He's directed to an even lower political advisor, and State's later press release closes contemptuously: "The Italian ambassador was informed that we had long expected Germany to carry out its threat against this hemisphere and the United States fully anticipated that Italy would follow obediently along."[12] Colonna had apparently had to be roused to make the State Department visit. Earlier that morning, when reporters rang the bell at his embassy, an aproned servant answered and announced, "The boss is still in bed."[13] Though by the end of the day the ambassador has rallied sufficiently to submit a list of ninety-three staffers and dependents to be repatriated, headed by himself, his wife, their Italian cook, and Hungarian maid.

Arriving back at his embassy, Hans Thomsen is his usual genial self. He motions to his automobile and asks the assembled reporters, "Somebody want to buy a nice car?"[14] One enterprising newsman telephones Bébé, whose anti-Hitler diatribes have confounded Washington for years. Like the age-old game of pealing flower petals while alternating saying, "He loves me," "He loves me not," she must finally make a decision. And she reveals that . . . she's sold her horse and will be returning to Germany. "'What else could I do' in an accent that smacked more of French than German," writes the reporter. "'Of course I shall go back with my husband. . . . It is in the Bible, you know, to go where one's husband goes. Is that not so? Yes.'" She voices regret at having to leave behind her beloved pets: 66 squirrels, flying squirrels, and birds. "War," she says resignedly. "It is so terrible. But it is, I guess, a power beyond human forces. I shall go back, yes, but I shall come back here again after the war is over and renew all my old friendships again." She hesitates, then adds in a low voice, "I wish all of you a merry, merry Christmas. Goodbye."[15] Though she doesn't quite leave everything behind. She takes her cocker spaniel to their temporary refuge.

The von Boettichers plan a quick little getaway, booking a train from Union Station tomorrow night to visit their pregnant daughter, her husband, and their two children in Buffalo. Who knows when or if they'll ever see each other again? The FBI gets wind of their plans and explains to the military attaché that no Axis diplomats can leave the District of Columbia without special permission—and that won't be forthcoming.

For the Terasakis, their reunion proves bittersweet when Hidenari returns to their apartment for the first time since December 7. Before her, Gwen sees a broken man. "His eyes that had been so brilliantly alive spoke an effable sadness," she wrote. "His career seemed to have gone for nothing, and the future held only the inevitable, violent doom of his beloved country for him to witness, an impotent and wretched spectator. He seemed to have lost all hope."[16]

But for one German couple, romance blooms. With all foreign nationals except the Japanese free to roam the city, second secretary and Gestapo agent von Gienanth calls his sweetheart, a German schoolteacher, from a pay phone at the Mayflower and proposes. An hour later she calls back to accept and boards a late train from New York. Since Washington DC law requires a three-day waiting period, the couple opts to marry in Virginia. A Swiss representative arranges for two FBI agents to drive them to nearby Alexandria. But since only a hotel room is available, a kindly agent volunteers his apartment, telling his wife to place two candles on their dining room table. An elderly Lutheran priest performs the ceremony before a handful of witnesses. One FBI agent congratulates the bride, saying, "We have watched your future husband for a long time and he is a very nice guy."[17]

Three neutral countries, known as protecting powers, are appointed to handle the Axis nations' affairs: Spain for Japan; Switzerland for Germany, Italy, and Bulgaria; and Sweden for Hungary. Many representatives from each country are tapped to begin their behind-the-scenes activities.

"The bulk of our work is with the Germans," says Eduard Feer of the Swiss legation, who'd personally hosted Hans and Bébé Thomsen when she first arrived in America nearly five years ago. "They are much more methodical, demand more details—particularly where finances are concerned."[18] In addition to overarching issues concerning frozen funds and repatriation, the vast majority of time is spent on a Herculean and thankless task. Hundreds upon hundreds of individuals have possessions large and small—homes, cars, furnishings, antiques, clothing, pets—to sell, lease, store, or give away. Not to mention bank accounts. The all-encompassing work comes to involve landlords, lawyers, accountants, retailers, storage companies, and more.

For several years federal agency memos about contingency plans for diplomatic detainment have circulated, but the surprise attack and near-instantaneous war footing catches the government unawares. It's a far different world than twenty-five years ago, when State Department Special Agent Joseph Nye personally escorted Ambassador Johann von Bernstorff back to Germany in 1917 during the World War. (Soon, references begin adding the roman numeral I, the term "Great War" fades, and "World War II" emerges to describe the latest conflict.) During those genteel times, a story goes that the ambassadors from England and Austria-Hungary were good friends, and neighbors, since their embassies stood across the street from each other. "Their bedrooms chanced to be so placed that they could see each other shaving in the morning," reported the *New York Times.* "When war was declared the friendship between the two men was necessarily broken, and the British Ambassador henceforth shaved with his back to the window."[19]

Now pressure skyrockets to relocate the Axis diplomats immediately, with priority going to the Germans since the Swiss legation informs the United States that its diplomats in Berlin have been moved to a once vacant resort, Jeschke's Grand Hotel, in Bad Nauheim, north of Frankfurt. There's also a local imperative, the arrival of a surprise VIP: Winston Churchill. He's currently streaming across the stormy, U-boat-infested North Atlantic aboard the *Duke of York* for an unannounced parlay with FDR, who's made it clear he wants the diplomats, especially the Nazis, gone before the prime minister arrives. On December 16 Berle puts on

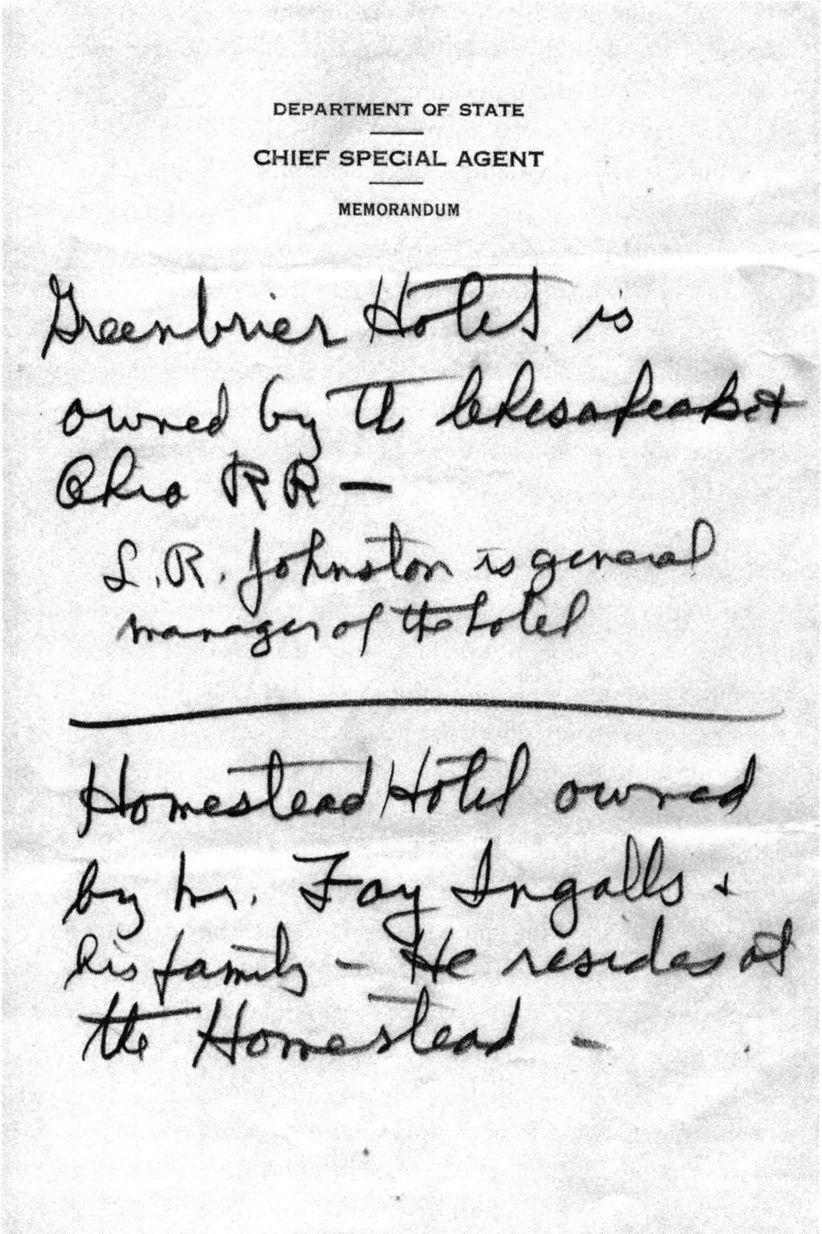

DEPARTMENT OF STATE

CHIEF SPECIAL AGENT

MEMORANDUM

Greenbrier Hotel is owned by the Chesapeake & Ohio RR —

L. R. Johnston is general manager of the hotel

Homestead Hotel owned by Mr. Fay Ingalls & his family — He resides at the Homestead —

**Fig. 24.** Handwritten note from Robert Bannerman specifying the two hotels initially chosen to house the Axis diplomats. U.S. National Archives and Record Administration, Record Group 59.

paper an idea that's already been circulating among higher-ups: that the Axis diplomats "should be held in some quiet and isolated place, but without the right of communication."[20]

State Department Special Agent Robert L. Bannerman is tasked with finding suitable accommodations: large, secluded, well-appointed hotels, near a rail line and reasonably close to Washington DC. And oh yes, available for immediate occupancy. He quickly narrows his search to two: the Greenbrier in White Sulphur Springs, West Virginia, and the Homestead in Hot Springs, Virginia, only a couple of hours apart. "The officials of these nations could not object to the class of accommodations offered by these two hotels," Bannerman writes to Thomas Fitch, chief special agent.[21] Such luxury hotels are essential for the government's number one goal of reciprocity, although reports insinuate mistreatment overseas by the Japanese of Ambassador Joseph Grew and his team (who later dub their spare quarters "Black Sulphur Springs"). Nevertheless Hull won't "be drawn into a contest in which he would have to out stink a skunk," and "there was a limit below which the United States Government would not stoop."[22] Besides, several members of FDR's Kitchen Cabinet are personally well acquainted with the hotels; Hull had even been staying at the Greenbrier in the summer of 1939 when Germany invaded Poland.

At the moment it's off-season at the Greenbrier, owned by the Chesapeake and Ohio Railroad, and the living is leisurely—unlike the frenetic pace of activity in Washington. On the same day that memos about relocating the diplomats are flying among federal agencies the hotel's consulting engineer, R. H. Patterson, writes to General Manager Loren R. Johnston. A lifelong hotelier, the courtly sixty-four-year-old Vermonter has managed high-end properties in Vermont, Pennsylvania, and Florida. No stranger to catering to the rich and famous, he once refereed a golf match of a foursome that included John D. Rockefeller Sr., then the world's wealthiest man. He joined the Greenbrier in 1928. Wintering at his home in Fort Lauderdale he's confident that acting GM George O'Brien has all well in hand. Patterson writes that electricians, plasterers, and painters are doing standard maintenance and repairs, and a team has rebuilt a suspension bridge on the golf course. "This was a rather lengthy job," he writes, "because the timbers had to be hewn out of standing red

**Fig. 25.** Greenbrier manager Loren T. Johnston. Courtesy of the Greenbrier.

oak."[23] The hotel's handful of guests includes James Moffett, chairman of the board of Standard Oil; professors from Catholic University and Harvard University of whom the latter, the FBI later notes, "maintains close friendships with persons of note, such as Sumner Welles"; and an elderly New York woman with her full-time nurse and companion.[24]

On December 17 O'Brien receives a telephone call shortly after lunch from Bannerman, inquiring about its immediate availability. "Well, that was very short notice and exacting information," reads the hotel's subsequent summation of the internment. "So the management got busy and concluded that The Greenbrier had an opportunity to serve our Government at a time when they needed it most."[25] Then Bannerman phones Fay Ingalls, owner of the Homestead in Hot Springs, Virginia. It was more "in the nature of a command," recalled Ingalls in his post-detainment report, *A Journal of the Sojourn of the Axis Diplomats at the Homestead* (misspelled "Sourjourn" in the original typescript).[26]

At first plans are to move the Germans to Hot Springs, and on December 17 Long asks for an allocation of fifty thousand dollars as an initial outlay for the detainment and repatriation. Yet by the next day, for reasons unknown, the destinations are switched. On the morning of December 18, less than twenty-four hours after the request, the Greenbrier answers the government with an unequivocal yes. Or as Loren Johnston later puts it, "We immediately enlisted."[27]

A scant thirty-six hours later, with an onslaught of workers hurriedly building guard booths and erecting lighting, the Greenbrier transforms from ghost town to boom town. With Hans and Bébé Thomsen leading the way.

# 10

## Fenced Inn

If you're going to go, you might as well go in style. Above the fold on the *New York Times* front page—the lone photo on the cover—stand the Thomsens in front of the rundown embassy. He wears a bowler hat and a wide-lapelled, double-breasted topcoat open to show his shirt and dark tie. He clutches not one but two briefcases, a folded newspaper and box tucked under one arm. She's in a stylish dark fur chapeau, wearing a full-length mink coat and holding another. He looks stoic; she stares intently at someone or something out of view.

On this crisp, cold morning of December 19, 1941, quite a crowd has gathered: press, police, and the public. Bébé moves all about, saying farewells to several teary-eyed friends. One reporter misses their sobs while editorializing with a spot of snark: "Tear detectors yesterday failed to catch a single drop of brine among the well-dressed throng, abounding in fur coats and smart hair-dos, with dozens and dozens of bags, boxes and bundles, piled picnic-style into their special buses."[1] This initial contingent of 150 German and a handful of Hungarians boards buses for Union Station, all except the Thomsens, once described as "one of the most attractive couples in the Diplomatic Corps."[2] Although that status has ended rather unceremoniously, they're still chauffeured to the station in a limousine—albeit with a federal agent behind the wheel.

Also making front-page news today is Thomsen's fascist friend Laura Ingalls. Arraigned yesterday for being an unregistered German agent in contravention of the Foreign Agents Registration Act of 1938, she couldn't post the $7,500 bond and was sent to jail—far less luxurious surroundings than where the diplomats are heading. (The obscure act, used sparingly over the ensuing decades, was the basis for charges against Michael Flynn, Paul Gates, and Paul Manafort, advisors of President Donald Trump, in 2017.)

The fiery flier has now audaciously refashioned herself as an anti-Nazi spy, a preview of her forthcoming legal defense. "I didn't take orders from the German government," said Ingalls, neglecting to mention that she did accept cash many times from von Gienanth. "I was carrying on my own investigation, even if I overstepped."[3]

Later this afternoon FDR hosts a cabinet meeting marked by a wide-ranging discussion of wartime and economic matters. Attorney General Francis Biddle brings up von Boetticher's request that "his insane son be allowed to stay in a hospital in this country to prevent his being chloroformed if he were sent back to Germany."[4] Afterward the president informs Biddle that the subject caused Secretary of Labor Frances Perkins so much distress that he feared she might throw up.

Police motorcycles escort the buses to Union Station where the well-dressed, well-heeled group boards an eleven-car all-Pullman special train. One young secretary confides to a reporter that she'd packed her bathing suit in anticipation of a coastal destination but will now have to figure out how to get skis. On the long ride Friedrich von Boetticher buries himself in the *New York Times* while Olga works halfheartedly at a crossword puzzle. Hildy watches the passing wintry landscape, dozing and eavesdropping. One woman announces she's heard there's a fat shortage in Germany, so she's brought along a dozen jars of face cream to use for frying food. Others talk about nylons, the latest thing in stockings, that they'd brought; Hildy herself had packed a dozen. Another woman jokes about their upcoming exclusive cruise to Europe, closed to others, which Hildy doesn't find terribly funny. But she does find something terribly ironic as the train roars through the Lynchburg station where she'd always gotten off to go to college. From chasing boys and chairing the Christmas dance committee to captivity at the Greenbrier, a mere hundred miles but worlds apart from her former collegial college life.

Else Arnecke enjoys the train's first-class accommodations and fine food, noting that the "colored" waiters in the restaurant car wore white gloves. "The world goes down in elegance," writes Arnecke.[5] Also aboard are three State Department men: Spruks, who'd squired around Queen Elizabeth and King George VI back in the summer of 1939, and John O'Hanley and Edward Poole, who'll become the on-site agents at the Greenbrier and Homestead, respectively. When the train arrives in early evening, the passengers assemble on the wooden platform of the tiny White Sulphur Springs station. Hildy von Boetticher glimpses, looming close by, "a white palatial-looking building bathed in a mass of flood-lights. . . . Our elegantly upholstered, flood-lit cage."[6]

What the detainees don't know is that a vexing question rages behind the scenes: who'll guard them long-term? Yesterday the FBI informed State and the attorney general that its oversight would end once the detainees boarded the train. A proposal to call in the army was rejected because enemy nations might construe that as akin to internment in a concentration camp. Late calls to the West Virginia state police produced a stopgap solution: twenty state troopers. With negotiations ongoing with the Department of Justice's Immigration and Naturalization Service (INS), it's suggested that the state might have to deputize citizens to provide protection when the troopers need relief. "If decision on the protective feature is not promptly forthcoming," writes Special Agent Thomas Fitch, "it would be advisable to have the Department telegraph the Governor of West Virginia asking him to further continue the guard of State Police."[7]

The arrivals walk the short distance to the hotel. Dietrich von Knoop, four-year-old son of a German commercial attaché, recalls memories of that day more than three-quarters of a century later: the gigantic hotel, the guard shack at the entrance to the grounds, and especially the pistols worn by the state troopers. The hotel was quite familiar to his parents; they'd vacationed there several months before. Even with so many guests

**Fig. 26.** Dietrich and George von Knoop. Courtesy of the von Knoop family.

en masse, the veteran staff efficiently registers everyone and delivers all baggage to their rooms. Only one problem emerges: an agitated forty-six-year-old Hungarian woman who insists upon sharing a room with her thirty-one-year-old brother, an unusual arrangement prohibited by law. Soon she's reported to be crying every day and on the verge of a nervous breakdown at the thought of being deported. The Thomsens receive especially cushy quarters: a suite that includes a living room and two bedrooms, each with a bathroom, that normally rents for forty-four dollars (the equivalent of $760 in 2019) per day without meals.

With no precedent to guide it, the start-up detention experiences considerable growing pains. Thomsen designates Wilhelm Tannenberg, first secretary, to handle day-to-day matters. Within days the chief of the border patrol informs his men of a comprehensive presidential regulation. "No alien enemy," it reads, "shall have in his possession, custody or control at any time or place or use or operate any of the following enumerated articles." The list includes firearms or component parts, ammunition, bombs, shortwave radio receiving sets, transmitting sets, signal devices, codes or ciphers, and cameras. Plus a catchall ban on any papers, documents or books that may contain invisible writing, and photographs, sketches, pictures, drawings, maps or graphical representations "of any military or naval installations or equipment or of any arms, ammunition, implements of war, device or thing used or intended to be used in the combat equipment of the land or naval forces of the United States or of any military or naval post, camp or station."[8]

For years Nazi agents like von Gienanth and others have trafficked in print information. Seemingly arcane technical manuals and journals can contain valuable facts and figures to gauge an enemy's infrastructure and production capabilities. The United States, for example, now mines such materials under the auspices of Librarian of Congress Archibald MacLeish at the direction of Donovan who's serving at the vaguely titled Coordinator of Information, which later morphs into the OSS. Soon the FBI prohibits the purchase of any current periodicals, a blanket hotel ban that enrages the detainees.

Despite the fine trappings and "detainment" nomenclature, it's still an imprisonment. Constantly changing rules and regulations make for

**Fig. 27.** One of the guard shacks on the lawn of the Greenbrier. Courtesy of the Greenbrier.

an uneasy atmosphere, not just for the detainees but staffers. "Everybody in the place, including the employees—perhaps more particularly the employees—is under close observation at all times. There is evidence of some discomfort in certain directions," writes the hotel's consulting engineer, R. H. Patterson.[9] Monitoring developments from Florida, Loren Johnston reiterates confidence in his staff but offers to come back anytime if the situation warrants: "I know of no reason why the organization won't work perfectly. I am rather glad that we are having the present experience at White Sulphur. It will teach us all that all is not beer and skittles. It will also tend to impress upon us the fact that this is still America and still handles vital things in an efficient manner."[10]

When the White House publicly announces the Greenbrier and Homestead as locations, a caustic front-page commentary runs in the *Bath County Enterprise* in Warm Springs, Virginia: "Careful, brother, careful!

If the intermittent blackouts over the past week have frayed your nerves and stimulated your irritability, take a bromide and calm yourself. Better take two bromides just in case you see a Jap, or maybe two Japs, or even a hundred of the little 'yaller' inhabitants of the Land of the Rising Sun which is due for an eclipse in the not too distant future."[11] The paper notes that the blackouts were unintentional, the result of sleet storms that caused ice-coated tree limbs to fall onto power lines.

The imminent arrival of the Japanese, however, is deliberate and most unwelcome.

While the Germans are settling into their posh new digs, Kato remains at his bare-bones detention camp in Gloucester City. Yet he makes the news thanks to a former colleague who uses an ancient Greek word to describe what's happening in Washington today: *metamorphosis.* "A year ago," writes columnist Jack Stinnett, German newsman "Kurt Sell, Masuo Kato and I could walk into the White House and the President's press conference with no more than a grin of recognition from the man who manned the door. . . . Now I have to say 'friend' and prove it before I can get past a couple of bayonets into that outer White House sanctum where your only passport is a nod from the knowing secret service."[12]

The times have changed, but Kato's services are still in demand. INS Chief Supervisor Willard F. Kelly phones the camp to ask him if seven Japanese detained at Ellis Island are accredited correspondents as they've claimed. Kato knows them all well and vouches for their professional backgrounds. After reading that the Japanese will soon be sent to the Homestead, he asks the camp's director to allow him and three fellow detainees to complete personal matters left undone after their hasty, forced departure: "If you kindly give us a permission to let us stay in Washington for day or two on our way to the South for those purposes, we should appreciate very much. . . . Needless to say we pledge ourselves to observe all the laws and regulations of the United States during our stay in Washington as elsewhere in this country."[13]

Up the chain of command it goes, and two days later permission is granted by Lemuel Schofield, special assistant to the attorney general. Further attesting to Kato's knowledge of how to work the system, he writes to Felix Morley, president of Haverford College and a former editor of the *Washington Post.* Morley, who coincidentally had spoken at Hildy von Boetticher's graduation from Sidwell Friends three years ago, writes back to the camp's director. He recommends Kato, whom he notes "praised the very humane treatment here at this Station and expressed the hope that the American correspondents in Japan would receive like consideration from his people."[14]

Meanwhile his people at the Japanese embassy, though still cramped, are in better spirits. Once-frozen funds have been released, so food and supplies are plentiful. So too are deliveries of trunks and suitcases in anticipation of their forthcoming journey. A G-man inspecting a grocery shipment examines some small dark objects and exclaims, "Not bombs, after all. Just eggplants." Reporters congregate outside, eager to report any and every detail. When the FBI drives away one young male staffer, a dogged investigation determines his destination: a downtown clothing store to buy a pair of drawers for Ambassador Nomura. His size? Unreported.

Wives and children previously stranded at home are finally allowed to move in, with Gwen Terasaki the last to enter. Hoping to avoid the press, she asks her FBI driver to circle the block several times to ensure all is quiet. Mariko races inside, but Gwen, holding their poodle, Pechy, by a leash, is waylaid as it heads toward a tree to relieve itself. "I yanked him, dripping, into the Embassy," she wrote, "and to the butler's horror, across the hall. I had planned to enter my internment with more dignity."

Several days later a ten-foot Christmas tree is delivered. Gwen and Mariko enjoy its lights, and Mariko happily announces, "'I'm glad there's Christmas, mama, even with the war.' I assured her there would always be Christmas."[15] While Gwen's reassuring her daughter, Takeo Iguchi's little brother Norio doesn't believe it. He bursts into tears upon learning that he won't be getting any presents this year. So his mother approaches an FBI agent and offers him money to buy the lad a gift. The considerate agent does just that, buying a toy at a local department store. The boy is overjoyed, but his father is quite irritated by the unruliness of his youngest son, who a family friend nicknames "Diaper" because of his spoiled behavior. A little Japanese girl, carrying a doll, is asked if Santa

Claus brought it to her and she nods. "Yes, last year," she says. "So you believe in Santa Claus?" she's asked. "I used to," she replies, "but this year the FBI wouldn't let him come and I am not so sure."[16]

Back at the Greenbrier, the Germans enjoy a huge Christmas tree decorated with red apples and white candles, the latter a tradition that eschews electric lights. "They make a most beautiful picture—the branches bending and turning as they swing over the candle flames, crackling briskly: the soft drop of wax on the white paper underneath the trees."[17] Hans and Bébé Thomsen hand out presents. But holiday or not, some locals are mightily upset by the arrival of the enemy into their little mountain town of 2,093 inhabitants. "We, and I speak for every person in our town, are happy to have this privilege of doing our part during the war crisis," insists Mayor William Perry, who also doubles as the hotel's purchasing agent. "Our whole tradition here in White Sulphur Springs is one of patriotism and support of our government."[18]

The mayor's pronouncements notwithstanding, stiff opposition forces a sudden public meeting at the county courthouse. The task of soothing recalcitrant residents falls to Spruks, but afterward many still fume that the enemy is given such posh accommodations. Such rage spills over into public view as many newspaper editorialists ignore the traditional seasonal salutation of "good will towards men" and let loose their venom. "Over at White Sulphur Springs, the regular clientele has been chased out so that the delicate bluebloods representing Hitler's superior Nordics will not have to breathe the same air of plebian Americans whose habits of paying their bills and cussing an enemy to his face show plainly they are not born to the aristocracy," reports the *Charleston Gazette.* "Here is a West Virginia resort . . . given over to as deceitful and rascally a flock of hired bravos as ever worked the doublecross."[19]

For the next six months Spruks heads State's administration of the detainment, working closely with the Greenbrier's on-site agent John O'Hanley. Born in Newport, Rhode Island, Handsome John (as the girls called him in high school) served in the navy in World War I. He worked in the railroads and for brokerage houses before joining State. O'Hanley and Spruks get on like gangbusters, doing unsung and often tedious work on myriad issues that'll range from serious to silly. He takes it as a badge of honor when, right after their arrival, Swiss representative Feer tells him, "O'Hanley? You must be thick-skinned."[20] The FBI, which blanketed the diplomats when they lived in DC, assigns three agents to each hotel to handle security, monitor phone calls and mail, and recruit informants. Agents cycle in and out, with two key players emerging: John Lawler at the Greenbrier and Roy Morgan at the Homestead. Alabama-native Lawler joined the FBI in 1935, serving in Buffalo and Los Angeles field offices. Returning to DC he worked as an administrative aide to Hoover before being appointed head of the Richmond, Virginia, field office.

West Virginia–native Morgan, who received both undergraduate and law degrees from the University of Virginia, is an even more key overseer. He practiced law before joining the FBI and after a ten-year stint was assigned to head up the detainment, first at the Homestead and later at the Greenbrier. "He was a typically easy-going and good-natured American," recalled Takeo Iguchi, "who usually greeted our family with a friendly smile."[21] His pleasant demeanor belies the steely inner drive of a dedicated G-man.

"The Bureau," Morgan writes to his agents, "is intensely interested in intelligence information from the internees, and it is the duty of all agents to secure this information in the most proficient manner possible."[22]

The third group of federal agents involved in the detainment are about to receive an unexpected and perhaps unwelcome Christmas present.

# 11

## Moving Daze

Patrolling America's borders with Mexico and Canada is arduous, oftentimes dangerous work. Rough-hewn men toil anonymously in fly-speck border towns like El Centro, California, McAllen, Texas, and Rouses Point, New York. Off on Christmas vacation, some receive out-of-the-blue telegrams via Western Union:

> NECESSARY CANCEL YOUR ANNUAL LEAVE. REPORT DIRECT TO CHIEF PATROL INSPECTOR AUBREY S. HUDSON, HOMESTEAD HOTEL, HOT SPRINGS, VIRGINIA, MORNING DECEMBER 29 OR AS SOON THEREAFTER AS POSSIBLE FOR TEMPORARY DETAIL. PER DIEM FIVE DOLLAR AUTHORIZED.[1]

So overnight many self-described good old boys—who one hotel staffer calls a "pretty hard-boiled" lot—find themselves in high-end mountain-top resorts. It's a far cushier assignment that means covering a lot less ground, with little chance of getting shot at and far better grub. Plus in Hot Springs there's lots of shiny new equipment waiting: twenty-five flashlights, a thousand batteries, and four pistol-grip portable search-lights with handle, bulb, cable, and jack for car battery. Supervisors set the rules: "All officers whether in uniform or civilian clothing will at all times present a neat appearance and perform their duties in a dignified and efficient manner, adhering strictly to instructions which have been or will be hereafter issued."[2]

But the change in scenery is a bridge too far for some. Barely a week after arriving at the Homestead, one guard is playing cards one night with two off-duty hotel staffers at a local hangout. Drinks flow, tempers flare. He calls them "stupid hillbillies," follows them outside and breaks one man's nose with a blackjack. Cops arrest him, but State intervenes, fearing the impact of bad local press coverage. So charges are dropped; the guard pays the victim's hospital bill and is sent packing a week later. Other guards apparently haven't adjusted well either, as sixteen more leave then too.

To keep a tight lid on any and all leaks, the Greenbrier's border patrol supervisor—an old-timer who's soon to be replaced himself—sends out a memo: "You are hereby instructed not to discuss any matter whatsoever with anyone or write letters to anyone, outside the Immigration and Naturalization service, pertaining to the detainees or your duties in connection therewith."[3] The guards are soon hard at work examining new arrivals' luggage, confiscating cameras and shortwave radios, even inspecting all parcels delivered to store owners. The FBI's even more strict, confiscating and sending all mail and packages in locked pouches to Washington DC for inspection or censure. Their zealousness even extends to flowers, as one detainee recalls looking through a lattice to see withered flowers lying on the hotel mailroom's floor, perhaps a metaphor for how many will come to view their internment.

The detainees are a polyglot lot consisting of mostly Germans but several other nationalities too, and within there's a distinct social strata. From ministers to maids, counts to clerks, generals to gardeners, everyone's in the same (exclusive) boat. For some it's an accustomed life of luxury. For others, it's an eye-opening entrée into a new world—like the splendid dining room, with its rich burgundy carpet, ivory columns, two-tiered crystal chandeliers, and tables topped with crisp white tablecloths laden with elegant dinnerware. One night two detainees appear for dinner in sweaters. An elderly headwaiter reminds them of the strict

**Fig. 28.** State Department rep John O'Hanley with wife, Charlotte, after the war. Courtesy of the O'Hanley family.

**Fig. 29.** Swiss liaison Frederick Stocker and wife, Mary Anne, after the war. Courtesy of V. Elizabeth Powell.

jacket-and-tie rule, to which one replies, "What the hell are you talking about? This is just a concentration camp anyway." The headwaiter evenly replies, "Maybe a concentration camp, all right—but deluxe."[4]

The only outsiders allowed in are representatives of the protecting powers. With a comparatively small, overworked staff Charles Bruggmann reaches out to countrymen to serve as liaison like Frederick Stocker, a young Swiss eye doctor who immigrated to the United States last spring. Stocker immediately signs on and makes up for his lack of diplomatic training with fluent language skills and an engaging personality. Upon arriving by train at White Sulphur he's met by O'Hanley. "We immediately hit it off cheerfully," wrote Stocker in his unpublished memoir, *An Eye Surgeon Turns Diplomat,* "and found out that we both had a sense of humor, something very valuable under such unusual and tense conditions."[5]

O'Hanley soon needs that sense of humor when he receives a phone call from a man claiming to be Hans Thomsen who complains in broken English about the accommodations. He quickly realizes that the callers are two new agents from State who accompanied the latest contingent of detainees, and he facetiously nominates them to join the border patrol. A couple days later he receives a phone call from Bébé Thomsen—the real one, not an imposter—who complains that she can't regulate the heat in her room. "I looked through my belongings here," wrote O'Hanley, "and since I couldn't find my plumbing tools, I called the hotel plumber and I think he satisfied the lady." A humorless anonymous State staffer pencils into the margin, "OK—but did he fix the heater?"[6]

Spruks negotiates a flat daily rate of ten dollars per detainee, including meals, meaning two clerks sharing the same room pay the same as a minister occupying a suite. Neutral country reps also pay ten dollars. Children under ten, FBI agents, and border guards are charged five dollars a day. It seems like an equitable arrangement, but big boss Breckinridge Long objects. "I am a little shocked to find that the hotel is charging our 'guests' $10 a day but is willing to accept representatives of the Department of State and the Department of Justice at $5 a day," writes Long, a disagreeable combination: wealthy by birth, cheapskate by inclination. He suggests reducing the food choices as a way to grind down the price. "Somebody some day is going to want to know about these costs and it will be hard to explain."[7]

Long also grouses in his diary about wartime inconveniences, although gasoline rationing doesn't stop him from driving to his Georgian-style plantation house in Laurel, Maryland, where labor shortages have cut his staff to three from "the six or seven of yesteryears. And no more assistant butlers, housemen, kitchen helpers, footmen, etc. They are all in the army or in industry. So we can hardly have guests—two at a time—no one to attend to them."[8] Overseeing hundreds of men, women, and children whose lives have been uprooted and will soon be deported, poor Breckinridge Long must also suffer the galling deprivation of being unable to live and entertain in the style to which he's accustomed.

Back in DC, while Long pinches pennies, the three assigned agencies tussle over countless other concerns: most serious, some superfluous. In the latter category, a Mississippi hotel pitches its accommodations for diplomats. "Here is an aggressive business-getter," an anonymous State staffer pencils into the margins of its letter.[9] Questions arise over the now-frozen twenty-eight thousand dollars in Ambassador Colonna's personal bank account, yet another headache for a charge soon to become the most aggravating of detainees. A proposal by Hoover to raid the Japanese embassy in search of those potentially hidden radio transmitters is nixed. Finally, Biddle rules that von Boetticher's son, Friedrich, can remain in the United States as long as his father sets up a trust fund to pay all his expenses. But even that can remain a chip to be played, as the Germans discover when insisting down the line that a certain young woman who expresses an interest in staying must be repatriated. "The file with regard to the general's son is on my desk in Washington. It might disappear," says a State negotiator. "Oh, that is the way you intend to treat this matter?" asks his German counterpart, to which the American replies, "Precisely so."[10] In the end the girl decides to leave, and the boy stays.

Meanwhile the capital's social scene carries (and parties) on. While the mood is definitely subdued, it's still the holiday season. One hostess not curtailing her entertaining bemoans the uncertainty of college-aged offspring, with military service looming for the boys. "No telling what they'll have to face before this thing is over," she said. "We're going to give them all the fun we can . . . while we can."[11] Another prominent couple hosts a Cigarette Party, with a large hamper by the front door for guests to deposit packs that'll go to servicemen. On the diplomatic front no one professes to miss the Germans, while the sequestered Japanese never maintained a heavy social calendar anyway. Because American diplomats in Rome haven't been rounded up yet, the Italians in DC—usually the least newsworthy of the three major Axis powers—are still living in their homes and traveling about freely. But not for long.

In a city tired of hearing bad news, residents awaken two days before Christmas to a rare spot of cheer: Churchill is in town! He arrived last night, and by 10:30 p.m. an industrious company prints and begins selling one-cent postcards heralding the news. On his first morning at the White House, where he and his entourage are staying, the prime minister is astonished and delighted by breakfast. In wartime England there's a strict one-egg ration, but here he enjoys the works: juice, eggs, bacon, toast, and coffee. Churchill's post-Christmas address to a joint session of Congress draws a packed, rapturous audience that peppers his remarks with deafening applause and huzzahs. For the first time ever the Senate chamber allows not only a live radio broadcast but movie cameras, so all Americans can hear and eventually see the cherubic master orator decked out in a three-piece Oxford gray suit and dark bow tie. Aiming straight at the Japanese, prominent in everyone's minds, he asks, "What kind of a people do they think we are? Is it possible they do not realize that we shall never cease to persevere against them until they have been taught a lesson which they and the world will never forget?"[12]

The recent memory of Pearl Harbor still weighs heavy when, on the morning of December 29, the latest issue of *Life* magazine hits the newsstands. It shows the most comprehensive photographic record yet, even though authorities haven't disclosed the shocking hard numbers: 2,400 killed, 1,000 wounded. The story focuses not on the carnage of the decimated fleet but damage at the nearby military station: "First pictures of Jap onslaught show death & destruction at American base."

The same morning brings a terse statement from State that the Japanese diplomats are being moved to the Homestead today. A hostile crowd, with a sizable contingent of reporters and photographers, quickly forms outside the heavily guarded embassy. At 8 a.m. four buses and three limousines drive through the gates. Staffers begin filling one bus with mounds of baggage: trunks, valises, wooden crates, hat boxes, tennis racquets, baby carriages, and golf clubs—twenty-five sets, according to the tabloidesque *Times-Herald*, which will go unused when golf is prohibited. The paper adds there's no sign of any of the cases of whiskey that had been delivered before: "To have straightened out the collective hangovers acquired from so much drinking, the embassy would have required the services of an entire drug store."[13]

Assembled inside the large reception hall, everyone departing is told which number bus they should board. Nomura's farewell address expresses his sadness at being unable to help avert war. He praises both his staff and attachés and their country's stunning recent successes in battle. But he warns against complacency on the long road ahead: "We must remember. A rich man is spoiled by his wealth, a tactician by his tactics, a wise man by his wisdom, and a brave man by his bravery. We must be prudent to the end. . . . Since we are the representatives of the government and the people, we must maintain our dignity in advance or retreat, whether we stand or fall. I wish to add this is the best chance

**Fig. 30.** Gwen Terasaki (*in doorway*) emerging from the Japanese embassy, daughter Mariko ahead (*second from left*). Courtesy of DC Public Library, Washingtoniana Division.

for training our minds and bodies, especially for improving our minds. I wish you young people would not miss this opportunity."[14]

As the group files out, a photo in the *Evening Star* shows several women: Gwen Terasaki coming out the doorway while Mariko and other girls walk just ahead. Terasaki gamely tries to ignore the crowd's hostility and jeers: "One woman looked at me with stark hatred and made a vile gesture. Perhaps she had a son at Pearl Harbor."[15] Many male staffers doff their hats and bow low toward the embassy in farewell. After everyone boards the buses, the crowd boos even louder when Nomura, Kurusu, and high-ranking officials including Hidenari Terasaki emerge. Photographers ask the ambassador and special envoy to pose on the steps. Nomura refuses, striding straight to a limousine. Kurusu pauses briefly, but like Nomura his face is stern. Federal agents join the diplomats in their cars. The motorcade pulls out, police motorcycles leading the way.

"When we arrived at Union Station," said Takeo Iguchi, Mariko's classmate, "the looks of animosity and hostility on the faces of the Americans were palpable and frightening."[16] Gwen Terasaki looks away from the staring and shouting and popping flashbulbs of the photographers' cameras and spies the American flag fluttering atop the station. They board a special nine-car train that's soon gliding through the Virginia countryside whose cold, snowy landscape matches the detainees' dark mood. Terasaki notices one of the state's historical markers and realizes they're traveling through land where Confederate and Union soldiers fought three-quarters of a century ago. She feels a bond with those families torn apart during the Civil War: like them she's been forced to choose between conflicting loyalties, the land of her birth and that of her husband. Takeo too is forlorn, thinking of his classmates back in Washington enjoying Christmas vacation and presents and parties, friends he'll likely never see again.

Porters serve sandwiches for lunch, and soon agents including Poole, border patrol guards, and uniformed railroad police are passing through to confirm the passenger list. Since many travelers don't speak English, Mariko Terasaki serves as a volunteer translator. The agents reward her with chewing gum and candy and ask her to accompany them through the other cars. "I told her to go along and make herself useful," said Gwen, "and she went proudly off, jabbering first in Japanese and then in English, a happy nine-year-old go-between for the enemy adults."[17]

When the train arrives six hours later at the small station in Hot Springs, Virginia, another unfriendly crowd awaits. Gwen Terasaki realizes that these hardy mountaineers, many of Scots Irish descent, resemble the people she grew up with in nearby East Tennessee. In her later bestseller, *Bridge to the Sun*, she describes them as silent, but Takeo has a different memory. "When they spotted the American Gwen Terasaki in our midst [they] raised an ominous roar of booing," recalled Takeo, an eleven-year-old mature beyond his years. "The grace and dignity with which she bore this was impressive, though painful to witness."[18] Local fifteen-year-old Johnny Gazzola heard of the pending arrival on the radio and walked over. The disembarking women and children seem especially frightened. "I remember it being cold, gray [and] dark," said Gazzola, who later worked many years as a journalist and PR manager at the Homestead.

"They had so many guards you had to stand way back. Of course, a little kid like myself just got pushed back."[19]

The men walk the short distance to the Homestead while cars are provided for the women and children. As at the Greenbrier, everyone's room assignments and baggage are delivered smoothly. Nomura and Kurusu receive three-room suites, as does counselor Iguchi and his family. The Terasakis and most other families get two-room suites while unmarried staffers double up in single rooms. All are impressed by the hotel's luxury and scenic mountain locale. Some veteran staffers remember visiting when Ambassador Hirosi Saito and his family summered here five years ago.

Two days before the internees arrived, several FBI agents, led by Roy Morgan, met with hotel manager George Slosson Jr. The first of near-daily reports from on-site agents to headquarters (all headed "Memorandum for the Director") laud his cooperative nature and willingness to comply with all their requests. They inspect the premises and work from a list he provided to query all department heads. "If any mail, messages, or other information were given to them [by the Japanese] to smuggle out of the hotel, such information would be immediately made available to the agents through Mr. Slosson," wrote Morgan.[20] The FBI also gives the hotel's chief switchboard operator strict instructions: no incoming or outgoing calls without their approval; all calls can only be made by two designated representatives and the Spanish embassy, which is handling all Japanese affairs; and route every call to a room where an FBI agent can listen in. They neglect to inform her of the recording device in the room, from which disks will be forwarded to headquarters for transcription. Only Slosson knows that, and he's sworn to secrecy.

The same day the diplomats pull out of Union Station, Masuo Kato and three other journalists pull in from New Jersey. With the government acceding to his request, they're given a day to attend to personal affairs. With an immigration officer accompanying him, Kato makes the most of his short time. He lunches with the family he'd met on December 7 and arranges for their daughter, Hurley Fisk, Hull's secretary, to assume his apartment lease. Though Kato's married with two small children back in Japan, he and Fisk are quite close. A native Iowan, the head-turning redhead's universally acknowledged as one of the best-looking and most graceful gals of the secretarial set. Kato packs and does some shopping: long underwear and an extra pair of eyeglasses. "As far as I could see, no one showed the slightest interest in our movements except the immigration officer who was assigned to each of us."[21]

The day after the Japanese arrive, Fay Ingalls, who keeps a tight (and tightfisted) watch over his domain, writes to State: "The advent of these enemy aliens may be a temptation to misguided Americans to create disturbances and cause damage to the property of the Homestead." He believes the government will successfully safeguard all people and property, but adds he's been advised to buy more insurance. "For all practical purposes the only guest which we have is the State Department of the United States," Ingalls writes, "and I am assuming under these circumstances the State Department would be responsible for any damage which these Japanese guests may cause."[22]

Beyond the damage the Japanese have already caused at Pearl Harbor, many Americans remain enraged in insult-to-injury fashion by their luxurious accommodations. "May I ask," writes a Washington man to his senator, "why our government deems it necessary to pamper the delegation of Yellow Rats by housing them at one of the country's finest Winter resorts?"[23] Several weeks later, after the senator forwards his letter to State, he receives a detailed three-page response from the top, Cordell Hull, reiterating the noble principle of reciprocity. A tenet for which most Americans couldn't care less.

On the last day of the year State Department agent Edward Poole reports that all's going smoothly and he likes everybody, including Hidenari Terasaki, appointed as the Japanese representative ("100% cooperative"), and Spanish representative Don Joaquín Rodríguez de Gortázar ("quite a pleasant person"). Unlike O'Hanley, he even gets along "wonderfully well" with the G-men: "The agents of the FBI are gentlemen of the first degree. They have extended me the privilege of using their typewriter and other equipment."[24] Poole's harmonious beginning, at least with the border patrol guards, will end badly. Very badly.

Also on December 31 protocol chief George Summerlin ("Summie" to his friends) hosts a meeting of State employees representing several agencies with purposely obscure titles like Special Division, Foreign Activity Correlation, and Foreign Funds Control Division. Their discussion covers a wide range of thorny issues from mail delivery to telephone service to the settlement of enemy officials' personal debts before departure. However, any visions that may be dancing in their heads of a relatively short, harmonious detainment will be dashed, as negotiations to exchange U.S. diplomats held overseas will drag on for nearly six months. Reasons include ever-shifting demands and counteroffers, the niceties of diplomatic debate, multiple parties including neutral countries representing the warring nations, and inevitable delays involving the translation and transmission of voluminous paperwork among far-flung capitals worldwide.

On this busy December 31 Kato arrives at Hot Springs on a train with officials from Japan's New York consulate, swelling the number of internees to around 150. The detainment's a newsworthy story he was born to tell, but of course he can't publish a word. He's familiar with the Homestead, having vacationed here the last two summers. Town residents have pejoratively begun calling the hotel "Little Japan." Home from college for Christmas vacation, one local captures the tenor of the times in a note to a former beau, Lohr Vance. "Our 'little yellow friends' have taken over the Homestead," she writes, "and a queer feeling it is to see the hotel surrounded by armed guards! Of course it is exciting but not very pleasant."[25]

Back in White Sulphur Springs, a train from New York City brings thirty-six more arrivals. Among the Bulgarians, Hungarians, and Italians is a lone German: Paul Scheffer, the itinerant journalist whose transformation over the years from tepid Nazi supporter to outright critic has put him into a precarious position. At the Greenbrier he's reunited with old friend Margret Boveri, to whom he'd given her first job at the *Berliner Tageblatt* in 1933. Born to an American mother, she's also been freelancing in New York, but she's an ardent nationalist and determined to return to her native Germany. Scheffer knows his return would only end up with him swinging from a noose or facing a firing squad. Soon he's overheard telling friends that he'll commit suicide before he'll ever go back. Old friends on the outside worry for his safety too. Writer Dorothy Thompson, who'd known him since she reported from Germany and Russia in the twenties, writes in her diary, "To send him back to Germany is insane."[26]

As the New Year nears, the phone rings late that afternoon in the study of Frank Settle, minister of the local Methodist church. It's the FBI, asking if he'll conduct a Protestant service on New Year's Day at the Greenbrier, now home to more than 250 Axis country nationals.

"Yes," Settle tells the agent on the other end. "At the request of the FBI, I would preach to Hitler himself."[27]

# 12

## (Not So) Happy New Year

"Ein feste burg ist unser Gott, Ein gute Wehr und Waffen . . ."

Voices ring out from a congregation seated in a makeshift temple, the Virginia Room of the Greenbrier, as the pastor sings along in English: "A mighty fortress is our God, a bulwark never failing."

New Year's Day morning finds Minister Frank Settle leading a service for the detainees. His selection of Martin Luther's defining hymn of the Protestant Reformation seems especially appropriate. Despite the solemnity etched on so many faces, "they sang it lustily," he recalled forty years later. "No person with a semblance of sensitivity to human needs could face these distressed faces without feeling some of the anguish they experienced. And so we prayed together." When the service concludes he greets the attendees in reverse order of when he entered, ending with their highest-ranking official, Hans Thomsen, with Bébé alongside. So much fear and uncertainty lie ahead, yet in this moment there's no animosity between the citizens of two countries now at war. "I hate Germany and Hitler with all my might," one guard blurts out to Settle. "But working with these people, for my life, I cannot hate them!"[1]

Children run and laugh and play, oblivious to the gravity of the situation. Adults talk in subdued tones. A routine of sorts has settled in, with the hotel's rural locale—now blanketed in snow—and old-world elegance, fine dining, and shopping and recreation options somewhat mitigating their enforced stay. Only a handful of regular guests remain, as management quietly works to ease them out. "They had to make room," wrote Hildy von Boetticher, "for nervous diplomats, their indignant wives and their somewhat uncontrollable children."[2]

Yet despite a blanket ban on all outsiders, one enterprising reporter from Cleveland tries to bluff his way in. A couple of weeks ago he was playing Santa Claus in a benefit concert at a local hospital; now he's sending a telegram requesting a room for his imminent arrival. "Regret unable reserve accommodations," wires back Robert Parker, assistant to the general manager. "All available Greenbrier rooms temporarily taken over for German embassy personnel. Very sorry." Parker even leaves word with the doorman in case the reporter appears anyway, extending further regrets. "I sincerely hope," he writes, "that we may have the opportunity of having you visit us at a later date."[3]

The Greenbrier has to fend off not only reporters but poachers too. Not the kind that try to steal employees but rather their clients. Since the diplomats' arrival has also eliminated all group meetings and events, an established New York hotel goes fishing for business. Hearing that the Greenbrier will be occupied for the duration of the war, its sales director writes, "If this is so, would it be proper at this time for us to solicit any convention groups that might have been booked for the Greenbrier in 1942?"[4] Parker diplomatically replies that the diplomats are expected to stay for only four to six weeks. "We realize how talk and gossip is going around," he adds, "but I am sure Mr. Johnston would be interested in ascertaining who told you that the group would be here for the duration of the war. They may have some inside dope with which we are not familiar and naturally we would like to ascertain this full information for our own benefit."[5]

A week later the prospective poacher backpedals by claiming it was all secondhand information: an unnamed staff member had told him that some newspaper he never saw himself ran a story about the war-long timeframe. "Naturally, I did not want to embarrass Mr. Johnston or yourself by soliciting any of the things booked at the Greenbrier until I had official information from you that your conventions had been cancelled," he writes.[6] He closes by inviting Parker to stay at his hotel "as our guest" when he's next in New York—an offer that, one can only imagine, was graciously refused.

The Greenbrier and the Homestead have long been popular destinations for wealthy and well-connected patrons. They're so famous that sometimes their names weren't even necessary—simply a mention of their locations sufficed. "The White Sulphur, the Hot Springs and Atlantic City hotels are all well filled with pleasure seekers for Easter and Easter week," wrote the *Washington Post* a quarter century earlier, when even the outbreak of World War I couldn't deter the upper class from springtime vacationing.[7]

Last Easter time the *New York Times* profiled the pair, detailing their comforts and pleasures. It noted some differences, as in the dining room staffs: the Greenbrier's international mélange including Italians, French, and Greeks versus the Homestead's black waiters who balance food trays on their heads. (By the time the detainees arrive, the Greenbrier's waiters are largely German, a situation that causes a considerable stir and several arrests; the Homestead may have discontinued its long-established lawn race between waiters with trays on their heads, but its advertisements still feature the image of a smiling waiter balancing a tray.) Overall, the paper detected a subtle difference between the tenor of the two renowned resorts: a faint tinge of nostalgia for earlier, genteel times at the Homestead, snazzier overtones of the Riviera for the Greenbrier: "Perhaps it is a difference of tempo and melody. Jerome Kern for the Homestead with Victor Herbert echoes; Gershwin plus a smidgeon of Cole Porter for the Greenbrier."[8]

Yet today Easter and springtime are but distant memories. Frigid January temperatures keep most guests inside, where the athletically inclined turn to activities like swimming, Ping-Pong, and roller skating in a vacant underground parking garage. Nine-year-old George von Knoop enjoyed "excellent and desirable" swimming lessons from Greenbrier's legendary coach, Charles Norelius, a one-time Olympian for his native Sweden. He trained his daughter, Martha, the first American swimmer to win gold medals in two different Olympics starting in 1924 at age fifteen. Others take to Ping-Pong tables in the north wing hallway, known as the Celebrity Corridor for its portraits of past illustrious guests. Among the rotating display are movie stars Douglas Fairbanks Sr. and Norma Talmadge, publisher Condé Nast, baseball great Lou Gehrig, and General George C. Marshall, currently helming military operations as army chief of staff.

Some people venture outdoors, especially the dog-walkers. At least a dozen Germans have brought theirs along, including the Thomsens' cocker spaniel Peterkins, four dachshunds, a griffon, a terrier, and two police dogs (Wolf and Prince). Owners pay an additional dollar per day, though complaints soon knock that down to fifty cents. A hearty few skate on a frozen-over lake near the golf course. One day fifteen-year-old Lucy Buran, whose father owns the hotel's men's clothing store, meets a German couple while out skating. In fluent English they ask whether she knows how to do crossovers. When she admits she doesn't they teach her how to execute the basic forward and backward technique, which she soon masters. Lucy recalls them as "a handsome couple, beautifully dressed with wonderful manners"—an apt description of the Thomsens, and records show that Hans indeed bought Bébé a new pair of skates at the hotel.[9]

Small sentry shacks have been built that offer the guards some protection from the cold, which on many nights can dip well below zero. "Our guards now have little houses to stay in with a large lantern inside," writes one staffer, "so I hope they will not get frost-bitten."[10] Other new construction includes floodlights that stay on all night long, triggering complaints about disrupted sleep. "We are not prisoners, and I do not see why all this is necessary," says Bébé Thomsen, who also whines about nighttime guards talking loudly outside her bedroom window.[11] The men are asked to be more discreet, but the floodlights remain on.

Yet when it comes to disruptions, one far bigger than lighting is about to arrive: the Italians. Not that they wanted to.

Letting them roam free in DC while their Axis allies had been removed is causing the government a public relations nightmare. Attorney General Biddle writes FDR asking permission to "intern" (couching the word in quotation marks to reinforce its undesirable connotation) the

**Fig. 31.** The Italian detainees, with Colonna seated in second row, center. Courtesy of the Greenbrier.

Italians, Bulgarians, and Hungarians. Hull concurred: "Unfortunately, some of these officials have attracted attention in public places to such an extent that there has been public criticism of the liberal treatment accorded them."[12] So the order went out to the Swiss to convey to the Italians, putting Colonna into a snit. "Such observation appears to me completely unfounded," he wrote in a telegram to Rome. "Members of Embassy have abstained with greatest care from frequenting public places where their presence could be noted."[13]

To quiet the diplomatic storm State backtracks, explaining that the public criticism is less about alleged misbehavior and more about the policy of letting the Italians remain free. The response mollifies Colonna, but his far greater concern is their proposed destination: the Greenbrier. Colonna meets not once but twice in the same day with Bruggmann to protest being stuck with the Germans. After being under the Nazis' heel for the last several years, the Italians have been enjoying (and perhaps flaunting?) their freedom while their ill-natured allies were rounded up. But now, to be forced to join them? He argues strenuously for another hotel, any hotel, but is informed there simply aren't any other suitable and available options. When the deadline for departure is set, Colonna balks and angles for more time until he's told it's not open to negotiation.

So in the early morning hours of January 16, 1942, a familiar scene unfolds at the Italian embassy on 16th Street NW. Like the prior departures from the German and Japanese embassies, passengers and baggage fill buses that proceed to Union Station for a special train to White Sulphur. Leading an entourage of eighty, Prince Colonna and his wife ride in a private car accompanied by a State Department agent. But the third time's not a charm—and definitely not a swarm. Far fewer spectators and reporters turn out, and a bare handful of papers even report the story. At a time when war news fills every paper every day, both the *Washington Post* and the *New York Times* ignore it.

Yet both front pages, and virtually every other paper in America, do highlight a shockingly sad story: last night's crash outside of Las Vegas of a plane carrying screen star Carole Lombard, returning from a trip selling war bonds. Her husband, Clark Gable, charters a plane from LA to rush to the site, but his worst fears are confirmed. "She brought great joy to all who knew her and to the millions who knew her only as a great artist," writes FDR in a telegram to Gable. "She gave unselfishly of her time and talent to serve her government in peace and in war. She loved her country. She is and always will be a star, one we shall never forget nor cease to be grateful to. Deepest sympathy."[14]

On New Year's Day at the Homestead, there's no church service like at the Greenbrier. Instead, many detainees gather under the bemused watch of the guards to sing "Kimigayo," the Japanese national anthem:

> May the reign of the Emperor
> continue for a thousand, nay, eight thousand generations
> and for the eternity that it takes
> for a small pebble to grow into a great rock
> and become covered with moss.

They end by raising their hands and chanting "Banzai" three times. Their world, like that of their European Axis brethren at the Greenbrier, settles into a routine of luxurious monotony. Outdoor activities like skiing are prohibited, despite the nearby snowy slopes that look so inviting. Federal agents insist it's for their own protection, since anti-Japanese sentiment runs high and rumors of possible acts of retribution have spread. Though the snow eliminates any chance for golf, State still delivers a message forbidding it because the Japanese are not allowing U.S. diplomats in custody there to play. So the large indoor swimming pool becomes a popular destination at seventy-five cents per person, as do the nightly movies (thirty-five cents) such as *How Green Was My Valley* and *Swamp River*, although the newsreels that typically accompany films in theaters aren't shown. The hotel screens Charlie Chaplin movies and Bob Hope comedies for the children.

With detainees so eager for news of the outside world, reading takes on an outsize importance and becomes a favorite pastime. But on some days newspapers don't arrive. "A common rumor on such occasions," wrote Kato, "was that the Americans were holding the papers up so that they could prepare special editions for us, to minimize Allied defeats and play up Japanese reverses. This was patently absurd, but nervous tension was high on those days when the newspapers did not arrive."[15] However, the days of a missed paper now and again will soon feel like a minor annoyance when the FBI announces a ban in late January on all newspapers, magazines, and books, immediately turning the mood from tension to outrage. The only exception is that they can choose one newspaper; detainees at both hotels vote for the *New York Times*.

Other diversions include ping pong, billiards, and board games like bridge, mah-jongg, go, and shogi, but some adults disapprove of children playing cards in the lobby. They "scolded us and then reported us to our parents, warning them we were in danger of turning into delinquents or wastrels," said Takeo Iguchi. "Cowed, we folded our games but in my heart I frowned upon these busybodies for making such a fuss over such a trivial matter."[16] Eventually a courtyard is opened up for outdoor activity, and the kids merrily frolic and toss snowballs. But even that horseplay can have a downside. Hidenari Terasaki bitterly tells an FBI agent that the Iguchi children threw snowballs at his daughter "like the Japanese bombed Pearl Harbor. Since she had an American mother, Mariko felt they had been so unfriendly towards her for being half American by blood."[17] The animosity between Terasaki and Iguchi predates their children's squabbles, for Iguchi had replaced Terasaki as liaison after some of his countrymen complained. Terasaki thinks they were jealous.

During his stay Terasaki talks volubly with FBI agents on a host of war-related issues, offering opinions on events past and potential future developments. Reports of these conversations are dutifully typed up and transmitted back to FBI headquarters, which Terasaki undoubtedly realizes. So his practice of putting himself and his superiors in the best possible light is unsurprising. On the day he arrived he brought up the subject of Pearl Harbor with Roy Morgan, insisting Ambassador Kichisa-buro Nomura, Special Envoy Saburo Kurusu, and he knew nothing about it beforehand. "If the U.S. had seceded a little and put forth its hand just a short way, Japan would have reached out and grasped it wholeheartedly and would not have clung to all their demands," reads Morgan's recol-lection of Terasaki's talking-point comments, which further reiterate the official Japanese stance that China is "a very backward nation which will only develop through the efforts of Japan."[18] "Efforts," to everyone else, means bloody conquest. (In a postwar interview with Roy Morgan, Masuo Kato admits the truth: "China is the muddy swamp: once you get in it is hard to get out."[19])

He praises Kurusu to the heavens, claiming that the then-ambassador to Germany only signed the Tripartite Pact under duress. He describes Kurusu's recent afternoon address to male Japanese detainees in which the envoy suggests it will be a long, costly war, and Japan will probably lose. Study hard, Kurusu tells the young men, and prepare for the revolutionary changes that will follow. Hoover is so impressed by Mor-gan's report that he forwards it to Assistant Secretary of State Berle and officers at G-2 (army intelligence) and ONI. This is one of the director's favorite practices: when he likes an internal report he has it summarized and sent out, with a cover letter under his signature, to top government officials.

These memos do double duty: imparting useful information and reminding the recipient just how much the director of the FBI knows. Hoover's not the most feared man in Washington for nothing.

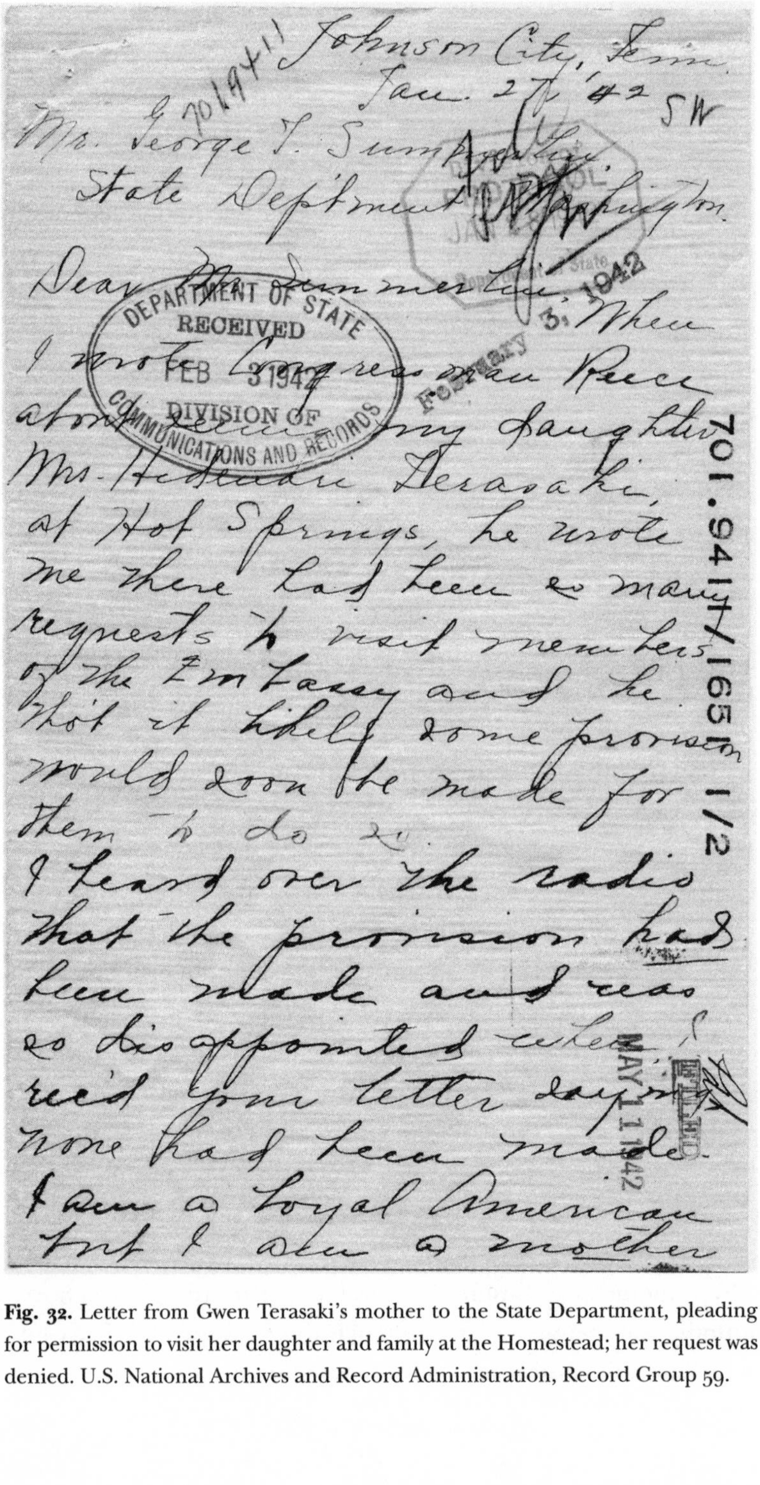

Johnson City, Tenn.
Jan. 27, '42

Mr. George T. Summerlin
State Dept. Washington

Dear Mr. Summerlin; When I wrote Congressman Reece about seeing my daughter Mrs. Hidenari Terasaki, at Hot Springs, he wrote me there had been so many requests to visit members of the Embassy and he tho't it likely some provision would soon be made for them to do so.
I heard over the radio that the provision had been made and was so disappointed when I rec'd your letter saying none had been made.
I am a loyal American but I am a mother

DEPARTMENT OF STATE
RECEIVED
FEB 3 1942
DIVISION OF COMMUNICATIONS AND RECORDS

February 3, 1942

701.9411/1651 1/2

MAY 11 1942

**Fig. 32.** Letter from Gwen Terasaki's mother to the State Department, pleading for permission to visit her daughter and family at the Homestead; her request was denied. U.S. National Archives and Record Administration, Record Group 59.

Terasaki has a counterpart at the Greenbrier who's even more talkative: Friedrich von Boetticher. The former Nazi military attaché is never one to turn down an opportunity to pontificate on war matters, whether in Europe or farther afield. In late January he predicts the fall of Singapore—which happens less than three weeks later. At the same time he acknowledges mistakes made by Germany in Russia but believes a spring offensive by a rested and freshly resupplied Wehrmacht, along with Russia's being forced to simultaneously face Japan in Siberia, will cause its defeat. Neither a Japanese front nor Russian downfall ever happens.

Aside from his pronouncements to anyone willing to lend an ear, von Boetticher has one overriding concern much closer to home: his hospitalized son, Friedrich. Right after Pearl Harbor he began lobbying to allow the boy to stay in America. His request was approved within several weeks, an extraordinarily fast response given the chaotic times and the United States' sudden wartime footing. It's a testament to his position, his influential military contacts, or a combination of the two. The approval comes with three conditions: establishing a seven-thousand-dollar trust fund to handle all the boy's expenses for at least two years; appointing his son-in-law, David Miller, a respected doctor, as guardian; and having his son register as an alien. Now von Boetticher wants to visit him at the hospital before repatriation, while Olga wants to visit Buffalo to see their new grandchild: exceptional requests given that no visitors are even allowed at the Greenbrier. Gwen's Terasaki's mother, Bertha, for example, pleads to be allowed to visit her daughter, son-in-law, and granddaughter at the Homestead and again asks her congressman to intercede. "Mrs. Harold has a good reputation," writes representative Reece, "and has not been suspected of disloyalty in any way. I should appreciate her being extended any courtesy which the situation may permit."[20] Their requests are rejected. Brigadier Army General Sherman Miles, whose career effectively ended after Pearl Harbor due to his mishandling of intelligence, volunteers a War Department officer to accompany Friedrich von Boetticher to visit his son, but that offer goes unanswered.

Most detainees, not as self-serving as von Boetticher or Terasaki, don't speak so readily to the feds on site. At least not intentionally. Agents have several surreptitious methods for obtaining information. One of the three FBI agents stationed at the Greenbrier speaks German, so he hangs about the lobby and other public places to mine idle chatter. A border guard who speaks German reports listening to conversations in the room adjoining his. Trying to get a glimpse of the man and women talking he slips a mirror under the door, but the space only allows him a glimpse of her "shapely and slender" ankles."[21] Suffice it to say, such crude attempts don't generate much, but there is a far more productive technique: the telephone. The detainees assume the phones are tapped and talk very guardedly, even on house phones. What they don't know is that the FBI doesn't have the equipment or the manpower to listen to internal calls. (Some paranoid detainees think their rooms are bugged, which they're not.) The FBI does record all long-distance calls made by the handful of Axis officials permitted to speak with the neutral countries' representatives handling their affairs and with U.S. government officials.

Behind-the-scenes equipment troubles cause some missed coverage, but local telephone repairmen soon get the system running smoothly, and conversations in multiple languages are taped and transcribed. The monitoring of long-distance calls pulls in hotel employees too. Once, when a man identified only as Ralph talks to a Jack about buying a portable radio, the FBI determines the potential customer—on behalf of a detainee, perhaps?—is the hotel's chief engineer "of whom nothing of a derogatory nature was known."[22] Nevertheless the call sparks an investigation of both men. Others ensnared by the phone surveillance are State and INS representatives. The FBI often gleans what its fellow agencies are thinking and planning, all the while, of course, keeping mum on what it's doing. "I know these three FBI men in the hotel by their first names, and they know me as John," writes O'Hanley to his superiors, "so wouldn't you think, since we're all working for the same Government, and towards the same goal, that they would at least co-operate a little bit?"[23]

The undercurrent of mistrust only intensifies and fuels nagging turf wars.

Most detainees, keeping plenty of secrets themselves, remain largely oblivious to their captors' infighting, but there's at least one shrewd observer of the rivalry between the FBI and State. "The two ministries," writes journalist Margret Boveri, "do not seem to love each other."[24]

# 13

## Watched While Waiting

While telephone taps provide occasional nuggets of valuable information amid mostly mundane matters, the best source of intelligence comes directly from informers falling into two discrete camps: employees and detainees. The FBI quietly reaches out to anyone and everyone on staff for what it euphemistically calls "services rendered." Bellboys, waiters, maids, housekeepers, telephone operators, clerks, valets, managers, store employees: no one's exempt. Masseurs and masseuses are considered especially valuable assets since their relaxed clients may be more prone to talking openly, albeit unwittingly.

But information comes at a price. Since many staffers earn meager wages and rely on tips—a prickly problem with the detainees that comes up time and again—bribes are essential to loosening tongues. "It is believed that if these people are not appropriately rewarded for their services that the services they have been performing will not be rendered us willingly in the future," warns Roy Morgan. "The hotel management and the personnel have a great respect for the Bureau and it is felt that if they are compensated for their services in a proper but conservative manner that this respect will be enhanced and appreciated."[1] His superiors agree and approve his request to have five hundred dollars deposited in a local bank in late January for the agents to spread around as they see fit.

Yet while informants may be lurking around any corner, the crown jewels of the recruitment efforts are the detainees themselves. Prospective informers' motivations vary widely: some genuinely oppose their countries' regimes; some have become quite Americanized and fear being sent home; some want money or crave attention; some want to settle old scores; the rest are some obscure combination thereof. At least one had spied previously, and given how riddled all foreign embassies were with informants getting paid by various intelligence agencies, there could have been more. Regardless, it's left to analysts back at headquarters to sift through the observations and opinions to uncover any truths or actionable information within.

FBI memos use code names, but since their confidential reports are for Washington eyes only, they sometimes include real names. Two at the Homestead are Kyusuke Hoshide, former clerk at the consulate in New York, and Kunichi Sasaki, former clerk to the naval attaché at the embassy. Both are married and have lived in the United States for more than twenty years. Hoshide, the most prolific, is recruited into Coordinator of Information, precursor to the OSS, to continue informing after he returns to Japan. A week before he sails, an FBI memo outlines his future communications and financial arrangements. At the Greenbrier there's German clerk Albert Schweikle, an informant from his first day at the German embassy last spring, and Italian journalist Piero Saporiti. All informants receive weekly stipends of around twenty dollars, and each hopes to remain in the United States. But agents never promise any special treatment, urging them to file the necessary applications if they wish. All four men wind up being repatriated. Many higher-level detainees speak with agents, but none are ever identified as informants. Journalist Paul Scheffer speaks openly and often. He never hides his desire to remain in the United States and soon takes a drastic step to make that happen.

Surveillance of the detainees, regardless of age, remains vigilant, as Takeo Iguchi's older sister Tatsuko discovers when she develops a toothache. Escorted by two FBI agents to a local dentist's office, she innocently reaches for a magazine on the waiting room's table. An agent jumps up and orders her to stop. Though the FBI insists that the agents are there for her protection, she realizes that they're actually wardens. "Our each and every move was under an almost pathological surveillance," recalled Takeo.[2]

That spying extends beyond the detainees to employees too. In early January all four hundred workers at the Greenbrier are fingerprinted. Since there are seventy-five border patrolmen, the FBI lets them conduct the interviews and add a lone fingerprint to the back of every employee's pass card. However, hotel personnel data is updated only every other year, and some employees skip their interviews. "Information was in many cases incomplete and, as was later learned, unreliable," wrote Morgan.[3] Nevertheless, the work produced enough information for INS to arrest three employees in the country illegally, with the border guards gloating that they caught people that the FBI had okayed. Apparently it's not just State that resents the FBI's heavy-handed presence.

Embarrassed by the guards' success, the FBI redoubles its efforts to monitor employees, from their immigration status to poor character to suspect loyalties. One day, for example, in conversation with Morgan hotel manager George Slosson mentions that his wife was born in Germany. This offhand comment immediately triggers a background check to determine her maiden name, when she emigrated, her political views, and whether any of her relatives are pro-Nazi. Results confirm that she and her husband are unquestionably loyal to the United States. Their conversation happened on the same day that Slosson dutifully turned in a glass slide dropped inadvertently by a detainee after a movie, proving that even someone providing such loyal service isn't above suspicion.

But sometimes suspicions don't pan out. Last year the local FBI office looked into a German waiter alleged to be a Bund member. The investigation suggested pro-German but not necessarily pro-Nazi feelings, with a hotel employee opining that the man was "harmless, unintelligent and overly talkative."[4] Locals also fall under suspicion, including a "raw-boned" White Sulphur Springs man described as a "village loafer and former bootlegger" who reportedly cursed FDR and said he hoped the war would last for twenty years.[5] Considerable pro-Nazi sentiments exist among some of the Greenbrier's sizable contingent of German waiters. Many converse with detainees in German. Some do small favors like smuggling out letters to mail or sneaking in contraband: all strictly verboten. Right after the internment began, General Manager Loren Johnston wrote privately that it might prove beneficial: "It will smoke out anything un-American, and those that might prevail anywhere about the place. I have always liked to feel that there wasn't anything of that kind prevalent, and I still hope so. . . . It is our first duty to see to it that anything not entirely favorable to our country should be immediately handled and straightened out. That, I shall do regardless of who it hits, because this is too good a country to have anything else prevail."[6]

The FBI launches a large-scale mission. It brings in more men and takes over the fingerprinting operation, conducting half-hour interviews with every employee: twenty minutes of questioning, ten minutes for fingerprinting and taking photographs. They comb through employee lists, homing in on a dozen or so suspect German waiters and compiling detailed profiles of each. One report contains an informant's recollections of one waiter's comments: "I'm a fifth columnist and I don't give a damn who knows it. . . . It would be better for the whole world for Hitler to take it over. Everybody would be better off if he did."[7] The FBI learns that one room in the servant's quarters is festooned with Nazi memorabilia, including swastikas, a portrait of Hitler, and propaganda. Here the men reportedly hold meetings and celebrate German victories. It's no secret that many luxury hotels employ foreign-born waitstaff. One former hotel guest from New Jersey questions this policy, writing to the State Department: "Obviously Teutonic, if you ask them their nationality, and I have, they invariably reply that they are Swiss. If this be true, then all I can say is that the German cantons in Switzerland have a terrific birth rate."[8]

Besides having a good sense of humor, this ordinary citizen also has extraordinary timing. For on February 9, 1942, *one day after he writes his letter*, the FBI and a detachment of West Virginia state police swoop in at dinnertime and arrest seven men: an Italian baker and six German waiters, including Joseph Krautlager, the man who'd openly rooted for a Hitler victory. Kept totally in the dark, neither INS nor State are given any notice until shortly before the arrests. The New Jersey correspondent

**THE HOMESTEAD**
**HOT SPRINGS, VIRGINIA**

*Dinner*

Cream of Chicken, Infante

Consomme, Double

Broiled Makerel with Olives and Anchovy

Roast Prime Rib of Beef, au Jus

Puree of Fresh Broccoli

Saute Potatoes

Heart of Lettuce, 1000 Island

Pineapple Pie

Chocolate Ice Cream

Coffee

Sunday, January 25, 1942

**Fig. 33.** Typical dinner fare for the Japanese housed at the Homestead. U.S. National Archives and Record Administration, Record Group 59.

offers a final suggestion: "If there is any room left on the boat which takes this German official group back, I would suggest sending back some of these 'Swiss' for ballast."

The loyalties of a handful of Greenbrier waiters notwithstanding, the Homestead faces a completely unrelated service issue: some of its black waitstaff are reluctant to serve the Japanese. Racial animus against blacks seems a Japanese trait. A story surfaces that one waiter was mightily tempted to pour coffee onto an especially condescending guest; in another telling, the waiter actually pours the coffee on him.

Disinclination and loyalties aside, there's one thing upon which everyone wholeheartedly agrees. Both hotels have reputations for culinary excellence, and neither disappoints. "I hope," jokes John O'Hanley, "that I don't put on about twenty pounds while here."[9] Yet the mouthwatering menus produce a most curious reaction from the Japanese: a request to cut back their options. Their official statement reads: "We, as members of the Japanese nation, feel that we too should share, though in a small way, hardships now being experienced by Japanese people at home. In view of the above, we should be grateful if the State Department would kindly have new arrangements made with the Hotel management whereby our daily meals may be made simpler."[10]

Concurrently, they make two more requests. First, they ask that their servants be relocated to eat in a separate dining room. Japanese culture echoes the upstairs-downstairs tradition of British aristocracy, though a British server waits unobtrusively to assist as necessary, while a Japanese servant serves and immediately leaves the room. Second, they request that the afternoon musical performances by a string trio be shifted from the main lobby to a more remote location. These requests, coming directly from Nomura through liaison officer Iguchi, are immediately put into effect. But the ambassador apparently feels that not all rules apply to him. Several weeks later, on-site State representative Edward Poole writes to his boss: "Hotel management informed me that the Japanese Ambassador Nomura, while dining in his room alone, had ordered certain entrees that did not appear on the menu, which were suggested by himself. Please advise the proper course to pursue in this case."[11]

In late January the Germans also have their menu choices reduced, though not by request. Rather, it's that old fallback on "reciprocity"—for the administration has learned that American diplomats being held in Germany are receiving minimal meals. So State orders a stateside cut-back in the quantity of choices, though the quality of the food remains unchanged. "The question of the amount and variety of the food was the greatest single cause of complaint among the members of the group during the stay at Bad Nauheim," wrote George Kennan, the embassy's first secretary.[12] Though they didn't know it, the American detainees also faced a potentially deadly problem that the Germans at the Greenbrier never encountered. British Royal Air Force pilots conducted regular bombing raids over Germany, and in late February U.S. Ambassador John Winant sent a telegram to Hull inquiring about the diplomats' exact whereabouts so the bombers could be instructed to avoid that area.

While Nomura's room service orders raise eyebrows, it's actually Hans Thomsen who causes the most problems. Initially, State arranged for free room service for all heads of mission, which Thomsen makes a point of informing each incoming minister. The detainees' ranks are swelling with arrivals from embassies in Colombia, Cuba, Guatemala, Mexico, and Panama—with the goal of assembling everyone in one central location for eventual repatriation. So many take advantage of the hotel's largess that Charlie Spruks, when notified by management, rescinds the no-charge option. Now each room service delivery incurs a charge of twenty-five cents per person. "This is a particularly heavy blow to Dr. Thomsen," writes FBI agent Lawler, "inasmuch as his wife has been confined to her room much of the time she has been here, and has had most of her meals served in her room."[13]

John Lawler's report catches the eye of the director who quickly sends a letter—marked "Personal and Confidential, By Special Messenger"—to Adolf Berle. Hoover cites a "confidential source of information, who is close to the German mission," who surmises that the reason for Bébé Thomsen's spending so much time in her room is because she's distraught at the thought of returning to Germany. The source believes that her previously espoused anti-Nazi feelings are also causing considerable marital strife, though Hans Thomsen is held in high regard by the Hitler regime and "will undoubtedly be decorated by the German Government upon his return to Germany in appreciation of the work he has done here."[14] This prediction turns out to be 100 percent accurate; within days of Thomsen's return next spring, with his wife, the führer himself presents him with a prestigious award.

The FBI never reveals this source's identity, though he—memos confirm it's a man—obviously has both access to and a keen knowledge of the German mission. In his letter Hoover notes he's not on staff and in a subsequent letter identifies him as "a former German journalist."[15] This informer also divulges that Friedrich von Boetticher once asked him to relay any information of a military intelligence nature that he might come across during the course of his reporting; the informant refused. This information, combined with his astute analysis and characterizations of the embassy's top Nazi officials, clearly point to one man: Paul Scheffer.

Which makes perfect sense, given his vow about not wanting to go back to Germany. Providing information to the FBI is the lone avenue open to an increasingly desperate man that might allow him to curry favor among decision makers and positively affect his fate. Scheffer's intellectual vigor and worldly experience, having lived in or visited and reported on dozens of countries on three continents, arguably makes him the scholarly equal or better of any German detainee. But it's also made him powerful enemies within and without. In some U.S. quarters he's still wrongly suspected of being a Nazi supporter; others dislike his vocal anti-communist stance, one that's fallen out of favor now that the Soviet Union is a U.S. ally. (Never mind that the Soviets have many spies in America, including one who penetrates into the upper ranks of OSS.)

"There is goodwill in Washington," writes Scheffer, "but at the same time, a conspiracy. In the Department of Justice, Biddle, emphasizing conspiracy of press, radio attacks, all with same material and tenor: spy, Goebbels agent. Goebbels I have seen once, in 1933, at a garden party. It is all alarmingly funny."[16] In short, he has few influential friends and fewer options. Time is growing short. Several dozen other detainees, mostly Hungarians, have also applied to remain in America but none face such momentous consequences as Scheffer if their pleas are rejected.

Most detainees focus on living in the moment and making the most of their enforced stay before returning to uncertain futures in countries at war. So there's plenty of entertaining and socializing, which occasionally leads to unexpectedly humorous moments. One night Bébé Thomsen, a longtime devotee of tarot cards, invites friends back to their room. She shuts off the lights and shuffles the cards before laying them out, repeating the process over and over. Suddenly there's a loud knock at the door: it's the guards, convinced that the lights going on and off must be some kind of spying signal. Here, in a remote mountain village?! Once when chief clerk Roy Sibold, Johnston's righthand man, casually mentions Bébé to Hans Rabe, a twenty-year-old embassy clerk, he replies, "Oh, her? Well we don't have anything to do with her."[17] His tone suggests that he and some other detainees think she's a bit daft.

Another time a strange request comes from outside. A Los Angeles man mails several photographs of Ambassador Colonna to State and asks if they could have him sign and mail them back. "I realize that during these delicate times a request of this kind might look a bit like I was favorable to the enemy," he writes. "On the other hand, my loyalty cannot be questioned and my only desire is to have Ambassador Colonna autograph my picture and the enclosed card for my collection."[18] Ten days later—never let it be said that the government isn't efficient—his request generates a terse response: "It is contrary to the practice of the Department to comply with requests of this nature. The enclosures to your letters under acknowledgement are returned herewith."[19]

Meanwhile, relations between the Italians and Germans are anything but cordial; their mutual animosity is palpable. The Germans' smug superiority—well remembered from the prewar embassy years—quickly resurfaces, with snide comments flying from both sides: taunting questions about the Italians' military capabilities, retorts about Germany's stalled, and some imply failed, invasion of Russia. Swiss liaison Frederick Stocker occupies a rare role, an outsider equally comfortable in this cloistered world. Invited to many cocktail parties he discovers that after a few drinks, with him speaking high German, some forget he's not one of them and reveal a bit too much. The pretty wife of one Nazi official, for example, complains bitterly about how Washington was the most disagreeable city in which she'd ever lived. Suddenly her husband speaks up: "'First, don't talk with your mouth full. Second, you don't know what you are talking about. And third, you will get a spanking,'" recalls Stocker of her husband's response. "The original German, of course, sounds more dramatic."[20]

One weekend Stocker's wife, Mary Anne, visits, and dining the first night she singles out a cultured woman. "Now there is a real lady," she says, "the one wearing that simple but elegant black dress and the beautiful pearl string." That lady is Princess Colonna, who takes an especial liking to Mary Anne and tells her of their previous visits to the Greenbrier. She suggests outings that she and her husband should take, excursions that are off-limits to the detainees, whose activities are limited primarily to indoor pursuits, of which dining becomes a favorite pastime.

The excellent food is served professionally, albeit with a contentious undercurrent: the absence of tipping. This lack of compensation generates continual grousing among waitstaff and management. Behind the scenes memos and conversations go back and forth. Finally the Germans and Hungarians begin paying a lump sum weekly that's distributed among the waiters. But the Germans do it under duress, arguing that it's really State's responsibility. Wheels turn slowly, but eventually the Axis diplomats are reimbursed. Even the three on-site federal agencies agree that their men should be tipping too, and they do, with reimbursement again coming from their employers.

Yet solving one problem leads to another: how about the bellboys and maids? Don't they deserve compensation too? The Greenbrier estimates that its bellhops have transported some five thousand pieces of baggage since the detainment began, many of which are heavy trunks and boxes. "The bell staff is made up of loyal, colored American boys, many of whom have been with us from twenty to thirty years," writes assistant manager George O'Brien. "I am sure that they are within their rights in expecting gratuities of some nature on the basis of that which would be comparable to any other first class hotel."[21]

# 14

## Quiet Desperation

At first-class hostelries fine dining is unquestionably de rigueur, as is another attribute: high-end shopping. The Greenbrier offers a diverse array of goods and services including men's, women's, and children's shops to dress everyone in the family from head to toe, hats to shoes. A linen shop carries home goods; a drug store, everyday essentials and sundries. Plus there's an antique shop, gift shop, florist, newsstand, candy store, beauty shop, and barber.

"One could find an entire new outfit to wear," writes Else Arnecke. "Shoes, only the best. A beauty salon. In the antique shop, everything exquisite—including the prices. Plus their famous drug store. In short, everything that a person needed or dreamed about."[1] Men's store owner W. W. Buran, who also owns the men's store at the Homestead, does a brisk business selling bolts of fine wool and even orders trunks and suitcases for the detainees to transport their purchases home. His wife makes friends easily, and while talking one day with an Austrian house-keeper she asks her to describe her native country. With a thick accent and a wave of her hand, the woman replies, "Gone vith the vind"—an allusion to the *Anschluss*, Germany's swift takeover of Austria in 1938.

Out in one of the cottages is the Doll House, home to beautiful toys and dolls often fashioned by owner Pet Sullivan, a bit of a local eccentric who always dresses in red.

Money is no object since embassy staffers are still on the payroll. Back on January 4—priorities, people!—Stocker and a Swiss attaché arrived with thirty-five thousand dollars in cash (the equivalent of $545,000 in 2019) for Tannenberg to distribute. So with nowhere else to spread their cash around, the detainees do it here. Big time. Hildy von Boetticher noted the shops' not-so-subtle transformation as savvy businesspeople began to cater to their needs: "The Greenbrier's Fifth Avenue shops were gradually restocked to resemble a village general store: shoe leather, steamer trunks, tins of coffee, butter and tea, woolen underwear, yard goods. It was a last frontier station for the internees equipping themselves for war. The merchants profiteered because shopping had become an obsession. Besides, everyone had his monthly salary to spend. 'What's new in the shops today?' was the first question at breakfast."[2]

With detainees flush with cash, it's no surprise that stories of hoarding soon surface. It starts with a report that one woman bought 50 pounds of coffee, 5 pounds of cocoa, and a 5-pound can of marmalade. Inquiries made to Perry, the hotel's purchasing agent (and the town's mayor), report that a previous order from other detainees was for around 40 pounds in total of coffee, Sanka, Postum, cocoa, and tea. These obviously aren't for current consumption but to take back home. Other merchants report runs on items reportedly scarce in Europe, including silks, woolens, soaps, face cream, and toothpaste. The druggist reports that Klem, a powdered milk, is a big seller. Investigations suggest that the reports of hoarding have been overstated, but nevertheless State issues a directive banning any more large orders. Each country's liaison in turn sends out a memo informing their charges of the new rule. Some merchants begin imposing limits, like allowing each detainee to buy a maximum of twelve bars of soap, six sheets and six towels, three dresses, three suits, two pairs of shoes, and so on. Still, other than items that involve specific sizes, any determined detainee can easily circumvent the rules by enlisting friends and family to make purchases for them. And it's hard to believe that, say, the druggist is actually keeping a list of who's bought how much soap.

**Fig. 34.** First Lady Eleanor Roosevelt cutting a birthday cake alongside reporter Hope Ridings Miller, president of the Women's National Press Club. Library of Congress, Prints and Photographs Division, Harris and Ewing Collection.

Hoarding is actually a far wider concern throughout the United States, as grocery store shelves are being stripped bare of essentials like flour, sugar, lard, canned goods, soap, and toilet paper. In February the phenomenon produces a humorous aside when Eleanor Roosevelt attends a meeting of the Senate Ladies Red Cross and takes questions from the audience. "I have been very much disturbed by the hoarding I have seen going on in Washington," says Henrietta Hill, wife of Democratic Alabama Senator Lister Hill. "What do you think we can do about it?" Roosevelt looks aghast, gulping and sputtering, until a friend of the questioner comes to the rescue. "Mrs. Roosevelt," she says, "Mrs. Hill did not mean what you think she did, that is just her Southern accent. She meant H-O-A-R-D-I-N-G, not W-H-O-R-I-N-G."[3]

Limits on purchases are an inconvenience, but another, far more serious issue flares up every day: mail, or rather the lack thereof. Being cut off from the outside world isn't easy, but not being able to communicate in writing (nor speak on the phone) with friends and family is infuriating. All incoming mail and packages received at the hotels—and there's plenty—is sealed in rotary-locked pouches and shipped off to FBI headquarters. Any outgoing letters, which must be submitted stamped and unsealed, are forwarded in those same pouches. But it's apparently a one-way street because nothing ever comes in. Even inmates in Sing Sing are allowed to receive mail, complains one Italian. Another remarks that he preferred Ellis Island, a temporary internment locale for some before arriving here, because there he received not only mail but visits from his wife.

Is the volume of mail and packages simply overwhelming the FBI staff of censors, or are they purposely moving at a glacial pace from orders on high? The on-site agents don't know, and in their memos they try to gently prod headquarters into showing results sooner rather than later. They're feeling the heat every day from their increasingly exasperated charges, a situation that's exacerbated by the quick and efficient handling of official diplomatic mail by the hotels' State Department reps. They keep detailed records of each piece and deliver it promptly to either the protecting powers or the detainees' liaisons, though this type of correspondence is never opened or examined. Morgan notes that Masuo Kato has received special permission from State to send and receive mail after having it censored. He trades dozens of letters with Hurley Fisk, the young woman who rented his DC apartment after he was interned. Intriguingly, Kato also writes one letter to her boss, Secretary of State Hull, which despite due authorial diligence appears lost to history.

While the mail mess festers and causes continual ill will, the draconian new edict banning all newspapers except the *New York Times* triggers even more of an outcry. Spokesman Wilhelm Tannenberg calls the prohibition "preposterous." The Germans ask, unsuccessfully, to add the *Washington Times-Herald*, Cissy Patterson's anti-FDR rag. Boveri recalls that a black market occasionally produces a verboten copy of a *Time* or *Harper's* or *Newsweek*. Since everyone is allowed to listen to the radio, the ban seems both spiteful and futile. Journals and some books are another matter, since many can contain technical material that might aid the Axis's war efforts. Children's books are exempt, but even schoolbooks and foreign language dictionaries are out. Tannenberg smartly introduces the idea of reciprocity since he's heard Americans in Bad Nauheim have formed a literary circle, so they obviously must have access to reading matter there. Pushback comes from Breckinridge Long, who suggests that the FBI allow some softening for "innocuous books of fiction" and "histories of the United States . . . providing the latter does not concern itself with the active participation of America in the war or scientific developments or economic problems."[4]

John O'Hanley adds a typically droll coda: "All the news that is fit to print is in the 'Times,' so why stop a man from selling the other newspapers?"[5] The arbitrary periodical ban and missing mail depress just about everyone, but their unhappiness pales before that of one detainee whose situation is so precarious that he takes shocking action on Sunday, February 1.

"Mr. Paul Scheffer, a German newspaper man had a fall in the North Wing corridor of the hotel at approximately 1:30 p.m. today and late this afternoon was taken to the C&O Hospital at Clifton Forge, West Virginia," writes O'Hanley. "[Previously] S[c]heffer is alleged to have made the remark that he would commit suicide before he would set foot on German soil again."[6]

That day both border patrol inspector Harry Helmke and FBI agent John Lawler write memos recounting the incident to their respective bosses. In addition, later that day Malcolm Grove, the guard who reportedly witnessed the fall, is interrogated by a senior patrol inspector, with another serving as stenographer. "I saw a man walking across the corridor," begins Grove, "and I saw him stub his toe and fall. He caught his toe on the edge of the heavy mat. I waited for him to get up and then when he didn't get up I ran up to see about it and he said he was hurt pretty bad." Grove phones Helmke, the inspector in charge. Asked if anyone else was in the immediate vicinity, Grove replies, "No, sir. I didn't see a soul around when he fell. There was another fellow came right after."

That other fellow was Hans Thomsen. Only Helmke, in his memo, writes that when he got the call,

> I hurried down as quickly as I could, rushed thru the door and was the first one there, and found a man stretched out near the main north door. Before I could inspect him closely or ask him about his injury a guest came out of this same entrance known as Dr. Thomsen, and he immediately kneeled down across the injured man from me. He asked him a few questions in German [which Helmke understands]. The injured man then got Dr. Thomsen by the lapel of his coat and pulled his ear down to his lips and whispered something to him that I could not hear. Dr. Thomsen seemed to be awfully excited.

Helmke leaves to telephone his supervisor and the medical department, which is closed. He asks the operator to find Dr. George Caldwell, the hotel's doctor, and returns to the corridor where Scheffer is still lying. "At this point," wrote Helmke, "a young German doctor whose name I don't know came out of the door and rushed to the injured man, and made a hasty examination."[7]

FBI agent Lawler's memo offers a third recounting: "According to Dr. Hans Thomsen, who was an eyewitness and standing near the scene of the accident, Mr. Scheffer appeared to have had a spell or fainted, as he fell completely forward and it did not appear to have been an accidental fall. Mr. Scheffer was immediately examined by the German doctor." That man is detainee Carl Sennhenn, who'd been rejected last year for induction into the U.S. Army as unfit for duty. Although he married an American and had a young daughter, no family members accompanied him to the Greenbrier, suggesting that the couple had divorced. Sennhenn, according to Grove, diagnoses a broken leg and gives Scheffer a shot of morphine. Helmke doesn't mention that but notes that Scheffer pulled the doctor down by the lapel of his coat, just like he did with Thomsen, and whispered something in his ear which Helmke again couldn't hear. Sennhenn jumps up and runs off. Helmke gets an overcoat to cover Scheffer, who pulls him close and whispers in German, instructing him to go to his room and take some papers from near his typewriter. "Hurry, hurry. Go on," says Scheffer, who's obviously in much pain.[8] Later on Helmke and Lawler and retrieve his papers.

Three accounts, many inconsistencies that begin with two mind-boggling coincidences. With some 560 detainees, 600-plus employees, and 75 guards, one guard happens to be in the right place at exactly the right time to witness one person's fall? And then the first person to arrive on the scene is . . . the German chargé d'affaires?! *Unglaublich—* incredible. Except Grove claims Thomsen was there first, and Helmke said he was. Lawler said Thomsen was an eyewitness even though Grove said he alone saw the fall. Grove and Helmke say it was an accident; Lawler writes that Thomsen said it wasn't.

Late that afternoon Scheffer is transported to the hospital, where doctors diagnose "a number of small fractures in the right acetabular cavity including a fracture of the rim at its lowest point."[9] Translation? A broken hip. The next day Dr. Caldwell brings O'Hanley two letters: one addressed to him, the other to Scheffer's wife, Nathalie. Scheffer asks O'Hanley to please deliver hers as soon as possible so she won't be too frightened after hearing about his fall. "The shock will be reduced somewhat if she sees that I am capable of writing myself," Scheffer scrawls. "Excuse this rather shaky letter. I am under the influence of a number of hypodermics. I am very grateful to you, Paul Scheffer."[10] The next day, Tuesday, the chief supervisor of the border patrol, W. F. Miller, writes a memo to Lemuel Schofield, special assistant to Attorney General Biddle. In summarizing the events he notes many discrepancies and adds, "There may be something fishy about the matter."[11]

Fishy? How about fictitious? The reason the many reports don't add up is because they're concoctions, slapped together to hide the truth: Paul Scheffer jumped out a window, perhaps a low one, to either commit suicide or injure himself so badly he'd avoid expulsion to Germany. His desperate gamble works but comes at a steep price. He lives, he isn't deported—but he's crippled and suffers for the rest of his life after doctors botch his treatment.

No one has ever reported this story until now, but documentation unearthed in several archives is clear. The papers from Scheffer's room contain drafts of two letters he wrote but never sent to Thomsen. Their endings are worded slightly differently, but the message is the same. "For a long time," Scheffer began,

> I have been convinced that I would not be equal to the comedy which I would have to play in case I should have to return to Germany. . . . To work under the circumstances which exist in Berlin . . . which would not leave me anything but continuous hypocrisy and ambiguity and action contrary to my better knowledge and conscience, that surpasses my powers [and] would be a sorry ending to a respectable life.
>
> In order to give weight to my conviction I shall cease the taking of nourishment. I most sincerely regret causing you, Minister, and the Embassy, embarrassment and bring discord into the harmony which has hitherto characterized the Greenbrier group. I ask that under all circumstances this letter be considered irrevocable.[12]

Scheffer must have quickly realized that starving himself to death, if he wasn't force-fed to be kept alive, could drag on for many unpleasant months—with no guarantee that, in the end, the authorities wouldn't simply carry him aboard ship. So he never sent the letters to Thomsen and instead decided to risk it all. That the authorities covered it up is no surprise since a detainee's suicide, or attempted suicide, could have had disastrous consequences. Germany would have screamed bloody murder, even if the Nazis were likely to murder Scheffer themselves upon his return. America would have looked incompetent or complicit in the eyes of the world. So it was far better to concoct a cover-up because, otherwise, heads would have rolled. And besides, who was there to investigate? Reporters were banned, and the handful of friends like Boveri who suspected the truth kept their thoughts to themselves.

So stories circulated only on the grapevine. An unpublished memoir, though, undiscovered for nearly half a century, reveals the truth—or at least a major part of it. Swiss liaison Stocker, who left the Greenbrier shortly before the incident, never mentions Scheffer by name, but the man he describes is unquestionably him: a close friend of journalist Dorothy Thompson, a man who lobbied vigorously for his release and faced torture and death if forced to go home. (Thompson's papers detail her longtime friendship with Scheffer and indefatigable work on his behalf.) Negotiations for exchanging detainees were already bogging down with a niggling, tit-for-tat checklist. Keeping a German journalist without the ambassador's consent would have undoubtedly meant the Germans would swap out an American journalist under the concept of reciprocity.

"So it was decided that the man had to leave the country and to return to Germany after all," wrote Stocker. "A few days later he jumped out a window, probably in an attempt of suicide. He did not die but he broke both legs and suffered multiple other injuries which made transportation impossible. . . . I do not remember whether he eventually got well. I rather believe that he died soon afterwards."[13] Though Stocker got the last part wrong, he confirms that Scheffer's so-called accident was a premeditated attempt at suicide or inflicting severe bodily harm.

Untrue stories have a pernicious way of spreading. Several months later two greenhorn reporters, with neither proof nor documentation, repeat a rumor that one detainee committed suicide: a fiction that takes on the aura of truth simply by dint of publication. In truth, the day after his fall, spirits at the Greenbrier soar as mail's finally delivered, setting off great cheer among his fellow detainees. Meanwhile, Scheffer lies on a hospital bed, in great pain, drugged and alone—save for his twenty-four-hour guard.

When he finally returns ten days later, friends welcome him back. "We hosted a great reception for him," wrote Margret Boveri, "with poetry and funny gifts. But he was too exhausted to notice."[14] Soon a select group of younger Germans are gathering around his bedside for thought-provoking discussions about contemporary history like an examination of Ernst Jünger, a complex and contradictory German war-hero-cum-writer. Scheffer's literary salon offers a welcome alternative to the interminable succession of gossipy cocktail parties.

But the host remains in limbo and in great pain.

# 15

## *Life* at the Homestead

Life goes on at the Homestead. And now *Life* wants in too.

Last summer, long before the detainment was even a distant glimmer, the powerhouse magazine—reaching thirteen million weekly readers, 10 percent of America's population—proposed doing a story on the resort. Management immediately accepted, "realizing the inestimable value such publicity would have in developing future business." An editorial team descended and created an "evergreen," an article that can run whenever there's a hole in an issue to fill. Shortly after the Japanese arrived, manager George Slosson learns that time has come. So he asks the State Department for its approval: "We regard this as an unusual opportunity [for] which no reasonable amount of money could purchase."[1]

The federal agencies in charge invariably have a simple answer to any out-of-the-ordinary requests: no. Every press request so far has gotten that knee-jerk denial. But here State's in a bind: the story's already written, and to deny a hotel that's stepped up to host, house, and feed the enemy would seem mighty churlish. So it nixes the magazine's request to do a new photo shoot but reluctantly okays the story, knowing it's bound to have repercussions. Edward Poole snags an advance copy and fires off an early warning to his boss, detailing eight inaccuracies in the tight five-hundred-word piece; the dozen prominent photos previously taken, without a Japanese in sight, are fine. Entitled "The Homestead: A Great Hotel Entertains Jap Diplomats as Patriotic Duty," the story runs in the February 16, 1942, issue that hits the newsstands the previous Friday. The backlash starts the same day.

"As a patriotic American for many generations," writes a railroad executive to Under Secretary of State Sumner Welles, wouldn't "any old wooden shack be good enough? . . . Why coddle German and Jap prisoners who are all bitter enemies of our country, and who would ruin us if they had half a chance."[2] Readers inundate the magazine with complaints, incensed by the FBI-ordered removal of an American flag and amenities like free nightly movies and access to the famed Homestead Club. Some object to its gym: "Homestead gym, filled with queer machines invented by Sweden's Dr. Gustav Zander, was enjoyed by Jap children, who were bored by cold weather and FBI surveillance."[3]

Slosson's angry too, at the article's inaccuracies. He drafts a telegram to *Life*, demanding to know who provided them such erroneous information. He runs it by an attorney for the hotel, who suggests softening the language, something Slosson has no interest in doing. He winds up refuting several points: movies are not free, the Homestead Club is closed, and children are not allowed in the gym. Most importantly, an American flag still hangs in the lobby as it always has. At the suggestion of INS another flag was removed from the Japanese quarters "because of possible complications," a phrase that was penciled into the telegram to replace a more incendiary reason: "for fear that it might be desecrated."[4] No need to give *Life* another opportunity to fan the flames. Even in retirement, thirty-five years later, Slosson remained bitter: "The people who got my cork a little bit was '*Life*.'"[5]

Another anecdote, retold in a book published a quarter century later, suggests there really wasn't any need to fear bad behavior by the Japanese. "A small boy ran under the American Flag that was and still is displayed on a staff projected from the balcony in the main lobby," recalled an assistant manager. "His mother, the wife of a Japanese diplomat, called, 'Georgie, take off your hat—you're under the American flag!'"[6]

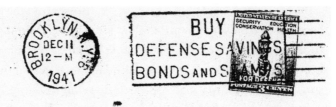

The Dishonorable

    Japanese Ambassador Nomura,

        Japanese Embassy,

           Washington, D.C.

**Fig. 35.** One of the cards from everyday Americans incensed by the attack on Pearl Harbor; many were intercepted by the FBI and never delivered. U.S. National Archives and Record Administration, Record Group 59.

Barely six weeks after Pearl Harbor, though, it's hard to overstate the public's animosity toward the Japanese. "More Monkeymen Caged" reads the title of a front-page story in the *Bath County Enterprise* that runs shortly after the *Life* piece. Since the Japanese were moved from their embassy, all incoming mail has been diverted to the FBI, which weeds out the insulting and obscene messages. "Liars—backstabers, to bad your innocent citizens—including women and children—must suffer. From all USA citizens," reads one scrawled postcard. A letter addressed to "The Dishonorable Japanese Ambassador Nomura" reads, "You back-stabbing, underhanded, smiling assassins, when we get through with you and yours, you will wish you had never copied the Hitler gangster. . . . Remember this, you dirty, stinking, underhanded, double-crossing snake, and take this message back to your stupid emperor."[7]

The FBI brings this mail to State, which sees no good reason to deliver it to the Japanese, so it doesn't. While such vituperation never rises to this level in government memos, distrust of the Japanese clearly flows through certain quarters of the Roosevelt administration. Those thoughts never surface publicly, especially given the delicate ongoing negotiations to achieve the end game: the exchange of diplomats from both sides as soon as practicable. "The Japanese will be mean-spirited and dangerous when their military reverses begin," opines William Langdon, a veteran in State's Division of Far Eastern Affairs. "If we do not get our people out of their hands before this situation begins, it is quite conceivable that the Japanese may decide to hold our people as hostages."[8]

Such disparaging sentiment isn't unusual, nor is the occasional whiff of racism. The day the Germans arrived at the Greenbrier, Loren Johnston obliquely compared them to the Homestead's Japanese. "Confidentially," he wrote to a staff member, "I would say our class of patronage over the next few weeks may be a little better than our neighbors. What do you think?"[9] Yet this kind of veiled comment pales before the blatant racism expressed by another State employee on the same day Langdon writes about the Japanese being "mean-spirited." "The German and the Italian Governments can be expected to accord more civilized treatment to our personnel than the Japanese Government," wrote Maxwell Hamilton in a memo marked Strictly Confidential. "I shudder to think of American

**Fig. 36.** A group of the Japanese detainees, with Hidenari Terasaki (in white slacks) in middle of front row. Courtesy of the Greenbrier.

officials and American nationals in the hands of Japanese once the veneer of civilized conduct disappears."[10] (Career foreign service officer Hamilton, who was fluent in Mandarin and had several postings in China, served as U.S. ambassador to Finland after the war.) As barbarous as Japanese treatment of American prisoners of war becomes, they never systematically murdered more than six million Jews and millions more Soviets, Poles, Serbs, Roma, gay people, and people with disabilities, as the Nazis did.

By the end of February the numbers of detainees are quickly rising, reaching 350 Japanese plus 673 Germans, Italians, Hungarians, and Bulgarians at the Greenbrier. Arrivals from consulates in Chicago, Los Angeles, New Orleans, Portland, Oregon, San Francisco, and Seattle bolster the Japanese ranks, as do envoys and families from embassies in Argentina, Brazil, Cuba, Mexico, Panama, Peru, and San Salvador. But there's one place on earth from which no consular staff will ever join them: Hawaii. Convinced that at least some there had a role in the attack on Pearl Harbor, the administration agrees to keep them incommunicado until repatriation. The position isn't sheer vindictiveness, since Tokyo is in constant contact with the Homestead through the Spanish representatives, and messages there could be passed along. So in early February, twenty-three staffers and their families—including spy Takeo Yoshikawa, still known by his alias, Tadashi Morimura—sail from Honolulu to San Diego aboard the USS *President Hayes*, whose passengers also include many survivors of the attack. Officials wisely keep the diplomats separated.

In San Diego they board a special train to a tiny station in Dragoon, Arizona (population: 40), and are driven one hundred miles into the desert. Their trip receives not a hint of publicity; neither railroad officials nor train personnel have any idea where these Japanese, whose baggage has been stripped of all labels, came from. Their destination is the Triangle T Ranch, a far-flung retreat for elite guests like the Rockefellers and Vanderbilts. Even its owners aren't informed of their guests' origins. A local army captain gets wind of their arrival and visits the isolated compound of a few cottages and main house now surrounded by a new barbed wire fence. He's stonewalled and refused admittance by a border patrol guard. On February 26 the *Tucson Daily Citizen* runs a brief item about the detention, offering few specifics about the occupants other than their nationality. State immediately intervenes and convinces the paper and its rival to run no more stories.

For the next ten weeks the government pays $1,260 per week to house and feed the prisoners and nine guards. Completely cut off, the Japanese play tennis, croquet, and ping pong. Guards put fuses onto boxes and mount them on the fence, telling the prisoners they're being photographed. Twice a week Edward Bailey, the State Department agent, takes their shopping lists that "read like a Sears Roebuck catalogue" and goes shopping in Tucson. One guard recalls coloring Easter eggs for the children and hiding them among the cacti, for which a black cook scolded him. "Oh, it is good for them," replied Roland Fleagle, "and it will give them something to do."[11] An FBI agent interrogates the envoys who universally deny having done any espionage, which he knows is a lie. "Quite likely," wrote Berle, "the Japanese consul deserves to be shot but we should undeniably risk the life of one of our men, without gaining very much save abstract justice."[12]

Yoshikawa defiantly stonewalls his interviewer, who notices that he's missing his left ring finger: a telltale sign of membership in the violent ultranationalist group Black Dragon. True believers in the divinity of the emperor and haters of Westerners, the members severed their own fingers so they could recognize each other. The spy denies membership but offers no explanation for his missing digit. Twenty years later, after his role has been exposed, he tells a U.S. military interviewer that for a brief moment, he "held history in the palm of [his] hand."[13]

Unbeknownst to the detainees at the Homestead, before they even set one foot on the property Fay Ingalls was insisting that they be gone by April 1. "While we could profitably take this business during the quiet winter months," he wrote in his post-detainment report, "with the only loss the interruption of our long history of continuous operation and a certain amount of ill-will from those who did not understand the situation and felt we were favoring enemy aliens, it would be ruinous to The Homestead if our spring season, the time of year when we must make money to carry us over the full period, was to be lost."[14]

Never afraid to work his contacts, Ingalls personally brings his case to the capital and visits both State and the FBI. At the latter he meets the bureau's number two man, Clyde Tolson, Hoover's special friend. With thinly disguised exasperation G. Howland Shaw, Hull's assistant secretary, writes to Ingalls in early February: "As I have told you, every effort is being made to repatriate these officials with a minimum of delay, but the difficulties confronting the Department are, however, no less real, and I regret that I can write you no more encouragingly. . . . No commitment can be made at this time as to the actual date of removal of the Japanese from The Homestead."[15] State encourages Ingalls, with his stature and industry experience, to suggest alternative hotels, which he does. So a renewed search to find a suitable new establishment begins—no easy task, and one later complicated by citizens who lobby furiously once word leaks out that the hated Japanese might be coming to their community.

But for the time being, even with the swelling numbers it's a harmonious

**Fig. 37.** Tower and front entrance, Homestead Hotel. Historical Society of Washington DC, Clarence Hewes Collection.

blend at the Homestead. Many people, unaccustomed to living in such luxury amid such natural beauty, quickly adjust to their pleasant present. Several pregnant wives wind up contributing yet more arrivals, like Akira Yamamoto, Gwen Terasaki's former neighbor back in DC. Since Yamamoto speaks no English, Terasaki assists at the delivery by the hotel's doctor. On the morning of January 23, Yamamoto and her husband welcome a daughter they name Izumi ("Little Spring"). One of the black waiters asks to see her, and when he does he exclaims, "Why, ma'am, she's as cute as any baby I've ever seen!"[16] A maid remembers them fashioning a crib out of a dresser drawer.

Mariko takes swimming lessons from a "big red-headed lifeguard," while Gwen watches them frolic and play water polo to the tune of Strauss waltzes on a record player. Her classmate Takeo gets his lessons from one of the many navy men, proudly becoming the first boy to master the naval version of the sidestroke. He also goes in for more boisterous activity, sneaking up behind officers and trying to push them into the pool. He recalls one successful assault on a lieutenant commander who tumbles in with quite a splash. "But the Navy men did not take offense at my rowdy antics," he recalls, "and were quite indulgent with me."[17]

Impromptu groups form around language instruction in English, French, and Spanish. Some people study painting and poetry. Gwen Terasaki joins a fledgling glee club and teaches a tune that becomes a big favorite: "On a Bicycle Built for Two." Card and board games remain popular, and the long-awaited delivery of mail offers welcome diversion. Masuo Kato writes often to Hurley Fisk, the young lady who assumed his apartment lease. She vacationed in Florida over the Christmas holidays, and the box of citrus she sent arrives five weeks later. "It seemed strange," he marvels, "that an American friendship could have survived the bitterness of Pearl Harbor."[18]

Though only innocuous books of fiction and one newspaper are allowed, reading still remains a popular diversion. On the same day that Scheffer takes his fall at the Greenbrier, a story runs in a newspaper that Kato can't see. The story was written by a former colleague, columnist Sam Tucker. Tucker ran into a mutual friend who passed along greetings from Kato when he last saw him on December 6. "Well I hope that little Kato is not too unhappy in his present isolation and imprisonment," writes Tucker. "It would be impossible to hate him, or to imagine that he hates any of us Americans he has known. There have been too many beers enjoyed together over the oak tables of the Press club; too many hours of talk about the political and economic tangles of the world."[19]

Kato's view has now narrowed to a single source, the *New York Times*, yet he and his fellow detainees "get a fairly accurate window-glass view of American life, which encouraged us to believe that the war was not going too badly for Japan. We became aware of rationing, of the economic and political changes that were sweeping across the face of our enemy host."[20] One Sunday he's attracted to the lead story in the *New York Times Magazine* with a provocative title, "Are We Awake?" It's a cogent essay by James Reston, at the outset of what's to be a stellar, Pulitzer Prize–winning career, about how America must adjust to win the war. In it he quotes a recent column by Hope Ridings Miller, society editor of the *Washington Post*: "This town recently has given itself over to the most hectic round of partying anybody has ever heard of. Capital hostesses are entertaining right and left, as if it's the last time they'll ever be able to give a party."[21]

It's obvious nobody misses the departed Axis diplomats, but her column raises a chorus of respondents furious at the capital's carousing. Miller writes to its rescue: "Society for society's sake died a natural death on the banks of the Potomac when the first bomb burst over Pearl Harbor. Parties go on, yes. Celebrations-for-a-cause, if you will. . . . More jobs are cinched over dinner tables and around the town's wassail bowls than across any desk you can name. It should go without saying that tea and international treaties and understanding flow simultaneously and regularly at most diplomatic receptions here. . . . There are more ways than one to help defeat Hitler and the minions of Hirohito."[22]

Columnist Helen Lombard, the well-connected author of *Washington Waltz*, delves even deeper. She warns of foreign agents still afoot, gleaning crucial bits of information amid convivial cocktail and dinner party patter. "No one thing heard at any one place could properly be considered vital information to the enemy," Lombard writes. "But the composite parts picked up by groups of agents and forwarded to the enemy give a picture of the American production scene on which the Axis plots the curve and the tempo of its strategy."[23]

The same could be said of the FBI's modus operandi at the hotels, cajoling information from hither and yon. Informant Hoshide provides substantial material about the embassy's naval and military attachés' interest in U.S. military manufacturing capabilities for producing planes, tanks, and ships. One American on its payroll tried to get a job at an airplane factory, another visited the New York consul's office to report on gasoline production. Correspondents for official press agency Domei, like Kato, routinely vetted information obtained by the consuls before it was forwarded to Japan. Hoshide also reconfirms that Hidenari Terasaki was in charge of all propaganda and names Americans and U.S. companies that helped prepare pamphlets and other literature. The FBI makes a thorough search of Terasaki's room, copying select documents "of sufficient importance to warrant translation."[24]

Nothing escapes the bureau's narrowed eye. It even takes away a book of nursery tales, *The Little Tortoise That Ran Away*, undoubtedly bought for their daughter, Mariko. No secret messages or coded material is found, but for good measure agents further examine it under a microscope—no microdots are detected.

As March arrives and the weather turns milder, everyone's eager to spend more time outdoors. Enamored of baseball, the men put together an eight-team league and play games regularly. However, since the outbreak of the war a push-pull relationship has roiled the military and civilian ranks, and now the military imposes mandatory daily calisthenics. Out walking one morning the Terasakis pass some men, women, and children dutifully, though somewhat raggedly, taking part. A lieutenant orders them to join. Hidenari refuses. When the officer begins lecturing him, Hidenari slaps him in the face. The man indignantly asks if the group will let him get away with such an affront. No one answers, the Terasakis stroll on—and attendance at the workouts drops off sharply thereafter.

Kato recalls being required to take both an exercise class and another superfluous class in anticipation of their forthcoming journey home by ship. "We were also taught flag signals, to the utter irritation and annoyance of most of us," he writes, "particularly since neither then nor later could we understand any reason why we should learn them. The more liberal elements were sharply resentful of such practices, but there was only minor friction because no one was certain just where he might stand later if he openly opposed them."[25] Many of the younger boys have a much more positive opinion of the military. Takeo recalls learning about a naval attaché recently arrived from Panama: "When we heard that he had been spying on the movements of U.S. Navy ships through the Panama Canal, he became the hero of us kids."[26]

Ever mindful of the importance of education, the adults organize a school just like the detainees are doing at the Greenbrier. So many teachers, recruited mostly from the younger ranks of the diplomatic corps, volunteer that it boasts a ratio of one instructor for every two students. The curriculum includes language, mathematics, geography, and history. The latter is taught by a diplomat who delivers ultranationalist Japanese doctrine. "As a result, I became brainwashed in this ideology," writes

Takeo. "I came to believe that because the Yamato race was superior and Japan was a divine land, we could never be defeated by the Americans and the British, and that we were destined to become the leader of Asia."[27]

The detainees are buoyed by news of Japan's continued advances in the Pacific. As the Philippines crumble FDR orders General Douglas MacArthur to depart Corregidor. Japan bombs the Australian city of Darwin in the single largest air attack on the country ever. In the Battle of the Java Sea, Japan defeats an Allied strike force and sinks many British and American ships. Malaya and Singapore fall, the latter occurring the day before the Homestead, by coincidence, removes sugar bowls from the tables due to a sugar shortage. "Ho," complains one detainee to a waiter. "We take Singapore, you take sugar bowl?"[28]

Another detainee, from the former legation in Mexico City, learns the hard way about the hotel's efficient infrastructure. Trying to burn papers in his room's bathtub, he triggers its automatic sprinkler system and causes a minor panic. After a staffer responds and shuts it off, two FBI agents arrive to discover the man "standing in a pool of water, drenched to the skin and looking like a drowned rat."[29] (One unconfirmed embellishment has him holding an umbrella too.) While the embarrassed envoy cowers in a corner in his wet BVDs, the agents remove several singed but unburned papers with writing in Spanish.

Apparently neither hell nor high water keeps the FBI from fulfilling its duties.

Thanks to media embargo, the story never gets reported. Yet occasionally an intrepid reporter ferrets out a story. Lombard adroitly contacts a Spanish attaché, one of the handful of outsiders allowed inside, who describes a scene right out of *The Mikado*. He reports that Japanese diplomats have rediscovered their heritage, walking around the grounds in colorful kimonos and waving fans. Another spot of local color disappears, this one from the nation's capital, when the annual Cherry Blossom Festival is cancelled in early March. Last year alone the event attracted one hundred thousand tourists celebrating the "good will and high esteem held by the people of Japan for the people of the United States."[30] This year those lofty sentiments are in short supply.

Meanwhile the two highest Japanese representatives, Kichisaburo Nomura and Saburo Kurusu, replay over and over their failed mission that culminated in a tongue-lashing by Hull as Japanese planes rained down bombs on Pearl Harbor. With so much free time each lives in a regretful fog of could've, would've, should've. Kato frequently strolls the grounds with both men, and one day Nomura tells him, "I am just like a living dead man."[31] For his part Kurusu, with an American wife and being well versed in American parlance, knows that the word *quisling*—coined for Norwegian Nazi sycophant Vidkun Quisling—has come to mean traitor. Now he fears his own name will become a new Americanism: "the double Kurusu." Both realize there's no middle ground as the world views them in only two ways: as duplicitous conspirators who knew all about the attack or as dupes betrayed by their own government. Out walking one day, a young Japanese envoy discovers words scrawled inside an unmanned guardhouse: "I don't know which one is Kurusu, but I'd like to wring his neck."[32]

While Americans unquestionably despise the Japanese, one minority group doesn't begrudge the detainees their fine treatment at the Homestead. Rather, it chafes under the inequity of America today. "We ought to accord citizens of hostile countries all courtesy and humane treatment possible, regardless of the attitude that country's leaders assume," writes B. T. Gillespie in the *African-American* newspaper. "But certainly this country should open its avenues of comfort, civil rights and decency to its black citizens whose sweat and toil have meant so much to its progress." Blacks make up a large percentage of the Homestead's staff, although they're rarely welcomed as guests. "If President Roosevelt," continues Gillespie, "expected less of colored soldiers than of whites, or if government taxes were lessened for colored citizens, there might be some argument for discrimination. Colored Americans want to, and will, help America win the war, but they likewise want to win the peace and comfort that is expected to follow."[33]

A sign of the times that captures the United States today: an illustrated advertisement in the *Evening Star* for a "Darkey Hitching Post."[34] The thirty-nine-inch-high cast iron figure of a capped black man on a pedestal costs thirty-five dollars at a downtown department store. At the

Greenbrier, an incident confirms America's inherent racism and double standards. On February 25—the first day Japanese Americans in Los Angeles are being relocated—a border patrol agent at the employee entrance notices an unusual bulging from the beltline of sixteen-year-old black dishwasher Walter Lacy. A search reveals an unloaded .32-caliber revolver plus six rounds of ammunition and a large knife. Unable to offer any reason for smuggling in the weapons, which are strictly prohibited, Lacy is arrested and rushed to a local justice of the peace. He pleads guilty to carrying concealed weapons and is fined fifty dollars and sentenced to six months. He's driven to the Greenbrier Country jail in Lewisburg to begin his sentence. The timeline, from arrest to trial to conviction to incarceration? *Less than two hours.*

"Justice moves quickly in West Virginia" is how FBI agent John Lawler sums up the event. Justice, or injustice?[35]

Either way, it's certainly not the kind of incident that'll merit a mention in the local press, let alone a national publication like *Life*. With the backlash from its magazine article still smarting, the *New Yorker* comes a-calling. The well-respected publication proposes a three-thousand-word article about the detainees at the Greenbrier "that would undoubtedly detail the excellence of the treatment of enemy diplomats."[36]

Despite this unorthodox advance promise of positive editorial treatment, three words scribbled in the margins by an anonymous State staffer provide the answer: no, no, no.

# 16

## "But Still They Complain . . ."

Last month Mary Florentina Harrington turned seventy, so there's undoubtedly little the chief housekeeper hasn't seen during her twenty-eight years on the job. But now, getting called in to see Mr. Johnston? Sure, he's a gentleman and well liked by the staff, but still, he's the *boss*. And after their meeting he asks her to write a letter addressing some guests' complaints? Now there's a first.

Harrington responds dutifully and beautifully, detailing the record of cleaning, vacuuming, and using carpet sweepers. "But still they complain," she writes of two guests, referring to them obliquely by their room numbers. A check of the register reveals the malcontents: Prince Colonna and his second in command, Alberto Rossi Longhi. "No. 619 [Rossi Longhi] has been overheard to say that we have only one vacuum cleaner for the whole house. For my part I would not feel obligated to tell him that we have many Hoovers and four large drum vacuums." Reluctant to openly confront a customer, Mary instead notes that letting the children eat in their rooms, which are jammed with so much baggage, often hinders a thorough cleaning. Wear and tear's visible on both the guest and public rooms. "Some parents give their children too much freedom. I realize that they are active and under restraint here and it is hard on them, but it is unfair to criticize the hotel."[1]

But criticize they do, and about more than room cleanliness. Several weeks ago Colonna telegrammed Rome requesting that the Swiss ask for four additional changes beyond "hygienic conditions": better menu choices for children, allowing children to take daily extended walks, expanding the outside area for all, and increasing reading matter to include nonpolitical books and magazines. A week later the German delegation, again through the Swiss, makes the same demands. Memos fly among State Department divisions weighing in theoretically, long distance, but it's John O'Hanley on-site who offers a keen firsthand perspective.

He talks to a chef who readily agrees about the food: "The mothers should order whatever they like for the children and the kitchen would be glad to prepare it," writes O'Hanley. Expanding the outdoor space and allowing for children's walks require approval from INS and the FBI. O'Hanley thinks it's a "splendid idea," adding that the children would delight to see the ducks and swans on the lake, and suggests horseback riding might also be permitted. But that sticky question of cleaning remains. "Mr. Rossi-Longhi said that he had a sore throat, attributed to the [dirty] rugs in the lobby but, on my word of honor, I saw him walking around in all the rain that day with one of his boys. I didn't mention this to him, of course."[2] Seems that Mary Harrington's not the only one to hold her tongue when Rossi Longhi spouts off. Yet O'Hanley patiently enlightens him about something the detainees never see. Having met many late-night trains, State's agent knows that every night the hotel's entire first floor is vacuumed and the floors and stairs washed and wiped.

Colonna's telegram causes such a fuss that a copy eventually circles back to the Greenbrier. Chief clerk Roy Sibold puts a copy into his pocket and goes up to see the ambassador and his wife, who like the Thomsens have a five-room suite with two bedrooms, private baths, and a sitting room. After some polite chitchat he asks if they're pleased with the hotel to date, to which Colonna responds that all's been "unsurpassable" and they couldn't be happier. "Mr. Sibold then produced the telegram to the Ambassador's embarrassment. Senora Colonna blew a fuse and forced the forthcoming apologies."[3] Once again, though, leave it to Charlie

**Fig. 38.** A young member of the Italian delegation lounging on Mother's mink coat? Courtesy of the Greenbrier.

Spruks to get in the last bon mot. "It is a great pity that the poor dears cannot stand the food at Greenbrier," he writes to his boss. "What will they do when they return to Italy where they can't even get spaghetti? The second point [about lobby cleaning] is well taken since we know the proverbial cleanliness of the Southern Italian, particularly before the time Mussolini forbid them emptying their night pots from the second story window down on the street."[4]

History and sarcasm aside, the Italians dislike being lumped into the same category as the Germans. "In their hearts I think the Italians feel that the Americans in Italy are almost free do to as they please," writes O'Hanley. "They don't like their own situation being comparable to the [shoddier] treatment of Americans at Bad Nauheim."[5] Americans in Rome are enjoying far more freedom than their counterparts in Berlin, yet as much as State believes scrupulously in reciprocity, it treats the Axis diplomats here equally because they're under one roof. Though maybe, with all the

Italians' carping—and Fay Ingalls's incessant badgering to relocate the Japanese from the Homestead as soon as possible—not for much longer.

The mood among the Italians and Germans has been strained for a while, especially as some Nazis openly ridicule the ability of Italy's military. At first there was some pretense at friendliness, with the groups frequenting each others' social events, but that time has long passed. When several Italians get into an argument with drug store employees that almost comes to blows, Germans begin "spreading the rumor that anybody and everybody could do whatever they want over the Italians."[6] An informant reports that privately most Italians are anti-Nazi but publicly espouse pro-Nazi sympathies. Colonna and Rossi Longhi are considered dedicated fascists loyal to Mussolini. The two countries' military attachés, Adolfo Infante and Friedrich von Boetticher, maintain cordial relations and discuss how they handled their respective duties. Though when Infante buys a pipe at the cigarette counter, his wife returns it the next day because she thinks it makes him look too Germanic.

In mid-February Hoover writes to Assistant Secretary of State Adolf Berle, suggesting that Infante's prewar spying wasn't as ineffectual as previously thought. He summarizes an informant's report that Infante forwarded to Rome considerable military information about airborne infantry, antitank weaponry, armored vehicles, British warships under repair in American ports, export of war materials, and more. At the same time, back in DC the Counter Intelligence Section of ONI holds a briefing on the Italian propaganda and intelligence system, whose nucleus had been thoroughly trained by German agents in the United States. "Although diplomatic representatives are no longer officially at work in the United States, it is certain that their propagandistic activities are still being carried on by non-diplomatic successors."[7]

About said propagandistic activities, the Germans, even sequestered in White Sulphur, soar back into the news as aviatrix Laura Ingalls goes on trial. The indictment repeats the name of her handler—Baron Ulrich von Gienanth—four times in four pages. Using the code name "Mama," the Gestapo agent paid her several hundred dollars a month for "disseminating certain oral and written information and matter for the purpose, among others, of influencing, persuading, and molding American public opinion."[8] When she proposed making a "peace flight" to Europe, he nixed the idea, according to Julia Kraus, the stout, middle-aged woman who introduced them and served as their go-between. "Keep up your America First work—it's the best thing you could do for us," Kraus recalls von Gienanth saying, adding that he suggested Ingalls enliven her America First speeches by joking about sending religion to Russia under the Lend-Lease Act. Her attorney, dapper James F. Reilly, mounts an audacious defense. He casts his client as a self-styled Mata Hari who only took the cash and spouted isolationist dogma to ingratiate herself with the Nazis so she could learn and expose their secrets. But her own writing punctures that counterespionage canard.

To Catherine Curtis, the isolationist fellow traveler who bankrolled her leaflet-dropping stunt over Washington DC, Ingalls had written, "I have always known that the best way to keep the United States out of war was to pray for, or aid a swift German victory. . . . Visit me in my little chalet near Berchtesgaden. (Hitler also has a chalet near Berchtesgaden—Editor's Note.)"[9] In her diary, Ingalls wrote, "The H.M.S. Hood sunk today. Sieg Heil!"[10] A New York plastic surgeon recalls that during an office visit she wore a silver bracelet with a swastika. In court Ingalls claims it's a Navajo Indian emblem, to which the prosecutor asks if the "Sieg Heils" and "Heil Hitlers" she'd written so many times were Navajo expressions too.

Yet regardless of her mindset or motivations, the prosecutors reiterate that the crime with which she's charged is not registering as an enemy agent. Taking the stand, Ingalls delivers a torrent of words that often precede her own counsel's questions and strike one reporter as "a reenactment of the fiery speeches she gave before America First Committee meetings."[11] In closing Reilly argues for acquittal but terms his client a "fanatic" and "egotist" and "a bit of a crackpot." The jury of ten men and two women takes a little more than an hour to deliver its verdict: guilty. "Well, it's Friday the thirteenth," notes an unrepentant Ingalls afterwards. "I accept [the verdict] with a feeling that I am a truer patriot than those who convicted me."[12]

Back at the Greenbrier, Hans Thomsen's not at all surprised by the outcome. Last January, after hearing a low-level staffer explain how the FBI had questioned him about the case in minute detail he was convinced, according to an informant, that the agency had an informant inside the embassy. That they did, as well as eyewitness accounts of several meetings between von Gienanth and Ingalls. What Thomsen doesn't know is that the FBI might've had even more ammunition had Charles Bruggmann acceded to a request by Attorney General Biddle to let the FBI search the abandoned embassy for additional correspondence from Ingalls. "The [Swiss] Minister expressed the feeling that to comply with this particular request would be a violation of what he considered a fiduciary relationship," writes Breckinridge Long.[13]

As the Swiss and Spanish diplomats remain very protective of the sovereignty of the deserted embassies they're representing, embassies of several neutral countries have become targets too. Fearing that Spanish strongman Francisco Franco is secretly helping Germany, British agents regularly break into the Spanish embassy in DC for its cipher codes. In March OSS gets approval to begin its own operation. Donald Downes, an oddball ex–British operative, approaches a prominent women's college and finds a Spanish teacher codenamed "Mrs. G." Eager to help her country Mrs. G is moved into a boardinghouse and quickly befriends the many secretaries from the Spanish embassy living there. At Downes's behest a large company creates an opening for a Spanish-speaking secretary and places a want ad in the *New York Times*. One day when the gals are all together Mrs. G "notices" the ad and reads it aloud. You're just perfect for this job, she tells one secretary, who promptly applies and lands it. To replace her at the embassy, she recommends her out-of-work friend. Voilà: the plant's in.

At her new embassy job Mrs. G tries to memorize a safe's combination behind her boss's back but can't get it to open. So, as instructed, she smacks its dial with a hard rubber hammer. To repair the now inoperable safe the Spanish call in a locksmith: another OSS recruit, a professional safecracker who'd spent considerable time in prison. Soon the safe's contents are being pilfered regularly, but the curtain falls suddenly. "We had taken all imaginable precautions," wrote Downes, "all except one: the possibility of betrayal by someone high enough in the American Government to know what we were doing."[14] That someone is Hoover, who's incensed that OSS, with no authority to operate domestically, is encroaching on the FBI's turf. (The FBI's regularly breaking into embassies too.) One night he orders a raid while Downes's men are burglarizing the Spanish embassy. The agents escape, but the jig's up. The next day, at the White House, Bill Donovan's hairsplitting rationale that embassies are technically foreign soil doesn't hold up, and the whole operation's transferred to the FBI.

Back in court the Nazis are dealt another defeat when Thomsen's slickest propagandist, George Viereck, is also convicted of violating the Foreign Agents Registration Act. Unlike Ingalls he was strictly a behind-the-scenes player, ghostwriting some of the Nazis' smoothest isolationist appeals. The prosecutor calls him "the American mouthpiece of the Nazis in Berlin, the American apostle of the murderous, lying rogues of the Wilhelmstrasse."[15] A key figure who appears to be collateral damage is staunch anti-FDR isolationist and New York Republican representative Hamilton Fish III, whose office used his franking privileges to send out at taxpayers' expense 125,000 copies of a speech Viereck penned for the late, rather simpleminded Minnesota Farmer-Labor Party senator Ernest Lundeen. "Not one bit of Nazi propaganda ever went out from my office with my knowledge or consent at any time," insists Fish, whose admitted bamboozlement appears to doom him to defeat.[16] Yet he improbably wins reelection this fall.

Tempers fray not only between the protecting powers and the FBI, but among the detainees. Unannounced room searches are always maddening, and one is sprung in mid-March. "Firearms should be removed, as gently as possible," writes Long, "but removed," though at least twenty well-hidden guns go undiscovered.[17] One evening, a newsreel—those are never shown at the hotel—unexpectedly precedes the nightly movie, prompting boos and hisses from the audience when it naturally puts the Allies in a good light. Morale plummets as rumored imminent departure dates come and go in vain. An informant reveals that the dispirited diplomats met privately and decided that Berlin has probably determined their significance to the war effort is minimal. Boredom sets in, and everyday routines seem, well, routine. "Daily swim, massage, beauty shop appointment, regular walks around the allowed piece of lawn no bigger than a riding rink, cocktails in room 364, bridge in room 248, a nightly movie with an occasional date," writes Hildy von Boetticher. "The routine was that after the movies everybody adjourned to the bar and after that, to somebody's room. That kind of invitation wasn't for the General's daughter, and perhaps it was easier for me not to be asked."

Yet amid the tedium comes something different, something exciting, at least for von Boetticher: the stirrings of first love. "I had never known love so delicate, sensitive and understanding," she writes of Joseph Fulop, a Hungarian cultural attaché who'd arrived last December on the same train as the von Boettichers.[18] He's twenty years her senior, far older than her drinking and bridge-playing pals. They first exchange glances while he dined alone in the restaurant. Soon they're meeting secretly: on a secluded balcony, or the roof, or occasionally in his room. Von Boetticher doesn't breathe a word to her straitlaced parents, who'd certainly disapprove.

Love's in the air too for another unlikely couple: a local waitress (and occasional FBI informant) and out-of-town border guard marry in early April. Also tying the knot is a Hungarian attaché and his recently arrived Russian fiancée. Those two countries may be at war in Europe, but here it's a peaceful Episcopalian wedding service. Heading his memo "These Charming People," lifting the title of Ghighi Cassini's gossip column, O'Hanley notes that "on their honeymoon they can't walk any further than a certain white line near the White Sulphur Spring, and all I want to know is after he carries his bride across the threshold of room 358 at the Hotel Greenbrier and Cottages, do we carry her as a guest of the State Department?"[19]

For some love's not beginning, it's ending. Like for an Italian couple with too much to overcome: his diehard fascism. While she loves him and has undying affection for her people and land, his politics are a bridge too far. Spilling out her heart to agent John Lawler, she reveals that she won't go back to Italy. "She is not a Fascist and never will be—there is nothing doing on that score," he writes. "She does not belong to the kind of woman who is blinded by love to the extent that they change their ideas."[20] He eventually returns to Italy on the first passage, but it's lost to history whether she stays behind or, like Bébé Thomsen, talks a good game but dutifully follows her man.

Some people facing future life-and-death unknowns opt for more transitory pleasures of the flesh. One-night stands are commonplace, with maids complaining they must change much bed linen daily "because of the resultant efforts of sexual intercourse." A German envoy from New York confides to his barber that he hopes his wife is delayed while at the hospital for a tonsillectomy since he's bedding a different woman every night. One night a German reporter tells his wife he's passing up the movie to play poker with a friend. Yet when she encounters that friend in the lobby, he knows nothing about any card game. She marches to the room of a secretary who she suspects is sleeping with her hubby. The young lady answers the door in the nude but denies her husband is there. She enters anyway, but her search proves fruitless. Later on it is whispered he was cowering in a closet; a smarter reporter might've concocted a more plausible alibi. Then there's the unmarried nineteen-year-old German girl from Colombia who becomes pregnant. Her parents try to persuade the hotel's doctor to perform an abortion, but he refuses.

The most salacious group story springs from a private birthday party for former first secretary Heribert von Strempel, a night which an informant describes to agent Lawler in great sweaty detail. Amid much drinking, "there was a continual switching and swapping of wives and a promiscuous handling of the private parts of the bodies of many of the outstanding diplomats' wives here." He claims that Bébé Thomsen and Hans Wolfram, a German journalist, went off to his room for half an hour; "he did not believe that they went for him to wash his hands."[21] The informant adds that while the Germans appear very correct and straitlaced on the outside, after they've had a few drinks they're the most promiscuous people he's ever met. Next month the hotel's medical department conducts 186 Kahn tests to detect syphilis, and 15 come back positive; the tests were probably done on employees, not detainees, but the report doesn't specify.

By mid-March new arrivals push the detainee count to more than 700, with more on the way. Spruks sails to South America aboard the SS *Acadia* to chaperone 250 Axis nationals back here to ensure embarkation from the United States. An old friend at the U.S. legation in Bolivia sends sarcastic regrets. "I wish that I could break away and meet you at Arica [Chile], unpleasant as the place is when the wind comes from the southwest off the guano island," writes the envoy, who assigns a Spanish-speaking subordinate "the unpleasant task of spending a week or so in Arica looking at the Germans and Italians snarl at each other."[22] For many new arrivals, plain country folks, the sight of the Greenbrier and its meticulously manicured lawn is wondrous. "It must be a well-trained bunch of sheep," exclaims one Ecuadorian, "that keeps this grass weeded and well cropped."[23]

In a major step forward for the tedious repatriation negotiations, the United States privately accepts Sweden's offer of a vessel, the ss *Drottning-holm*, for the initial transatlantic passage. More than a week later, after Germany hasn't responded, State asks the Swiss to inform them that if no reply is forthcoming U.S. officials will move the detainees from the Greenbrier because they can't be housed there indefinitely. That prompts the Germans to finally agree, claiming they didn't intend to complicate or delay the agreement. In truth they've been foot-dragging from the outset, happy to let the United States take the lead. But the bigger issue concerns not the vessels but the passengers: agents must undertake a painstaking, person-by-person examination, complicated by British demands to exclude "individuals possessing special abilities which could manifestly be used in furthering the enemy's war effort." That stance clashes head-on with the position of the United States and South American countries that their security is jeopardized by "the con-tinued freedom in those Republics of unscrupulous Axis agents" whose "continuing presence would be a menace to our hemisphere security."[24]

In short, it's a convoluted, contentious process with many sides, many angles, and few easy answers.

Back at the Greenbrier disagreements are cropping up not only between different nationalities but within them too. Among the diplomats arriv-ing from South America are many foreign nationals and dependents that the countries simply don't want. They run the gamut from ardent Nazis to people who have no connection to Nazism at all. One of the former is Colombian businessman Emil Prüfert, who writes Thomsen several letters dripping with Nazi condescension to be delivered to the German Foreign Ministry in Berlin. "Our border officials will have the pleasure of seeing a nice exhibition of native peoples from the jungles of Ecuador," writes Prüfert. "It is regrettable, on what extraordinarily remarkable criteria the people from Ecuador, for example, were selected to be sent away. Among them can be found pure Indian women, each with her own bastards, who here in the hotel have from the beginning comported themselves à la jungle, and certainly have not done credit to the appearance of Germandom."[25]

A lucky few apply for and receive approval to leave the Greenbrier for short trips. It's a rare privilege, indeed, given the blanket edict enforced from the outset and reiterated in a memo from the Department of Justice, under which both INS and the FBI fall. "When requests for exception to the rule come to you in the future from the State Department or any other agency, or from individuals, the answer should be 'no,'" wrote Lemuel Schofield. "In other words, our attitude should be that we cannot grant permission and the only person who can is the Attorney General."[26] Or in other words, cue the turf war between State and the other two agencies.

Special dispensation from on high is bestowed upon two individuals, both of whom bear all their own and their guards' travel expenses. First, Friedrich von Boetticher, accompanied by a border guard, finally gets to visit his hospitalized son near Baltimore. He finalizes trust fund arrangements and coordinates treatment with his son-in-law, David Miller, a doctor and the fund's trustee. Counselor Wilhelm Tannenberg calls the situation "a very pitiful case in that the deranged mind came about as a result of a fall."[27] Such boneheaded armchair analysis aside, young von Boetticher eventually rallies and proves his many critics wrong.

The other departee is Bébé Thomsen, who leaves on March 16 along with a border patrol agent and his wife for the University of Virginia Hospital in Charlottesville. This is quite unusual because every other person requiring hospitalization for tonsillectomies, infections, childbirth, Scheffer's broken hip, treatments of any kind, has gone to the C&O Hospital in nearby Clifton Forge. The reason for her hospitalization is vague. A single FBI report cites two radically different conditions: gastrointestinal problems, stemming from having been kicked in the stomach by a horse last fall, and severe depression previously described as caused by her apprehension at returning to Germany. Thomsen has also requested to be seen by a woman specialist as she doesn't trust Dr. Sennhenn, the German who first attended to Scheffer. Adding to the mystery, two days after their departure her guard reports that an unnamed Washington DC reporter (Lombard? Essary? Miller?) has made overtures to obtain a story about Thomsen: "Every attendant of the hospital," writes Lawler, "was instructed that under no circumstances or conditions should any statement be made relative to Mrs. Thomsen being at the hospital."[28]

Von Boetticher returns after four days but Thomsen, whose trip had been estimated to take three to four days, remains at the hospital for two weeks. While she's away every person who'd filed an application to remain in the United States is approved by State, with one exception: Paul Scheffer. With enemies in high places, his battle continues. An informant reports that Scheffer and Boveri have been tasked with writing an account of the Roosevelt administration to be presented upon the forthcoming arrival of the German diplomatic mission in Berlin.

While only approved detainees like Thomsen and von Boetticher have been allowed to leave the Greenbrier, agent Lawler has embarked on an ad hoc lecture tour. Over the last month he's spoken to three local Rotary clubs, a Lions club and a Junior Women's League meeting at which he modestly reports "the remarks of the Writer were apparently well-received."[29]

What's definitely not being well received are reports that the Japanese are to be relocated to a hotel in Augusta, Georgia. They're more than reports, actually, they're virtually a fait accompli as an intense State Department search in the last month has examined several hotels and zeroed in on one: Augusta's Bon Air. With on-site visits and estimates of lodging (cheaper than the Homestead!) and travel costs proving quite favorable, Protocol chief George Summerlin has okayed the move pending the approval of Justice. But the senators from Georgia, both influential Democrats, get wind and protest vigorously. The enmity toward the Japanese by the Georgia citizenry still rages, and it's enough to kibosh the deal. The day after Summerlin's memo, INS informs State that the plans have been dropped due to senatorial pressure.

Two weeks later, the real reason's revealed. "The FBI," writes Schofield, "objected to Augusta but have apparently now receded from their original position that they would object to any movement from Hot Springs."[30] How accommodating of the bureau to finally acquiesce to a move that State has been trying to orchestrate for several months. It feels more and more that the relations between the FBI and State are rivaling the animosity between the Germans and Italians.

# 17

## Twice Removed

Several young German boys are running all around the Greenbrier, proudly flashing their Junior G-Man badges for all to see. The Junior G-Men Corps is one of America's most popular clubs for boys, chock-full of secret codes and signals and activities. It was founded by ex-FBI agent Melvin Purvis, famous for having led the deadly manhunts for notorious bank robbers Baby Face Nelson, Pretty Boy Floyd, and John Dillinger. And just who are these lads proudly proclaiming they're Junior G-Men? Eight-year-old Dieter and five-year-old Folker Tannenberg, whose father is the German detainees' liaison.

While adults are weary of their confinement, it's been even harder on kids cooped up day in and day out for what's nearing four months. Some mischief-making boys have taken to pulling pranks like tipping over the sand-filled pedestal ashtrays meant for stubbing out cigarettes and cigars, marking or messing up furniture, playing with the elevators. One group armed with water pistols raided a meeting of German officials. An especially disconcerting trick is going into the public men's room toilet stalls, locking the doors, and then crawling out underneath, leaving management to figure out how to unlock them. "That's a new one on me," says

O'Hanley, "for I never heard of our American children doing anything like that."[1] Soon he finds out American boys can get into far worse trouble, when one of his sons' horseplay back at home nearly proves fatal.

No one knows quite how he learned about it, but Walter Winchell writes an item in his "On Broadway" column about the Junior G-Men lads, minus their names. It's a rare and relatively minor lapse in the government's blanket ban on reporting anything about the internment. With no reporters allowed in, a handful have cobbled together second-hand stories here or there for one-off articles like "Oh, for the Life of an Interned Diplomat," which its author slyly calls "a church-steeple [i.e., outsiders'] view of the not-too-dull, not-too-gay life."[2]

But bans don't stop rumors; if anything, they inflame them. The impending move of the Japanese has been an open secret for a while, and a Homestead ad that ran in mid-March left no doubts: "This Spring as always, The Homestead will be ready for you with its distinguished facilities for sports and recreation—expressly designed for those who know and appreciate the finest."[3] Across a short stretch of the Allegheny Mountains, the citizens of White Sulphur Springs—still smarting from the Germans' encampment—gird for battle. They know Georgia may not have halted General Sherman during the Civil War, but it just stopped these Japanese cold, and the West Virginia townsfolk aim for nothing less.

Word spreads quickly in this small town. The first tipoff comes on the morning of March 27, when the C&O Railroad drops off five empty baggage cars at the town's station. The news spread like wildfire. The next day the council calls a special meeting and issues a resolution that "doth hereby protest most vigorously to the Japanese Enemy Aliens being interned in or near said Town."[4] Always attuned to the community, Loren Johnston writes John O'Hanley just before the meeting that influential organizations and businessmen from not only White Sulphur but nearby Lewisburg and Ronceverte are preparing to protest. He states that he's made clear that under no circumstances is the Greenbrier to be included in any public protest or comment.

The resolution goes out to the governor and State Department through their congressmen, accompanied by a letter to Senator Harley Kilgore from F. E. Finks, president of the Bank of White Sulphur Springs. The protestors have done their homework, noting that hotels in several states besides Georgia have been approached unsuccessfully. "Since no other state would take them," writes Finks, "why should they be put off on our state for the duration of the war and ruin our town and county? . . . We realize that we are in War but feel there are thousands of hotels all over the country which would accomidate them."[5]

Up the chain of command it goes, but the response from Sumner Welles is exactly what they don't want to hear. His language could have been taken verbatim from the long-held justification of seeking similar treatment of American diplomats held abroad—reciprocity. Welles adds that since the exchange of Axis representatives is due to happen shortly, there's no need for apprehension about a long-term stay, and closes with a flourish: "This Government is confident that the townspeople of White Sulphur Springs will realize that the temporary use of the Greenbrier Hotel is a war measure, and that their patriotic support will greatly assist the Government in the discharge of its international obligations."[6]

Patriotism (or perhaps factionalism?) plays a part in the Italians' response too. Informed of the pending move, they face a delicate balancing act: privately they're delighted to finally be separating from the Germans, but publicly they can't admit that. So Rossi Longhi asks the Swiss representative for formal notification so he can lodge an official complaint to demonstrate complete faith in the alliance between Italy and Germany. Asked privately whether he thinks the move will ameliorate or worsen their situation, he smiles. "We'll know," he says, "when we get there."[7] On the last day of March, Loren Johnston writes a memo to employees in his elegantly expressive style. He acknowledges the difficulties of the last few months, salutes their courteous and attentive service, and reveals the forthcoming change. The Italians are out, Japanese in.

On April 2 the Greenbrier hosts an early dinner. Then 176 Italians, 52 Hungarians, 9 Bulgarians, and the detainment's lone Norwegian, a nursemaid to an Italian count, board two special trains for the overnight trip to the Grove Park Inn in Asheville, North Carolina. Originally assigned to remain at the Greenbrier, John O'Hanley—having done such a swell job—accompanies the Italians as they'd requested. The move, including

**Fig. 39.** Luggage piled high for the departing Italian detainees. Courtesy of the Greenbrier.

packing a sea of luggage into five baggage cars, goes flawlessly. Only a handful of spectators gather to watch their arrival. "Some of the women wore corsages or carried flowers," wrote the *Asheville Citizen-Times*, "and a number were dressed in what were described by those accompanying them to the inn as 'gorgeous' fur coats."[8] Private cars whisk away Prince and Princess Colonna and the ranking Hungarian and Bulgarian ministers and spouses; everyone else rides in buses. The caravan avoids the business district to attract as little attention as possible. Upon arrival the throng throws a monkey wrench into the hotel's prearranged room assignments when everyone, from ambassadors down to the lowest clerks, demands a private room. Nearby cottages are pressed into service, and the border guards who'd been living there are moved to an adjacent country clubhouse.

Problem solved. Are more coming? Do the Italians like pasta?

Meanwhile the industrious Greenbrier staff spends the next thirty-six hours cleaning up for the next mass arrival. On the morning of April 4, 331 Japanese depart Hot Springs on a 13-coach train. Two hours later "real guests," as the *Richmond Times-Dispatch* calls them, check into the Homestead to inaugurate its 176th season. That afternoon several hundred White Sulphur Springs locals watch silently as the arrivals walk or take taxis to the nearby Greenbrier, with police stopping traffic on U.S. Highway 60 so they can pass. Half an hour later all are inside and porters are busily removing a mountain of luggage. Edward Poole, replacing O'Hanley, arrives with the Japanese for his new assignment. Confounded by the move, Kichisaburo Nomura blames the Roosevelt administration for "dragging the embassy staff around on something akin to a 'circus tour.'"[9]

The government, however, sees the shift as a double-barreled win: it exposes the rifts in the facade of German-Italian harmony and removes the Japanese from the Homestead. Headlines like "Interned Axis Diplomats Parted by U.S. to End Row" and "Italians Moved Out, Rebuffed by Nazi Slurs" seem to validate its decision. But perhaps one long-distance newspaper editorialist understands the situation better than the boys at State. "Does anyone know," asks a prescient op-ed in the *Montana Standard*, "whether the Germans can get along with the Japs any better than they did with the Hungarians, Italians and Bulgarians?"[10] The government's soon to learn that its gambit more resembles putting out fire with gasoline—or *fires*, that is, because even before the inevitable squabbles comes a flare-up elsewhere from a very familiar source.

Two days after arriving in Asheville the Italians, on behalf of themselves, the Hungarians, and Bulgarians, hand the Swiss representative a long memo of complaints about facilities, service, and food: rooms not cleaned until after 2 p.m., maids who don't turn down the beds or leave fresh towels nightly. "Food is deficient in quality and quantity," the list continues. "Dining room service is most inaccurate and plates and silver are often dirty. . . . Food [needs to] be of a better quality, better prepared and more appropriate portions served. The diet at the Greenbrier was perfectly satisfactory as for quality and portions."[11]

O'Hanley's immediately on the case, agreeing that many of the complaints are justified. Shifting around a half dozen rooms helps alleviate the accommodations problems. He promises to investigate more thoroughly, adding, "The Italians have always been great for complaining, anyway, but on the whole it doesn't take a great deal to satisfy them."[12] Yet for him, these work problems disappear in a flash when he receives a phone call with devastating news: his oldest son, Peter, fourteen, was shot early this morning and is hospitalized in grave condition. O'Hanley departs immediately for his home in Rhode Island. Another agent, Bill Huskey, relieves him.

Billing itself as "the finest resort hotel in the Smoky Mountain region," the Grove Park Inn looms high above the city of Asheville. Surrounded by several thousand acres of timberland and accessible from only one road, it's perfectly situated for the detention. Opened in 1913, the palatial main building is made of uncut granite quarried from Sunset Mountain, where it sits. Hundreds of mules, wagons, pulleys, ropes, and workmen put the massive boulders, some weighing as much as ten thousand pounds, into place. It's furnished with hand-crafted American arts and crafts furniture and hammered metalwork by the renowned Roycrofters, four hundred handmade rugs imported from Aubusson, France, and Irish linen and curtains.

"It is unusual outside and inside, more like a country home than a hotel," reads a promotional brochure. "The gigantic [120-by-80 foot] lobby has nothing its equal in the world; it is built entirely of natural boulders. Its rustic nature blends well with the surroundings of the inn . . . with two huge fireplaces" that can burn twelve-foot logs. Border guard Mike Maffeo had worked at White Sulphur and accompanied the Italians to their latest home that's "just as swanky as the Greenbrier, a great big place. It had a fireplace as big as that wall there. They used to have a little donkey come in and harness him to pull the logs up on a pulley arrangement so that they could be swung into the fireplace."[13] The inn employs around 115 people, mostly locals and predominantly black, who are fingerprinted and issued identification cards. "The manager, the office force, and all persons working on the clerk's desk," reads an FBI memo, "are, of course, white. From casual inquiry it was stated that none of the employees have indicated any un-American tendencies."[14] His reflexive racism, reflective of the times, echoes the arrest and incarceration of that black busboy at the Greenbrier last February.

Not only does the Grove Park Inn pass the requisite FBI vetting, it offers highly favorable rates too: $8 day per adult for room and board, $5 for children under nine years of age and for federal agents. To avoid the previous brouhaha over tipping, State agrees upfront to pay weekly amounts: $9 to bellboys, $8 to maids, and $2.50 to telephone operators. The diplomatic groups pay waiters a flat fee of $1.50 per patron per week. "This is considerably less than was paid at the Greenbrier," writes special agent Robert Bannerman, "which was very favorably received by the diplomatic group." Shopping options are limited, with a beauty salon, a barber shop, and a cigar store that carries some druggist items. Yet it does boast the one-of-a-kind Homespun Shop, a salesroom featuring fine woolens made right on the inn's grounds by Biltmore Industries in a half dozen cottages. Management also arranges for a local department store to send in salespeople and merchandise three times a week. "It has been assured," writes Bannerman, "that the prices charged will be the regular prices and no advantage will be taken of the diplomatic group."[15]

Outside the steep terrain is crisscrossed by walkways and bridal paths, though nearby level areas have a clay tennis court and playgrounds. An eighteen-hole golf course at the foot of the mountain includes a swimming pool surrounded by a large fence. INS is amenable to arranging surveillance so detainees can enjoy the facilities. The guards who transferred from White Sulphur Springs and Hot Springs are augmented by a number of locals hired for emergency ninety-day service, a strategy that later backfires and causes considerable trouble. All outdoor lighting at the Homestead is disassembled, packed, and shipped to the inn. As for the guard shacks, it's cheaper to build new ones here than ship the old ones.

On April 17 O'Hanley calls with good news: his son is out of danger. Turns out he'd been accidentally shot by a friend while horsing around with a gun, an incident that "turned my mother's hair white overnight," recalled his younger brother Don, who'd been sent out shopping when the shooting happened.[16] While Peter's still recuperating in the hospital, he's well enough that his father plans to return. He arrives back on Monday, April 20, and writes to Fitch, his boss. "Please know that I appreciate all that you have done for me. It was the most trying period in my whole life and now that it's over with I lay awake nights thinking how fortunate we are that the boy was not shot between the eyes and blinded for life."[17] He closes by praising the job his fill-in, Bill Huskey, did and promises a report by week's end about the nagging problems at the inn.

The next day Charles Bruggmann again tells Breckinridge Long about the food complaints, and Long immediately fires off a memo to Protocol division chief George Summerlin: "It [is] incumbent upon us to take that matter up immediately and see that the food for which we are paying is wholesome, properly cooked and properly served. . . . I think this is quite important and call it to your serious attention."[18] Summerlin phones Fitch the same day, so again O'Hanley feels the heat. Undoubtedly the inn's current occupants would disagree vehemently with the description in its brochure: "Our cuisine delights even the palate of the epicure. Our menus are distinctive in their scope and variety, served in the most appetizing manner."

Immediately upon returning O'Hanley learns that food is the only issue still unresolved. Dirty table and silverware and room service have all been addressed. The night he gets back he dines on steak that "might have been all right on the dollar dinner at a Howard Johnson road stand, but I did not think it was a good one for this place," he tells manager Laurence Hollandsworth, who's puzzled by his new guests' attitude: "The hotel had always been complimented on their table, and he just could not understand what the trouble was."[19] The manager explains that their beef comes direct from Chicago, fowl from a local Armour plant, and milk and cream from one of the state's best, Biltmore Dairy. When O'Hanley asks to tour the kitchen, Hollandsworth immediately agrees. The agent discovers it's even cleaner than the Greenbrier's, with ample storage facilities for perishables. He's so impressed he arranges for Rossi Longhi to see it too. At lunch the next day an Italian woman approaches him and starts crying when describing the spaghetti and meatballs she'd ordered for her children, who ate very little and had been running to the bathroom ever since. So O'Hanley suggests that the main chef be sent on vacation and two Italian chefs among the group be assigned to run the kitchen. Hollandsworth refuses but asks his chef to allow these two to prepare spaghetti and sauce and another main dish. In short, O'Hanley writes, the food quality is first class ("the story of canned goods is just one of those rumors"); it's the preparation that's lacking.

Improvement does begin showing on several fronts. Rossi Longhi grudgingly admits that the recreation space here is far superior to that of the Greenbrier. A request is made to allow some diplomats and ladies to go shopping in Asheville. But one thing no one can change is the inn's massive granite construction, a characteristic that not everyone appreciates. "One individual," writes Hoover to Berle, "facetiously compared the hotel with the underground cell which was part of the setting in the last act of the opera 'Aida' in which Aida and her lover were entombed."[20] If nothing else, the man must get credit for having the buttoned-up director include a reference to an opera in a memo for undoubtedly the first and probably last time in his long career.

Once again the issue of finances comes to the fore: Prince Colonna's finances. Several months ago he'd begun lobbying for an exception to the rule that every detainee could take a maximum of $300 in cash upon repatriation. Colonna wants that bumped up to $5,000 for him and $2,000 for his wife. As head of the Italian delegation, he explains to Bruggmann, he's accustomed to entertaining and expects to do so aboard ship. On a voyage of eight or nine days, $300 apiece won't go so far, ignoring the fact that all room and board en route, like at the hotels, is already covered. Then when arriving in Europe Colonna fears he'll have no funds to allow him to get back to Rome—which again seems an absurd implication, that Italy would charge its countrymen for travel home. Nevertheless, the Swiss ask that State, in light of his circumstances, make some allowance for the prince. A couple weeks later the minister again brings up the question. "I told him," wrote Long, frostily, "that the regulation of the Government was $300 per person and that we were not disposed to make exceptions to the rule."[21]

But Colonna is nothing if not stubborn. Like the schoolboy who declares, "If I can't play, I'm going to take my ball and go home," he opens another front and triggers a major crisis. Out of nowhere the Swiss embassy in DC reports that in Berne, the Italian minister in charge of making arrangements for the repatriation has received an official communication from Rome. "The Italian Foreign Office," reads the cable, "is in full agreement with Prince Colonna's intention to leave the United States only after all Italian Nationals to be repatriated have started their journey. The note adds that the Royal Italian Government does not intend to compromise on this subject."[22]

Diplomatic jargon aside, this is the equivalent of a snit fit. But the prince is too clever by half, since his stunt infuriates the Swiss who've been handling the delicate back-and-forth negotiations for months. State official Joseph Green suggests that they ask "the Italian Foreign Office to telegraph Principi Colonna immediately, reminding him that the Swiss Government was the guarantor of the exchange and instructing him to cease his endeavors to obstruct the arrangements already made for the exchange."[23] In a follow-up memo, Green reiterates the seriousness of the situation: "We might conceivably be obliged either to give way to the insistence of the Italian Government and allow Prince Colonna to remain in the United States until the last of the Italian nationals has been repatriated or, alternatively, to carry him aboard the ship by force."[24]

Given how much of a royal pain in the keister Prince Colonna has been, there would undoubtedly be a stampede of government volunteers eager to carry him aboard kicking and screaming.

# 18

## A Feud Renewed

Back at the Greenbrier, it doesn't take long for cracks to emerge between the Axis power personnel now lumped together under the same roof. Or as one senator's wife puts it, "Leaving the Germans with their Axis partners, the Japs? It will be like tying two cats together to watch the fur fly."[1]

Two days—*two days!*—after the Japanese arrive FBI agent Roy Morgan, who accompanies them from the Homestead and replaces John Lawler (who goes to the Grove Park Inn) delivers the contentious news. "The Germans seem to be taking a dictatorial attitude toward the Japanese insofar as their rights here, the playground, and other activities," he writes. "Dr. Tannenberg has advised the Japanese pertaining to these matters and they are accepting these suggestions without any questions whatsoever."[2] Even Spanish liaison Joaquín Rodríguez de Gortázar is disgusted by the Germans' arrogance. The same day of Morgan's memo the Spanish embassy conveys a message to State: could it kindly ship five cases of Old Parr and five cases of Johnnie Walker Black Label, now stored in the cellar of the Japanese embassy, to the Greenbrier? The acquiescent Japanese are apparently being driven to drink by the Germans but, alas, State scotches the request.

The detainment represents the only time in history that high-ranking Axis country representatives have been forced to live cheek by jowl. It didn't go well for the Germans and Italians, and now relations are even more strained, albeit for an entirely different reason: racism. The Nazis clearly view the Japanese as inferior, an opinion shared by many other Western countries long fearful of the supposed "yellow peril." (These countries share anti-Semitism too: Breckinridge Long is an anti-Semite who furtively does everything in his considerable power to limit Jewish refugees.) Before the war the German and Japanese delegations never socialized with each other very enthusiastically, and that pattern continues at the Greenbrier.

Not with everybody, though, and certainly not all the time. But the Germans' innate feeling of superiority, always lurking just below the surface, is laid bare in a conversation between Bébé Thomsen and Brownie Carson, the hotel's nurse. Carson tells the FBI that she complimented Bébé's "masterly job in the reception line when the German officials were giving a formal reception to the Japanese dignitaries. Mrs. Thomsen said that such things were necessary for her to do in view of her husband's position."[3] Thomsen adds that she's been asked to host a tea for the Japanese ladies. Publicly she is cordial; privately she's mortified. "Mrs. Thomsen felt just the same about giving a tea for the Japanese as would Mrs. Carson, a native born Southerner, were she placed in the position of having to give a tea for a group of negroes."

Yet groupthink doesn't dictate every individual's life. People reason and act and make their own decisions regardless of their countrymen's general antipathy for another group. When the Italians were here, for example, Hildy von Boetticher's mother Olga struck up a friendship with Princess Colonna. The two traditional ladies met every day for tea, and not just because Olga was eager to brush up on her Italian. They were simpatico. A similar relationship develops between two strangers, Bébé Thomsen and Gwen Terasaki. They spend a lot of time together, trying to momentarily forget the predicament for which neither has a remedy, and their uncertain futures that lie ahead. Thomsen speaks openly about her aversion to Hitler and Nazism, and Terasaki finds her desperately unhappy. "She seemed to me," wrote Terasaki, "like a small bird lost from its nest."[4]

Meanwhile, an informant reports that Hans Thomsen has warned his countrymen not to criticize the Japanese and to tell him of anyone who does. The informant infers that Thomsen, like a lot of top Nazis, doesn't fully trust his ally, and the feeling, apparently, is mutual. Shortly after the Japanese arrive another informant reveals that an assistant military attaché assembled them outside and demanded that everyone refrain from talking to the Germans. He fears that any conversation is only a ploy to get them to reveal confidential information. It's a draconian request with which it's impossible to comply, and of course both sides still talk. But it illustrates the paranoia in which two supposed allies each fear the walls have ears.

And those walls do, at least as far as the FBI is concerned. Whether the talkers are looking to pass along information, curry favor, settle old scores, or simply gain attention, the FBI doesn't judge; it listens and passes everything along for its analysts to decipher. Like when Ulrich von Gienanth talks about the trouble with the diplomatic corps. With Hidenari Terasaki listening in, he opines that many good men with ability and initiative make mistakes, whereas those that do nothing rise rapidly in the ranks. The cumulative effect of doing nothing counts for more than taking a risk and doing the wrong thing. Terasaki agrees.

Neither of the Thomsens ever speaks a word to the agents save for a passing pleasantry, a reticence few other diplomats can claim. Friedrich von Boetticher continues to hold forth about military matters and offer predictions, yet he warns others "that they should not be seen talking to American FBI agents as that possibly would leave the wrong impression."[5] That kind of advice makes one of his subordinates call him a hypocrite, not to his face but behind his back to agent Roy Morgan. He calls von Boetticher nothing but an army "brass hat" who's deposited considerable money in a bank account in DC and plans to move back to the United States after the war. An informant recounts that von Boetticher privately believes America will invade France later this year. Though he thinks the attack will fail, in his view its objective would be to draw Nazi ground and air forces away from the Russian front. In actuality, he's somewhat on the right track: FDR considers a cross-channel invasion from England, an option many of his military advisors favor, but opts instead for a top-secret invasion this Fall of Vichy-controlled North Africa, the "soft underbelly" of the Nazi empire.

At least five interned Germans—reporters and officials high and low—and de Gortázar tell Morgan that soon Germany will re-attack and defeat Russia. All think it will happen quickly, except for von Boetticher, who warns of continued great casualties on both sides. In truth the war on the Eastern Front drags on for another year, ending with a devastating Nazi defeat at Stalingrad in early 1943 that will mark a turning point in the war in the Allies' favor.

A contrarian view comes from Paul Scheffer, now hobbled by his hip and leg injuries but hopeful because they've at least delayed his departure. He tells Morgan that a Japanese friend, a newsman, believes high Japanese officials want Germany and Russia to make peace. That way Germany could refocus on England while Japan would be reassured that it would not be attacked by Russia. Asked to name the officials discussing this matter, Scheffer demurs. His chronic physical problems persist: he repeatedly sees the hotel doctor and returns to the C&O Hospital for X-rays and examinations. Diligent Loren Johnston stays apprised of Scheffer's condition, writing medical director Guy Hinsdale: "Full and complete report upon pelvic case (broken) to Insurance Company, stressing fact it is one of the important diplomats and might have repercussions unless it has special care and attention."[6]

Now it's springtime and living is, if not easy, more agreeable. Mother Nature offers up a rejuvenating spring awakening. "Waiting for the hyacinth buds, the tulips, the columbine became the most important event of the day, at least for me," writes Margret Boveri. "In the end I knew every plant and could sometimes even overlook the white lines painted across the garden paths that barred our way."[7] She also enjoys the fine view from the roof, though not the less pleasant smells emanating from kitchen and laundry vents. The gently curving, colorful hills remind her of Ticino, the scenic Swiss region bordering on Italy, and she takes great pleasure in the beautiful sunsets and wonderful stillness.

The pool enjoys considerable use. Lucy Buran, daughter of the men's store owner, remembers a big difference between the two groups. "The Japanese were cut out of a completely different pattern," she said. "Their swimmers were mostly men, and their style very regimented, not at all leisurely."[8] They also did rigorous calisthenics. Both groups ask for permission to play tennis, soccer, and baseball. The latter is of special interest to the Japanese, enthusiasts who'd set up an eight-team league and played continuously at the Homestead. The tennis courts are readily accessible and easy to guard and are frequently used by men and women alike. Some ambitious youngsters earn pin money as ball boys. Baseball is another matter. An available field is about three-quarters of a mile from the hotel, large enough for both baseball and soccer. Bound by a creek on one side and a high, unscalable cliff on the other, INS feels it could be guarded by five men who'd be easily freed up by consolidating or relocating several existing guard posts.

The word comes back from State: "No baseball for the Japs."[9] This edict's later lifted and "no baseball" becomes "play ball," reflecting the prominence America's game held in prewar Japanese culture. An American teacher in Tokyo introduced Japan to baseball in 1873. "The game struck such popular fancy that it has reigned as the supreme sport ever since," wrote *Far Eastern Trade* in 1940. "Today the game is played throughout Japan in all seasons, and the Japanese baseball fan is just as avid and hit-conscious as any American who has sweltered in the bleachers."[10] Baseball later becomes a lifeblood for thousands of interned Japanese who create makeshift ballparks and fashion jerseys out of cotton potato sacks. The detainees don't go to such great lengths but organize their teams by the territories once represented by their consulates.

The short-lived baseball ban, like the ongoing prohibition of most newspapers and magazines, is unnecessarily spiteful and serves no real purpose. Especially the periodical ban since, as von Gienanth points out to Morgan, American magazines arrive on Goebbels's desk in Berlin within days of publication via the twice-weekly Pan American Clipper flights to Lisbon. The book regulations are eased, with detainees now allowed to order most anything unrelated to technical or economic issues. For her children Elenore von Knoop buys *The Wind in the Willows*, a book her family still has today. A shipment of racy Italian-language paperbacks includes titles like *Delores of the Seven Pains, Queen Margo,* and *The Delicious Blonde.* "Inasmuch as nothing of a political nature was discovered," writes Hoover, "the shipment was permitted to proceed."[11]

To brush up on his bridge game, von Gienanth orders a book by world-renowned expert Ely Culbertson. However, when it arrives the shopkeeper won't sell it to him, saying, "We won't teach you Nazis how to build bridges."[12] He goes to O'Hanley, the two have a good laugh, and von Gienanth gets his book. On a more scholarly side, Masuo Kato enjoys watching a group of swans swimming on a pond. One loses her mate and spends her days isolated from the rest of the flock, putting him into a philosophical mood about the nature of freedom. While he's not especially religious he orders a weighty three-volume set of Saint Thomas Aquinas's master work, *Summa Theologica.* Kato also opts for a more timely, less weighty subject with *The Japanese Enemy,* a new book by *New York Times* reporter Hugh Byas, which hypothesizes that Japanese aggression aims to establish "a position in the Pacific from which they cannot be dislodged, regardless of whether Germany is defeated."[13] Bringing the book back to Japan brings him trouble from the Kempeitai (military police), who force him to write a formal letter of apology.

Some detainees opt for soothing spa treatments, for which the Greenbrier is famous. Physiotherapy includes "tonic and Medicinal" baths, massage, colonics, ultraviolet, inhalations, and more. The Germans get along especially well with thirty-year employee Minna Schmidt, a native of Erfurt, who runs the baths. Men, interestingly, visit more than women, and business drops when some of the best customers, the Italians, depart. The Japanese aren't interested in the offerings at all. Hans Thomsen takes several diathermy treatments, but in his imperious way walks out without paying. "No doubt he expects to pay for several treatments when he has finished," writes medical director Hinsdale to Johnston. "I really feel it very embarrassing to 'bone' a man like Dr. Thomsen for services when I know perfectly well his credit is good. But if you think that we ought to make a practice of insisting on immediate payment after a service is rendered, perhaps that can be accomplished without giving offense."[14]

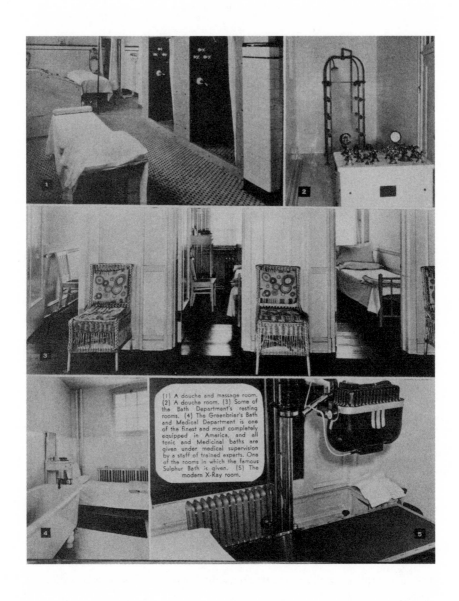

(1) A douche and massage room. (2) A douche room. (3) Some of the Bath Department's resting rooms. (4) The Greenbrier's Bath and Medical Department is one of the finest and most completely equipped in America, and all tonic and Medicinal baths are given under medical supervision by a staff of trained experts. One of the rooms in which the famous Sulphur Bath is given. (5) The modern X-Ray room.

**Fig. 40.** Spa treatment facilities at the Greenbrier. Courtesy of the Greenbrier.

Everyone continues to enjoy the fine food. Divorced from the shortages their countrymen are enduring at home, the detainees become so used to the cuisine that Kato jokingly notes that "steaks had reached the 'What, again?' stage." Years later, three Germans recalled everything fondly. Marie Fritzsching, a secretary, called the food and service "impeccable."[15] Rolf and Alfons Kleindienst, two young boys whose father was a consular secretary, said, "We always ate at the same table each night, had the same waiter and also were given double servings of sausages at breakfast."[16] Rolf picked up a lifelong taste for orange marmalade.

The Kleindiensts also remember the shopping. Just before arriving their mother sold their automobile, a 1937 Dodge, for eight hundred dollars and spent it all at the Greenbrier. Having been through World War I she bought sensible items that could be traded; she also bought a set of luggage that her sons were still using three-quarters of a century later. More options opened when detainees received permission to order from catalogs. Not only did this increase selections dramatically, it helped bypass what some felt was price gouging by the stores. Indeed, the owner of the women's store told agent John Lawler she'd sold two fur coats for five hundred dollars each, then admitted the next day she'd actually charged a thousand dollars apiece. Some merchants' complaints about letting their only customers order through the mail fall on deaf ears: Johnston "stated that if he heard any further complaints, that he was sick and tired of the conditions prevailing in connection with the concessions and would close every concession in the basement with the exception of the drug store."[17] When catalog orders arrive they're inspected by the FBI, and customers go to the hotel's post office and pay for the delivery in cash.

Beautiful spring weather, more sports and shopping and spa opportunities, continuous fine food. And now, a new sense of order upends the Germans' rather undisciplined existence, thanks (or maybe it's no thanks) to the Japanese. One day a blackboard appears in the lobby with a schedule in large Japanese characters of lectures for adults and lessons for children. Their regimentation shames the Germans into following suit, and both request separate classroom space, for which two cottages are designated. If memoirs can be believed, the German schools had many

**Fig. 41.** German children and adults outside their cottage schoolroom; Hans Thomsen standing in top row in light suit, Ulrich von Gienanth to his left. Courtesy of the Greenbrier.

founders. Else Arnecke teaches the ABCs, reads stories, and helps the littlest ones draw and paint. "Later, in Berlin," she writes, "I got a medal for my work. In Germany you get an award. In America, you get a raise!"[18] Hildy von Boetticher taps a German exchange student to help her with a class that has no books, maps, or teaching aids. She recalls drawing maps from memory. She puts Crimea in the Mediterranean, spelling it "Krim," which is German for the Crimea. "One child piped up delightedly, 'Now I know where Grimm's fairy tales come from.' So much for my efforts with German literature."[19] George von Knoop remembered studying German grammar since he'd only spoken English in U.S. elementary schools.

Von Gienanth teaches history and his wife, Karin, music and singing. Music is a favorite pastime that knows no boundaries. Both Japanese and German children, who rarely mix, gather around organist Nathan Portnoff every day. He plays a large, ornate organ with multiple keyboards, stops, and foot pedals that pump air across a bank of reeds to produce

**Fig. 42.** Japanese children and schoolteachers. Courtesy of the Greenbrier.

a big sound that fills the lobby. The children learn songs not only from him but from border guards. "Nearly every day," recalled chief clerk Roy Sibold, "one could hear children singing some good old American songs as they walked along."[20] Though sometimes a line must be drawn, even for music, like when a Japanese envoy from Cuba requests that his piano be shipped from storage in Miami. Thomas Fitch says no, suggesting to agent Edward Poole that he find a way to "explain this diplomatically to the appropriate Japanese representative."[21]

The animosity between the two groups bursts into clear view with the stunning news of Lieutenant Colonel James Doolittle's bombing raid, America's first aerial attack on the Japanese mainland. Though the attack inflicts relatively minor damage—industrial facilities hit, fifty killed—its psychological effects on a country starving for some good news are enormous. "Tokyo, Kobe, Yokohama BOMBED!" screams the front page of the *Los Angeles Times* on Saturday, April 18, a headline echoed nationally and internationally. Come dinnertime at the Greenbrier, the Nazis delightedly torment the Japanese by whistling shrilly to imitate the sound of a falling bomb, then banging their hands on their tables with a loud thump. Repeated over and over, the stunt never fails to elicit laughter from their side of the room and silence from the other.

Two days later the Germans again erupt, this time in celebration of Hitler's fifty-third birthday. The program begins with children singing a popular Nazi anthem, "Volk ans Gewehr." Then Hans Thomsen speaks at length, with several informants recounting his comments. He describes his earlier positions at the chancellery in Berlin, praising Hitler for his humanity, acumen, and memory. He calls Roosevelt Germany's "arch enemy" and voices "confidence in an ultimate German victory and the creation of a new order, not only in Europe but in the entire world where Germany will have the place to which she is entitled."[22] A boisterous celebration ensues that one waiter wryly describes as "a hell of a hail of heils."[23] Notified of the festivities Loren Johnston has a discreet word with Thomsen, and fifteen minutes later—a testament to Nazi law and order—the dining room's deserted.

A week later it's the Japanese detainees' turn to celebrate a birthday: the forty-first of Emperor Hirohito. Ambassador Kichisaburo Nomura holds court in remarks dutifully revealed by informant Kyusuke Hoshide. He begins by noting with regret that they must celebrate this birthday in enemy land and goes on to describe several personal audiences with the emperor. He praises his thriftiness, which is much greater than people know, and his punctuality, industriousness, and intellectual vigor. Hirohito eats but a simple dinner every day, far less sumptuous than what the detainees are eating here, and he warns of the shortages back home awaiting them. Nomura urges everyone to obey the officers and sailors on their journey home. The assembly ends with the singing of several patriotic songs and turning to the west and bowing in honor of the emperor. "For the information of the Bureau," writes Morgan, "the affair was very orderly in all respects and no disturbance or demonstration of any type was in evidence throughout."[24]

With monotonous, routine surveillance continuing day in and day out, and all indications suggesting the detainment is winding down, complacency sometimes sets in. But when chief patrol inspector E. J. Lincourt gets wind, he reads his men the riot act. "Concerning the procedure to be followed regarding persons seeking to enter the hotel, it is very evident that patrol inspectors have not been properly instructed concerning the matter, or are heedless of the instructions," he fumes, zeroing in on one prime offense. "Upon numerous occasions wives of the patrol inspectors on duty at some of the posts spend considerable time 'visiting' with their husbands. This practice must cease."[25]

Two days later he follows up with another memo specifying the qualifications for admission, reiterating that all truck drivers must show valid ID before delivering shipments. Anyone seeking hotel employment must be escorted by a guard. In respect to the latter, there are now two openings in the laundry department. For while it's been nearly three months since the FBI arrested those six German waiters, their clandestine investigations have continued. Now they've produced evidence that forty-seven-year-old John Bretz, a nineteen-year employee who'd worked his way up to laundry superintendent, is a Nazi sympathizer. Johnston immediately terminates him and his wife, Margaret, a fellow laundry employee for the last couple years.

More arrivals pour into the Greenbrier after the *Acadia*, overseen by Charlie Spruks, arrives from South America in New Orleans. The first of back-to-back round trips brings in 140 Japanese and Germans. Originally scheduled to accompany the Germans on their forthcoming trip back home, Spruks gets a telegram while en route informing him of a change in plans. "As there are a number of very important visits of distinguished foreigners scheduled within the next month or two," writes his boss, George Summerlin, "I do not feel that I can spare your services from the Division for the first trip to Lisbon."[26] That list of arrivals from on high includes the president of Peru, the first chief of state to visit wartime Washington; King George of Greece, who presents Spruks with an Order of George I medal, a high Hellenic honor; King Peter of Yugoslavia; and Queen Wilhelmina of the Netherlands. Yet after playing such a vital role and having gotten to know so many detainees so well, it must be quite a disappointment to Spruks not to see it through to the end. Not to mention missing a transatlantic voyage and a few days in the intriguing city of Lisbon. Frederick Lyon, Adolf Berle's executive assistant, takes his place.

Stateside, another place of lodging, the Gibson Hotel in Cincinnati, is pressed into service as a temporary home for another five hundred arrivals from South America. Once again it's State's ace logistics man, Robert Bannerman, who makes all the arrangements for travel and lodging. A high-rise downtown hotel, the Gibson presents an entirely different set of challenges. The detainees are housed in its top four floors, with guards manning all elevators twenty-four hours a day. While its ads tout the Gibson as "Famous for Friendliness," its employees—who are issued special IDs to travel to the upper floors—receive a ten-point memorandum, of which one is in all caps:

ONE OF THE GREATEST SERVICES YOU CAN DO FOR YOUR GOV-ERNMENT IS TO REFRAIN FROM TALKING ANY MORE THAN ABSOLUTELY NECESSARY WITH THE GUESTS. LIKEWISE, REFRAIN FROM DISCUSSING THIS MATTER WITH YOUR FAMILY, YOUR FRIENDS, OR ANYONE ELSE WITH WHOM YOU COME IN CONTACT. REMEMBER—A SLIP OF THE LIP MAY SINK A SHIP![27]

A long-term guest, forced to relocate for these short-term visitors, jots a facetious note to the hotel's manager:

Good luck, and here's hoping
That you'll still be in the pink
When the Japs are in the hoosegow
And the Nazis in the clink!

Back in Washington DC Henrietta Hill, wife of Alabama senator Lister Hill, gets the inside scoop about the Greenbrier: "My special spy tells me that neither the Germans nor the Japs are in a hurry to set sail for their native lands. They are too well situated here as the guests of Uncle Sam."[28] But on the ground, or more accurately high in the air, Kato offers wistful words that dispute that contention. "Many evenings we stood silently on the hotel roof and watched enviously as American cars swept by on the highway, free to go anywhere they pleased."[29]

Before they go, a final firestorm erupts in the press.

# 19

## Homeward, Unbound

To date the embargo on reporters at the hotels has been remarkably effective. So how exactly can a determined correspondent circumvent it? How about by visiting White Sulphur Springs and chatting up loquacious locals or, even better, the odd off-duty staffer willing to anonymously share a story about life inside the palace? And if buying a drink or two at a local gin mill might help loosen someone's tongue, why not?

Take those juicy but unverifiable stories, add a generous dollop of gossip, gussy it up in scandal-sheet style prose and what'd'you get? Five nationally syndicated pseudo-exposés that hit the streets beginning in late April. However, consider the source: ex-isolationist and virulently anti-FDR publisher Cissy Patterson, a self-described "plain old vindictive shanty Irish bitch."[1] If anyone has the will (and power) to put the administration in a bad light, it's Patterson. But of course she's out of sight, sending instead two callow reporters. One's a young man destined to forge a career in Hollywood, and he makes a great start by spinning some pretty wild and crazy stories.

Suicides! Escapes! Race wars! Spies! The series begins by describing the writers' stealthy pose: "They spent two weeks at the resort in the guise of vacationists; otherwise they would have been escorted out of town by the worried FBI."[2] This can be only one of two things: self-importance or self-delusion. Either way, while these "tourists" think they're getting the locals to spill the beans, they're being sold a bill of goods. One can almost hear the townsfolk chortling afterwards about how they played them there gullible city slickers. Yet by dint of publication these embellishments live on, repeated by subsequent generations of credulous writers who don't question the source material.

This author's review of tens of thousands of period documents from the FBI, INS, State, and other federal agencies failed to uncover a single page that confirms any of the reporters' fabrications, though it did unearth the contemporaneous response of Kay Bolger, owner of the Greenbrier's antiques shop and wife of its golf pro. "She was just so perturbed at the utter disregard for the truth by the writers, David Charney and William Wallace, that she just had to write to Mrs. Patterson," writes FBI agent Roy Morgan, "calling attention to the falsehoods and inaccuracies in the series of articles."[3] A half century later, a detainee decried a successive writer's repetition of "embroidered" stories like escapes, sirens going off, and "people wandering off the 18th hole on the golf course [when] we were even escorted to the tennis courts."[4]

Fantasies aside, the detainees do disappear for a night in early May. Or rather, they stay out of sight in their rooms as employees hold their annual springtime ball. It's a festive occasion the staff has celebrated since antebellum days, and the forced presence of hundreds of foreign guests isn't enough to derail their respite: a nostalgic night of music and fun and drinking and dancing in the ballroom of the hotel in which they toil 364 days a year.

The frivolity's short-lived for one staffer, waiter Alfred Nerz, who buys two magazines the next day. He slips them, unnoticed, to a detainee, but a suspicious newsstand clerk informs the FBI of his purchase. Immediately they phone him on his day off, and Nerz provides a written statement admitting his guilt. His reason? The detainee, a fellow Stuttgart native, had promised to visit his parents after getting home. Nerz hasn't heard from them in over a year and wants his folks to know that he, his wife, and eighteen-month-old son are doing fine. Nerz seems remorseful, but two complications arise. First, one of the magazines, *American Mercury*, features an article entitled "A Plan to Destroy Germany," exactly the kind of story the government wants to keep out of enemy hands. Second, an FBI investigation shows that Nerz was part of the group of waiters, some of whom had been arrested last February, that celebrated Nazi victories. He "is generally considered by the village people," writes Morgan, "to be the most dangerous of the foreign-born individuals in town."[5]

Meanwhile, after months of tedious negotiations, plans are emerging for the main event: repatriation. First up, the Germans and their European allies. Six trains—three from White Sulphur, two from Asheville, and one from Cincinnati—are slated to depart for Jersey City on Thursday, May 7, and from there they'll board the *Drottningholm* for Lisbon. A butler and a maid decide to turn their voyage into a honeymoon and are married by a local Catholic priest in the Virginia Room two days before leaving. A flurry of last-minute activity ensues. The Germans pack and repack trucks and bags, crammed with possessions from home and whatever they'd acquired in the stores and through the mail. But one particular item can't be packed: firearms that had been well hidden during previous searches. Wilhelm Tannenberg surrenders thirteen pistols confiscated from various embassy personnel, including a pistol and ammunition from Ulrich von Gienanth. The weapons will be carried aboard ship by Lyon and returned to their owners upon arrival. The Nazis outgun their Axis allies: the Italians turn in five pistols, including ones from Prince Colonna and Alberto Rossi Longhi, while the Japanese place third with three pistols and ammunition.

Kichisaburo Nomura gives Hans Thomsen a letter describing America's industrial mobilization to deliver in Berlin to Japanese Ambassador Hiroshi Oshima, who after the war will himself be interned temporarily in an American resort in Pennsylvania. Some German children present their favorite organist with a basket of fruit and a card that reads, "To our dear Mr. Portnoff." A few nights ago, while he was playing, Thomsen complimented a song's "pretty melody" and asked its title. The answer? "The White Cliffs of Dover," an unofficial wartime anthem in England. When Gwen Terasaki says goodbye to Bébé Thomsen, she gives her a small token

**Fig. 43.** Popular organist Nathan Portnoff and several young friends. Courtesy of the Greenbrier.

of their friendship, a corsage—though they'll never meet again. Hildy von Boetticher and her friends play one last tennis tournament against the Japanese, which in keeping with their previous matches, they lose. The night before departure—thanks to some unnamed but savvy movie buff— the Greenbrier screens a wartime epic of loss and romance and adventure, *Gone with the Wind.* "The final touch of irony," wrote von Boetticher. "All along I had felt like Scarlett O'Hara: in only one day all that was dear to me was blown away."[6] She recalled first seeing it with friends at college several years ago, and as then the Germans watching tonight react with strong emotion. The Japanese watch impassively; this Western drama's more unfathomable, and, besides, they're not going anywhere tomorrow.

The next evening, 422 German detainees assemble in the lobby. Despite some earlier rancor between them, many Japanese gather to say goodbye. A group serenades the Nazis with "Aikoku Koshinkyoku," a popular patriotic, militaristic song, and ends with three rousing cheers

**Fig. 44.** Departure day for the Italian detainees. Courtesy of the Greenbrier.

of "Banzai!" Thomsen delivers a short speech in German, concluding with an outstretched arm and crisp "Heil Hitler." Then it's off in an orderly fashion the short distance to the train station for the overnight trip. "There was no disturbance or demonstration which was objectionable or destructive in any way," writes Roy Morgan, "and the Japanese returned to their rooms and usual places of amusement immediately after the departure."[7] The next morning they arrive at the Jersey City station and board buses to the docks. From twenty-one train cars more than twelve thousand pieces of baggage are removed and loaded into the ship's hold. Inspections had confirmed that no forbidden items like cameras, radios, typewriters, or firearms had been packed. State orchestrates everything, excluding all other federal agencies like ONI, IRS, or customs that might delay the departure. No adult passenger may carry more than three hundred dollars; any excess is confiscated and placed in bank accounts for the duration of the war.

Last night Breckinridge Long worked late after summoning Berle's assistant Frederick Lyon from New York to discuss a last-minute "confidential oral communication to be made aboard the vessel": an offer so secret that he doesn't even describe it in his diary. Now, after hearing the detainees are on the docks, Long decides to unwind. He takes a noon train to Pimlico, where two of his horses are running. One disappoints but the other, a filly named Equipet, finishes strong on a muddy track to win the Carroll Handicap by a couple lengths. Stewards dismiss a challenge that the horse swept wide and drifted, and Long's presented "with a nice piece of silver plate as a trophy."[8]

Back in New Jersey the Coast Guard, INS, and local railroad and harbor police guard the route to which no visitors are allowed near. No streamers, no balloons, no flowers, no bands playing, no one waving goodbye. As the travelers queue to board, out of nowhere a young woman who somehow evaded security comes running up. "Don't leave me, Wilhelm!" she cries to a dumbstruck young blond man in line. "Please, please don't go without me. When will we ever see each other again?" She sobs uncontrollably as he hugs her, a bit embarrassed. The girl's escorted away, and up the gangplank they walk onto the steam turbine-powered *Drottningholm*.

Originally christened the *Virginian*, it made its maiden voyage in 1905 from Liverpool to Saint John, New Brunswick. On the fateful night of April 14, 1912, it was one of several ocean liners that picked up the *Titanic*'s distress calls. During World War I, while transporting troops, it was torpedoed by a German submarine. After the war the Swedish American Line bought and renamed it the *Drottningholm*. To prevent another submarine attack in the dangerous waters of the Atlantic, the ship's painted white with its name and the words "DIPLOMAT" and "SVERGE" (Sweden) in huge black letters on both sides of its hull. George von Knoop recalls "a stark white ship, heavily spotlighted" to deter attack, its dusk-to-dawn floodlights reminiscent of the unpopular lights at the hotels.[9] Despite sailing under a safe conduct guarantee signed by all nations involved, any transatlantic crossing—where more than two hundred ships were sunk in the first six months of 1942—is fraught with trepidation.

Nicknamed "Rollinghome" by previous travelers because of its tendency

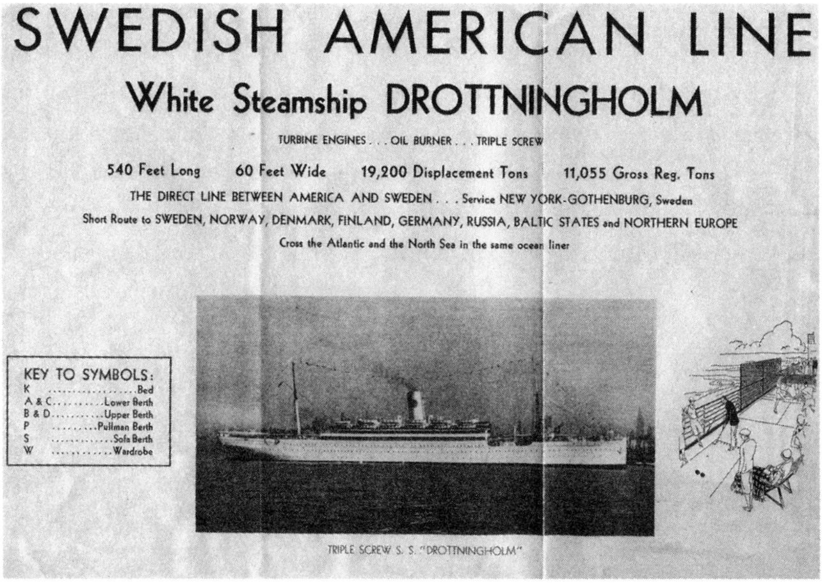

# SWEDISH AMERICAN LINE
## White Steamship DROTTNINGHOLM

TURBINE ENGINES . . . OIL BURNER . . . TRIPLE SCREW

540 Feet Long    60 Feet Wide    19,200 Displacement Tons    11,055 Gross Reg. Tons

THE DIRECT LINE BETWEEN AMERICA AND SWEDEN . . . Service NEW YORK-GOTHENBURG, Sweden

Short Route to SWEDEN, NORWAY, DENMARK, FINLAND, GERMANY, RUSSIA, BALTIC STATES and NORTHERN EUROPE

Cross the Atlantic and the North Sea in the same ocean liner

KEY TO SYMBOLS:
K . . . . . . . . . . . . . . . . . . Bed
A & C . . . . . . . . . . Lower Berth
B & D . . . . . . . . . . Upper Berth
P . . . . . . . . . Pullman Berth
S . . . . . . . . . . . . . . Sofa Berth
W . . . . . . . . . . . . . Wardrobe

TRIPLE SCREW S. S. "DROTTNINGHOLM".

**Fig. 45.** A brochure of the SS *Drottningholm,* which sailed to Lisbon with the Axis country detainees. Courtesy of George Borden.

to roll in rough seas, the liner is crammed to capacity with 948 German, Italian, Bulgarian, and Hungarian officials and nationals. Few happy reunions take place among the parties separated when some were relocated to the Grove Park Inn. Though Hildy von Boetticher has been looking forward to seeing Joseph Fulop again and had written him in Asheville, he's aloof. The reality of finally heading home to a world at war weighs heavily on everyone except the children. When one father tells his young son that the ship will take them to Europe, the boy replies, "Is Europe a big place like the Greenbrier?"[10] Many children, forced to get acquainted or reacquainted with their native language, are taught German songs every morning. But there's some backsliding. Dieter Tannenberg, who's probably not running around showing off his G-Man badge, entertains by singing a song he learned at the Greenbrier: "Deep in the Heart of Texas."

On the first day the captain orders an evacuation drill that proves utterly chaotic, with many passengers prematurely inflating their life jackets and impeding all traffic. It's so futile that no more drills are held.

The Nazis organize a fire brigade and a staff of stenographers and typists to issue directives. Between cramped quarters and a constant din from crying children to footsteps pounding down metal stairs, it's an arduous journey. Many feel pangs of *Heimweh* (homesickness). Margret Boveri humorously compares herself to adventurer Phileas Fogg in Jules Verne's *Around the World in Eighty Days.* Dietrich von Knoop, three-quarters of a century later, has one vivid memory of the voyage: the day a U-boat surfaced and sent over a raft. Its crewmen spoke in German to Hans Thomsen, standing on the deck, who confirmed that there were indeed German diplomats aboard. The raft returned to the submarine, which dove and disappeared.

While the Italians keep their distance from the Germans, Lyon approaches Colonna, scion of a royal family, with the diplomatic overture he'd discussed with Long: America is amenable to making a deal with the monarchy for Italy's surrender. "Lyon's message was that the United States regarded Italy as being in an entirely different category of enemy state," wrote professor James Edward Miller. "Left unsaid but evident was the offer to deal with the king. Speedy action to rid Italy of Mussolini offered the monarchy a last chance to survive."[11]

After its nine-day journey the *Drottningholm* glides into the Targus River estuary on a damp, misty morning and docks in Lisbon. "On the right was a chain of green hills," recalled Boveri. "On the left houses rose one above the other, pink between gray and yellow and white. Old ocher yellow fortification towers on the water, baroque palaces on the mountainsides, high against the sky, the cypresses of a cemetery in between. All so European: we could hardly remember anymore that something could be European. We were all a bit sentimental at the sight, unaware that we'd soon be torn apart and heading into different parts of Europe."[12]

Many of the arriving passengers claim to have no hotel accommodations and ask to stay aboard one more day. The ship's officials agree and feed them three more meals, stipulating that they must leave the following morning. The crew's exhausted, having worked nonstop sixteen-hour days during the crossing; now decks and staterooms must be scrubbed, fresh supplies brought aboard, and all Axis baggage unloaded. The next morning many Nazis demand to stay yet another day and are denied. They grouse but go, plunging from the isolated American resorts of yesterday into a teeming old-world temporary refuge. As the lights go out all over Europe, the City of Light is awash with espionage, double dealing, and opportunism. "River mist and fog often rolled in at night," wrote author Neill Lochery, "giving a distinctly noir movie atmosphere."[13]

Meanwhile, trains carrying the American contingent from Bad Nauheim arrive. Their trip had both good and bad moments. Shortly after departing Paris someone threw a rock that shattered a dining-car window and showered several diners with glass shards. Later that day, while steaming through the French countryside, a peasant working in a field suddenly began waving an American flag. The passengers were doubly impressed: by the man's courage and by an unseen intelligence operation that had conveyed what train they were on. When it comes time to board the *Drottningholm*, they're joined by other Americans including Admiral William Leahy, ambassador to Vichy France, who's bringing back the body of his wife, Louise, who passed away on the eve of departure after surgery.

Lisbon's German delegation turns out en masse to welcome their countrymen. Hans Thomsen immediately contacts the highest echelons of the Nazi government, as the diary of Joseph Goebbels, Reich minister of propaganda, attests: "Our diplomats and journalists have now arrived in Portugal," Goebbels wrote on May 18. "They gave exceptionally good interviews to the press, and described conditions in the U.S. in terms suited to our propaganda line. We helped a little in that respect, but in this way we can once again make a relatively deep impression on international opinion."[14] Like two sides of the same coin, on the same day Breckinridge Long wrote in his diary: "The Axis diplomats arrived safely at Lisbon, and so have ours. The press stories coming out make good reading and all seems to be favorable from the point of view of the Department's work in the premises—and give good insight of Germany and Italy as of the present."[15]

Thomsen gives a radio broadcast that offers a taste of the party-line propaganda to come. U.S. military production capacity has been greatly exaggerated, he claims, and most Americans don't support the war: "I am firmly convinced that the United States people, who would rather live in peace as far as their majority is concerned, would not benefit from Roosevelt's war."[16] "Roosevelt's war": this from the man who hand-delivered Germany's declaration of war to the State Department on December 11. Yet his strident voice is a lonely one, drowned out by a flurry of dispatches by Western correspondents. "FREED WRITERS REVEAL AXIS DISCONTENT: Italy Embittered by War; Germans Also Losing Faith" reads the headline and subhead of a front-page story in the *New York Times.*

But to the most important man in Germany, it's Thomsen's words that ring true. Lunching at the Wolf's Lair, his clandestine wooded compound in East Prussia, Hitler praises both Thomsen and Friedrich von Boetticher for their service in America. Yet like so many leaders, he habitually cherry-picked information he found most favorable. In the late thirties, for example, Hitler "believed a bizarre tale . . . that national socialist sentiment was so rife in New York that taxi drivers, on recognizing a German fare, inevitably said Heil Hitler!"[17] He announces his intention to soon reward them personally and to later appoint them to postwar positions worthy of their capabilities. "I shall hold Thomsen, in particular," says Hitler, "for a post of exceptional difficulty."[18]

Lisbon's elite often travel twenty minutes west to the fashionable seaside resort of Estoril—later popularized by British operative Ian Fleming, who was stationed there briefly during the war, in 007's *On Her Majesty's Secret Service.* Friends in Estoril throw a dinner party for the von Boettichers on a terrace with a magnificent ocean view. Their hosts mistakenly believe they've been deprived of food, insisting they take plenty of cream with their strawberries. But what the von Boettichers really hunger for is the news of which they've been deprived while living in isolation in the United States.

On another night Hildy makes news of her own. In their hotel an acquaintance from the Greenbrier introduces her to an enthusiastic compatriot. He shows great interest in her life in America and, on the spot, offers her a job in Lisbon as "an international radio broadcaster." Delighted by her incredible good fortune, she rushes to her parents' room, where her worldly father explains that the man's undoubtedly from the propaganda ministry—and the job will entail delivering Nazi

**Fig. 46.** Friedrich von Boetticher and Hans Thomsen being honored by Adolf Hitler. Bundesarchiv/Militärarchiv, Freiburg im Breisgau.

propaganda in her perfect American English. Shattered, Hildy learns the first lesson of survival in a dictatorship: be careful of everyone you talk to, stranger or friend, and eventually realizes that her father perhaps saved her from becoming another Tokyo Rose or Lord Haw Haw. Her father had a clear-eyed view of reality. "General von Boetticher loved America as few men have loved it," wrote his son, "but when the trumpet called he became an enemy of the United States. That was his duty as he saw it, and that was the law under which he lived."[19]

Arriving back in Frankfort the diplomats receive a heroes' welcome: an ostentatious display with flags, flowers, speeches, and songs before a rapt crowd of officials, storm troopers, and Hitler youth. As von Boetticher watches disbelievingly the kind of show she'd only seen previously in newsreels, she's thinks it "a meaningless display of party pomp." The ceremonies conclude with everyone receiving "identity cards, ration cards, clothing coupons, soap coupons, cigarette coupons, housing permits, permits to establish ourselves in the town of our choice, and permits to buy a railway ticket to get there. With this life-sustaining documentation, we became established as ordinary members of *das Deutsch Volk.*"[20]

Which her father and Hans Thomsen certainly aren't. Shortly thereafter Hitler personally awards both men a prestigious Knight's Cross of the War Service Cross "for special services rendered as a diplomatic representative of the Reich."[21] It's just like Paul Scheffer had predicted to the FBI at the Greenbrier: loyal servants of the Führer get rewarded. "The general," wrote Helen Lombard, "had hardly stepped from the train when Hitler pinned a medal on his chest."[22] At a subsequent reception a Nazi official simultaneously lauds the newly arrived envoys and denigrates their captors. "You have survived the storm," says State Secretary Ernst von Weizsäcker. "With uplifted heads you have done your work, untroubled by death and the devil, inwardly serene in your faith in Germany and its leader. If, across the ocean and under the barrage of hostile propaganda and lies, you have survived; if you have observed our enemies conducting their war of words, you will discover that here in Germany there prevails a war of deeds. Here you see no 'American way of life.' . . . Here you will hear no 'fireside chats.'"[23]

Back at the Greenbrier—where most every American would dearly love to experience such an "American way of life" with all the trimmings—the Japanese host a reception for two high-profile guests: Spanish ambassador Juan Francisco de Cárdenas and Minister Juan Gomez de Molina, who've driven in from a stay at the Homestead. More than a dozen detainees attend, including Hidenari Terasaki and former heads of missions in Canada, Cuba, Mexico, and Panama. Kichisaburo Nomura thanks the Spanish for their fine representation of Japan's interests. The ever-vigilant FBI notes that the visitors arrived in a private car, not an official embassy vehicle. Its subsequent inquiry reveals that the two were traveling with two unidentified women and thus used a private car to keep this suggestively salacious information from embassy staff. Roy Morgan forwards this spot of Spanish intrigue to the regional FBI field division office in Richmond for further investigation.

Since the initial group of Nazi diplomats departed the Greenbrier, several hundred German diplomats and nationals have arrived from

South America. The Japanese had always felt the Germans who preceded them from DC had been given the choicest rooms. Now they're incensed that the newly arrived Germans have been given those same rooms. In particular, Saburo Kurusu's eager to move into the Thomsens' old suite, now occupied by another diplomat heading the German delegation. "The Japanese here have little use for the Germans," writes Morgan, "and feel that they are superior and should be entitled to accommodations better than those furnished the Germans."[24]

Their demand that this "nobody" in Thomsen's old room be relocated goes nowhere, just like the increasingly discontented Japanese.

# 20

## Perplexing Passage East

So how do these blasted rumors get started, anyway? Just as the detainment's winding down and Loren Johnston can finally begin to focus on the Greenbrier's future sans foreign detainees, a letter arrives on June 1, 1942, from a local bank. A cashier's inquiring about the forthcoming sale of "furniture, rugs and draperies that have been in any way treated badly by the Foreign Element," asking to stop by "to look at this spoiled property with the view of buying it."[1] Through what surely must be gritted teeth, Johnston replies with his usual restraint and cordiality—and anticipates by eight months Humphrey Bogart's reasoning for his move to the title city in Warner Brothers' forthcoming classic *Casablanca*. "I believe you must have been misinformed," he writes. "We have suffered no damage to furnishings or equipment, and there are no articles of any kind for sale. . . . It would please our Government very much, I am sure, as it would us, if you would stop any further publicizing of this [erroneous] report."[2]

While Johnston delivers this most gracious slap in the face, the grimy white *Drottningholm* sails back into New York harbor in a steady drizzle. Exhausted but delighted to be home, the passengers stand on deck as a crowd of several hundred waits anxiously on the pier. After a tense ninety-minute delay, a black-shrouded casket containing the body of Ambassador William Leahy's wife, Louise, who'd died after abdominal surgery, is lowered to the pier. A naval honor guard covers it with the Stars and Stripes; Leahy silently descends the gangway and enters a car. Only after they've driven off are the 908 passengers allowed to disembark, a weary crowd of "diplomats, babies, old and young men and women, dogs, pet turtles and even two captive crickets."[3]

Later that afternoon in Washington DC, tensions run at a fever pitch. Charles Fahy, the U.S. solicitor general, has proposed halting the exchanges because certain agents of Germany may have been allowed to depart on the *Drottningholm*'s first trip. An irate Long convenes a meeting of a dozen representatives of agencies including State, FBI, ONI, and G-2. After an hour of heated debate it's determined that Fahy's young assistant had been working off an old list from which many names had already been struck. This has become a thorny issue that'll complicate the upcoming Japanese exchanges too: not diplomats but dubious foreign nationals whose repatriation may work against U.S. interests in the long term. "Justice seems to have the idea," fumes Breckinridge Long, "they have to supervise all my activities!"[4]

Screening passengers for the next departure of the *Drottningholm*, one man from Mexico is discovered to have hidden plans for a submarine escape hatch, stolen from the Portsmouth Navy Yard, in the toe of a shoe. He's detained and spends the duration of the war in an internment camp. On the same day the ship departs for Lisbon with 950 nondiplomatic Axis country nationals, the Battle of Midway erupted in the Pacific, where the Japanese have a huge advantage in naval and aerial forces. But having cracked the Japanese radio code the United States pinpointed the fleet's location and launched thirty-seven bombers from the USS *Enterprise* that destroyed two Japanese aircraft carriers. By day's end two more carriers were obliterated, halting the advance of the Imperial Japanese Navy. In military parlance, "operational initiative" in the Pacific effectively passed from Japan to America.

Back at the Greenbrier the Germans have come and gone, and the Japanese are itching to do the same. As soon as possible. But complications keep cropping up. Lists of potential nondiplomatic passengers have been circulating for months among the two countries and their respective protecting powers, but many names are still in limbo. Some people don't want to go back; others can't be located. That latter category also serves as subterfuge for U.S. intelligence agencies objecting to certain individuals by falsely claiming their whereabouts are unknown. "The exchange with Japan is nearly on the rocks," writes Long. "They have asked guarantees [for] about 700 individuals being included. I cannot guarantee—today. So I am postponing. The intelligence agencies are objecting to various of those the Japs insist on. I am trying to patch up a list which may be satisfactory—but which I doubt."[5] When an ally weighs in with yet more objections, an exasperated Long asks an assistant to "please thrash it out once more with the representatives of the British Embassy."[6]

While the last-minute wrangling continues, a lightning bolt blindsides the Americans as Ambassador Nomura announces he won't leave until the list problems are resolved. "I feel that I have failed in my responsibility if I departed for Japan before equitable adjustment of the discrepancy has been made," reads the telegram sent to the Spanish ambassador he hosted the week before. "It would even be necessary to postpone the departure of the exchange vessel until a satisfactory agreement shall have been made."[7] As was the case with Prince Colonna, Nomura actually has no standing since his official position ended with the declaration of war. Long calls his position "preposterous" and asks de Cárdenas to convey to Nomura that he's not under the direction of his government but rather the *American* government, and if need be he will be "escorted" on board. To make matters worse, the nettlesome U.S. intelligence services raise new objections to fifty-one individuals slated to sail. "Justice calls this a 'repatriation,'" writes Long, "and does not seem to understand that in an 'exchange' you have to give up something to get what you want."[8]

With the exchange still teetering on a tightrope, the Japanese government postpones its grant of safe conduct while State awaits a final list of Americans to be repatriated from China. Long, who learns that the Spanish ambassador had been soliciting the advice of Nomura "as if he still had authoritative voice," suddenly breaks the impasse by allowing the Japanese to leave the Greenbrier for Jersey City.[9] Like a shrewd poker player, he's calling his opponent's bluff—but does he have an ace up his sleeve? Time will soon tell. The rank-and-file detainees know nothing of the high-level, high-stakes machinations and welcome the long-awaited news: we're going home!

Since the Terasakis aren't able to take Pechy, arrangements are made for Gwen's mother, Bertha, to come for the poodle. When she arrives Gwen asks if she can meet her to say goodbye, if only for a moment. The answer? No. So she goes to the roof and sadly waves goodbye. "I remember the flutter of Mother's pink handkerchief," she wrote, "and the forced calm of her voice calling up to me: 'Goodbye, darling, keep a stout heart!'"[10] Afterward she and Hidenari and Mariko go back downstairs, wash up, and go to the dining room for a dinner they cannot eat.

Late at night on June 10, two trains carrying 407 Japanese leave White Sulphur. They arrive the following hot morning and board the MS *Gripsholm*. But J. Edgar Hoover plays the ultimate trump card—national security—to unilaterally ignore a signed international agreement and order a search of about a third of the seven hundred nationals brought from internment camps throughout the U.S. FBI and Customs agents force many men and women to disrobe, and in virtually every case they discover cash in excess of the three hundred dollars permitted. Through the Spanish embassy the Japanese government vigorously protests the rigorous examination of passengers' bodies and baggage. Contraband uncovered includes a thousand-dollar stock certificate, photographs, correspondence, address books, and an expensive nautical watch. Yet through all the plots and subplots Long can't help but again interject his tightfistedness into the mix by nixing the sending of two telegrams, one of which could have been placed aboard a previous *Drottningholm* voyage for free. "It will cost three or four hundred dollars," he writes. "I do think we have to take these matters into consideration."[11] Some miserly things just don't change.

Aboard ship the 1,100-plus Japanese include the Honolulu exiles from Dragoon, Arizona, who regale their countrymen with firsthand accounts of the attack on Pearl Harbor. One ugly scene flares between a drunk commercial consular officer and U.S. officials. No matter how patiently

**Fig. 47.** The MS *Gripsholm* carried the Japanese detainees to Lourenço Marques, East Africa. Courtesy of George Borden.

they speak to him, he becomes increasingly belligerent. "It was repulsive and embarrassing behavior," recalled Mariko's classmate, Takeo Iguchi. "Luckily the American mass media were not on the scene; if they had been, it would have provided them with great material."[12] Everyone receives a stateroom assignment according to rank: Nomura and Kurusu land cabins on the A deck, but the one preceding them goes to Tamon Mayeda, former director of the Japan Institute in New York. Established to foster Japanese culture in America, it had shuttered two days before the attack on Pearl Harbor, a minor story buried in the *New York Times* beside a far more noteworthy feature with the headline "Japan confident talks will go on." His choice cabin, writes FBI agent Roy Morgan, "indicat[es] that Mayeda, although not a diplomat, is treated with greater deference than Kurusu and Nomura."[13] The Terasakis receive a nice cabin with three bunks and a small shower they're cautioned not to use because of water restrictions.

The weather's stiflingly hot and muggy, with nary a hint of a cooling breeze. There's nothing to do but wait and bake and gaze at the harbor traffic and New York City skyline. Nights are restless or sleepless between the intense heat and piercing whistles from passing boats. Rumors fly as no one can answer the only question on everyone's lips: what's the holdup? The answer is Long's ace up his sleeve: by boarding the Japanese but keeping the ship anchored, he's putting the onus on Japan to keep its end of the exchange. Deprived of newspapers and radios, the passengers stew for eight sweltering days until, finally, on June 18, they feel the welcome throb of the ship's engines. The pilot flag goes up and the *Gripsholm* moves slowly out of the harbor. Passing the Statue of Liberty, Takeo recalls visiting it with his American classmates several years before. Shortly after transferring to that school, he'd joined them in singing the "Star-Spangled Banner" and saluting the flag. One of his women teachers came over and gently explained, "You are Japanese, so you don't have to salute the American flag."[14]

The ship's bound first for Rio de Janeiro to pick up four hundred additional Japanese from Brazil and Paraguay. Then it's onto Lourenço Marques in Portuguese East Africa, dashing the hopes of some that the exchange point would be the scenic isle of Tahiti in French Polynesia. (Today Lourenço Marques is known as Maputo, capital of Mozambique, which gained its independence in 1975.) The *Gripsholm* is a newer, bigger, grander ship that the *Drottningholm*. Named for a fabled sixteenth-century lakeside Swedish castle, it was built by the Swedish American Line in 1924 and soon dubbed "The Floating Palace" for its deluxe appointments and first-class accommodations. Even its second- and third-class staterooms rival the first-class trappings of other ocean liners. One of its most famous passengers was enigmatic film star Greta Garbo, who was greeted by thousands of fans upon arriving in her native Sweden on a 1932 voyage from New York. A typical luncheon menu offers mutton stew, fried bluefish meunière, boiled potatoes, coleslaw and fresh fruit: not quite the Greenbrier or Homestead, perhaps, but none too shabby.

Starved for news, the passengers get a sense from some Swedish crew members of the war's progress, and it's not good. Whispers spread about the defeat of the Japanese navy at Midway, which punctures the high spirits of the naval officers who nevertheless assume authority over their countrymen by organizing flag signaling and lifeboat drills and submarine watches. In sum, a general nuisance tolerated by the ship's bemused Swedish crew that tells Kato, "This is the safest boat in the world."[15] Though the *Gripsholm*'s also lit from late afternoon to dawn to alert submarines to its diplomatic cargo, it's still an uneasy passage for passengers ever fearful of attack. What would make them feel even worse, if they knew, is that despite cruising along they're not home free yet. Because the ships slated to carry the American detainees from the Far East have *still* not sailed as previously agreed. Long alerts the navy to stand by: at his order, it'll intercept the *Gripsholm* and escort it to port. If the situation cannot be resolved, he's prepared to have its passengers returned to the United States and sent to internment camps for an undetermined stay.

As the ship nears Rio, Long readies his plan. "We [will] get our hands on 403 more Japs there which may count in the scales if we need them," he writes. "I am prepared for emergency measures if necessary."[16]

On the same day Long shares his frustrations in his diary, the phone rings back at the Greenbrier. It's the Bernard Fur Shop in Washington DC, calling for Bébé Thomsen. The downtown furrier, located across Connecticut Avenue from the Mayflower, is told that she returned to Germany some time ago—alas, a good customer gone for good. With the Japanese having now departed too, the government begins to transfer all remaining detainees to the Greenbrier and wind up the Grove Park Inn's involvement: a short-lived decision that's reversed next month. Meanwhile several dozen remaining detainees hoping to remain in America, overwhelmingly Hungarians but also including correspondent Paul Scheffer, reverse the commute by traveling from White Sulphur to Asheville for their enemy alien hearings in a North Carolina courtroom.

The hearings are not open to the public. With little advance notice few witnesses attend, though noted columnist Dorothy Thompson comes down from New York to speak vigorously on his behalf. Nevertheless his application is tabled, and on June 11—the same day the Japanese boarded their ship—he's transported to Ellis Island and immediately hospitalized. Another friend signs sponsorship papers and surmounts considerable bureaucratic hurdles to have Scheffer released so he can move back into his old apartment at the Fairfax Hotel on New York's East Side. Four months after his fall he's in constant pain, on crutches or in a wheelchair. The muscles have contracted so much that one leg is now three-quarters of an inch shorter than the other. Newly retained doctors determine that the botched treatment, exacerbated by previous arthritis in the hip, makes his condition very serious.

In late June Scheffer finally has corrective surgery, with the hopes that his muscles and nerves will knit with his new Lucite hip socket. But a long convalescence lies ahead, along with the weight of considerable doctors' and hospital bills. From the hospital he writes Thompson: "Bound as I am from many directions in my fracture bed, I hope in a week's time to get into a more normal frame [of mind] and even make a token rise from this mattress. . . . I have stayed here to fight against Hitlerism and to live as a free man, but it has come to my being forced to fight for my own liberty and even my good name."[17]

His wife, Nathalie, offers to pawn an heirloom emerald ring and some Persian rugs, and begs friends for a loan to help cover his medical expenses. A handful of friends, including Dorothy Thompson, banker Shepard Morgan, and Ham Armstrong, well-respected editor of *Foreign Affairs*, pool money. Even Bill Donovan and Allen Dulles of OSS contribute two hundred and one hundred dollars, respectively, asking only that their gifts remain anonymous. Their belief in Scheffer's anti-Nazism is so unwavering that they offer to put him to work if his medical and immigration issues can be solved. Scheffer remains an enigma, with influential friends on one side and powerful enemies on the other. Unfortunately for him, it's the latter at Justice that have ultimate authority over his immigration status. For now he remains both in limbo, legally, and under surveillance. Shepard Morgan notes with some disgust that an assistant attorney general on the case, an Austrian immigrant, has been in America four years less than Scheffer.

Back in DC, OSS pulls off another audacious break-in. This time the target's the Vichy French embassy in advance of Operation Gymnast, which was later renamed Operation Torch, the invasion of North Africa that'll put American boots on the ground for the first time in World War

II and subsequently trigger the detainment of French diplomats led by Gaston Henry-Haye. The unprecedented land, sea, and air offensive requires vital naval codes locked in an embassy safe, and a meticulously planned, months-long operation springs into action. An ex–British operative, beguiling American Betty Pack (code-named Cynthia), had begun an affair last year with Charles Brousse, a married French press attaché who fell in love and agreed to help. Bribing a night watchman who perhaps vicariously enjoys his compatriot's affair *avec cette belle jeune fille américaine*, they'd been regularly having nighttime trysts at the embassy. But cracking a formidable ancient safe in a narrow timeframe had foiled two previous attempts, including one that involved drugging the guard and his very vocal companion, an Alsatian dog.

One late June night the amorous couple tries a third time. Inside, with a finely attuned sixth sense, Cynthia suddenly begins undressing and urges her lover to do the same. As he enthusiastically joins in, a door swings open and the guard's flashlight rakes the room, landing on Cynthia: naked save for a single strand of pearls. The guard apologizes and hurries off. They open a window and in climbs a nimble safecracker known as the Georgia Cracker, actually a Canadian sprung by the OSS from a prison in Georgia. This second crack at code room door and safe succeeds, and off he heads with two thick cipher books to be photographed by OSS agents waiting in a nearby apartment. Several agonizing hours and many smoked cigarettes later, the safecracker reappears. In go the books, fingerprints are wiped clean, and the exhausted couple leaves.

But later they'll reappear in a most unlikely place.

Back on the high seas, as the *Gripsholm* nears Rio the clouds hovering over this round of repatriation finally lift. The Japanese liner *Asama Maru* leaves Yokohama, bound for Singapore, where it'll join the Italian liner *Conte Verde*, slated to leave Shanghai soon. Combined, the two ships will bring the Americans to Lourenço Marques for the long-awaited exchange. On July 2 the *Gripsholm* arrives in Rio, where the passengers can again only gaze longingly at the bustling city, far more picturesque and exotic than New York and at nighttime a grand illuminated spectacle. Atop a mountaintop a massive statue of Christ the Redeemer overlooks all. The ship not only takes aboard three hundred Japanese and Thai diplomats and nationals but considerable provisions for the long voyage ahead: six thousand turkeys, many tons of beef, pork, vegetables, fruits, beverages and, much to the children's delight, six thousand quarts of ice cream. Food's so plentiful onboard that Masuo Kato gives his cabin boy a dozen cans of fruit, generosity he comes to regret when wartime shortages later make such food unobtainable.

A commotion occurs on the bow of a vessel docked behind, a navy minesweeper where U.S. sailors wave their fists and make threatening gestures. The Japanese military attachés glare back silently. In the morning they discover the minesweeper's forward cannon has been turned toward the *Gripsholm*, and the crew showily demonstrates loading and firing the weapon. There's another demonstration too but this one's of love, not war. One Japanese has been forced to leave his Brazilian girlfriend. After a tearful goodbye on the wharf, the young man stands silently on deck, gazing at the girl and her parents, who remain through the long night. At dawn, as the ship slips away, the girl gives him one last desperate look, climbs into a car, and drives away.

On the long voyage across the Atlantic many passengers become seasick, including Gwen and Hidenari Terasaki. They're brought meals by their unaffected daughter, Mariko, who proudly reports the dining room is largely empty. She also takes lessons to brush up on her Japanese and delights in playing ping pong and defeating most adult opponents. She and her father win a doubles tournament. Like at the hotels, many adults pass the time playing bridge, poker, and roulette. Overall, the ship's crowded, stuffy, and short on water, requiring passengers to handwash their clothes. Gwen recalls that many cabins came to resemble Chinese laundries with clothes hanging everywhere. In the beauty parlor a pretty young blonde does a brisk business giving manicures to young Japanese men eager to hold her hand. She receives many mash notes including one that reads, "Blonde Nordic daughter of Neptune, give me your smile."[18] Mariko's amorous classmate Takeo has no luck with a beautiful Thai girl who boarded in Rio. "I had my precocious eye on her, hoping to win at least a smile, but she completely ignored this inexperienced twelve-year-old," he writes.

On the morning of July 20 their thirty-three-day sea voyage ends as the *Gripsholm* glides into the hot, sleepy port of Lourenço Marques, which fleetingly stirs to life when ships arrive. Several dozen mostly battered freighters and tankers from Axis, Allied, and neutral countries fill the harbor. Red clay banks blend into a dusky landscape of muted purples and lavender from shore to sky. While the Japanese can only gaze out, reporters like Kato vie to be the first to file a story. The Portuguese-speaking Domei correspondent from Rio bribes a policeman to take their dispatches to be wired, but his efforts were in vain because a Portuguese reporter in Lourenço Marques filed a story as soon as the ship arrived. Allowed to disembark the next day, they're delighted to be back on dry land, even if it's still some eight thousand miles from home. Everyone passes through a big iron gate at the end of the docks manned by two friendly Portuguese soldiers.

Hard alongside the wharf sits a squalid neighborhood crammed with bars, restaurants, and casinos eager to part tourists from their cash. Beyond stands a plaza, or *praça*, and streets filled with shops in one- and two-story buildings of yellow or red brick often topped by ornate rooftop marquees. Sidewalks are paved with elaborate black and white stone mosaics in the shapes of sea serpents, snakes, sharks, and whales. Residential homes stretch beyond on wide streets, with patios and palm trees and thick hedges of bright flowers. Those bursts of color extend to the garb of the native women, dressed in vivid primary-color calico that contrasts sharply with men in faded rags often stitched together from gunny sacks. Amid the locals in this untroubled "picture of peace" are a mélange of foreigners from continents near and far.[19]

The Japanese eagerly descend upon stores selling a cornucopia of products including beauty supplies like face cream, soap, talcum powder, razor blades, and hairpins; foodstuffs from local bananas, citrus, and nuts to imported Heinz and Libby canned goods; and shoes and cloth-ing including Arrow shirts and Interwoven socks. Barbers and beauty salons do brisk business. Gwen Terasaki buys toilet soap, British woolen underwear, and a case of Portuguese wine. Soon there's a procession of agile African men bringing back the passengers' new possessions nimbly balanced on their heads—a skill the Japanese may have seen previously at the Homestead, where black waiters are renowned for carrying meal trays the same way. Takeo's excited by a trip to a zoo to see lions, giraffes, leopards, and elephants. Yet while neutral Lourenço Marques offers welcome liberation after months of captivity, the residents' viewpoint is decidedly not neutral. Everywhere are posters and photos of King George VI, Winston Churchill, and even Generalissimo Chiang Kai-shek, with nary a glimpse of Emperor Hirohito or Adolf Hitler.

The next morning the *Conte Verde* and *Asama Maru* arrive, with most Japanese exuberant or near tears at the sight of the flag of the rising sun. Yet the Americans receive a far warmer welcome. As they pass an old tanker, the captain sounds its whistle. "Up the masthead ran a brand new American flag which he had saved for the occasion," wrote ex–prisoner of war Norman Briggs, a Standard Oil executive captured in Hong Kong last December 8. "Did we ever let loose! Absolutely everyone on the 'Asama' shouted at the top of their lungs, waving hands, handkerchiefs, coats, shirts, everything we could lay our hands on! It was one of the greatest thrills of my life."[20] Other ships join in, an impromptu celebration of whistles blasting and crewmen flashing the V for Victory sign while the Japanese watch silently. Tugboats position the *Asama Maru* just ahead of the *Gripsholm* and the *Conte Verde* behind. Like the Japanese before, the Americans must spend their first day on ship, "like Israelites in sight of the Promised Land,"[21] wrote Phyllis Argall, a teacher and journalist imprisoned while working in Japan. As each side warily eyes the other, crewmen from the *Gripsholm* cheerfully toss apples and oranges and packs of American cigarettes to the grateful new arrivals.

The next morning, before the exchange begins, "swarthy" locals push a backbreaking line of boxcars one by one along the narrow-gauge tracks running alongside the pier. They sing lustily as they labor in the hot sun. "The bossman did nothing but sing," writes Associated Press newsman Max Hill, "slapping his palms against frayed knee-length trousers with a sure, confident rhythm no white man could match."[22] When the cars are finally in place, the Japanese descend the gangplank on their ship's bow, walk on the outside of the cars and ascend the *Asama Maru*'s bow. The Americans descend on the stern, walk inside and board the stern side of the *Gripsholm*, which immediately acquires the nickname "Trip

Home." Both sides glimpse the others' harsh glances and thumbed noses while passing by the breaks between boxcars. Wearing ragged and torn clothes, the Americans clutch their meager belongings in suitcases and cardboard boxes tied up with whatever rope or twine they could find. To a man, and woman, they're thin and haggard. "The Japanese got off with snappy new American clothes, nice matched leather luggage," wrote Briggs. "They looked well fed and happy. The women particularly looked very stylish with new hats and matched outfits. They surely presented a far different sight than we did."[23]

In town over the next several days, each gets ample opportunity to take a closer look at the other, but their initial animosity remains undiminished.

# 21

## Home Aghast

Separated by five thousand miles and more than a month's time, the exchanges of the Germans and the Japanese share one curious attribute: a corpse. In Lisbon, Ambassador Leahy was bringing back the body of his wife. Here in Lourenço Marques, a casket lies on the docks with the remains of Sotomatsu Kato, former Japanese ambassador to France. Last February he reportedly suffered a heart attack after opening a window at the embassy in Paris and plunged to his death. Rumors abound over this most mystifying demise. In an odd coincidence, soon afterward U.S. papers ran a photograph of him standing directly behind William Leahy shaking hands with Vichy French leader Marshal Pétain. The Terasakis knew Kato quite well; not only had he been Hidenari's superior in Washington DC when they wed in 1931, a newspaper had mistakenly run his photo opposite Gwen's in lieu of the actual bridegroom's. "Come," Hidenari tells her, "we must go down on the dock and keep our old friend company until he is brought aboard."[1]

That night the local German and Italian consular officials host a party for the Japanese. Having been cooped up for so long in the same place with the same people, a change of locale and new faces seems promising.

But it's a gloomy night, according to Gwen, who compliments the ranking Nazi diplomat for "play[ing] his part with a crisp perfection" but faults Kichisaburo Nomura's attempt to respond in German as "incomprehensive to Germans and Japanese alike." Most of all she's troubled, as she has been for months, by her husband's dark mood. "Terry was withdrawn and remote," she writes. "I was fearful that he might say something bitter to the Germans which would make trouble, but he hardly spoke during the whole evening."[2] Many couples dance until late but with little spontaneity or joy. Saburo Kurusu remembers the night quite differently, praising the elaborate banquet served by crew members shanghaied from German and Italian ships in the harbor: "We enjoyed ourselves to our heart's content that night."[3]

In town the two sides can't avoid each other. Occasional minor squabbles break out, but a heavy police presence keeps the situation well in hand. Most interactions are limited to feigned avoidance, icy stares, or stilted conversation. "We looked across and through each other," wrote Norman Briggs of an encounter in a restaurant with several Japanese. Max Hill warns Masuo Kato of the many Kempeitai posing as crew members aboard the *Asama Maru* that'll undoubtedly keep a close eye on the passengers returning from the United States—a taste of life ahead in a rigid totalitarian state. In America the detainees had more than their share of shadowing FBI agents, but they never displayed a particularly menacing presence.

One incident does attract worldwide attention. With the passengers on both sides having been incommunicado for so long, reporters thirst for even the slightest news. They pounce on an event from the first day when, as Ambassadors Nomura and Joseph Grew passed each other on the pier, Grew tipped his hat and continued on without pausing. Now, the story continues: when Nomura informally invites his counterpart to meet, Grew immediately rejects the offer. Stories with headlines like "JAP ENVOY REBUFFED" run 'round the globe, with Americans universally approving of the snub. "Informed interpretation," writes the *Evening Star*, "is that the admiral was eager to pour into the ear of a highly-placed American the story that would clear him of any complicity in the celebrated diplomatic double-cross of last December."[4]

Neither man comments publicly, but Nomura's private diary shows a marked turnabout: from unabashed praise about the attack in the days immediately after Pearl Harbor to self-pitying hindsight. "Since my arrival in Washington last year, I devoted body and soul to Japanese-U.S. diplomatic adjustment," he wrote. "It was truly a thankless task. Yet, just as a doctor does everything he can for a patient whose fate is already determined, it was a matter of course that I, as a retainer, honored the Imperial command and struggled to the bitter end."[5] Any such supposed remorse is short-lived, vanishing even before he arrives back in Japan.

On Saturday, July 25, the Japanese depart aboard the two ships for the last leg of their journey, which at its end will have circumnavigated three-quarters of the earth's surface and touched four continents. Just before they sail a couple dozen Americans approach and wave goodbye. Some even bow in the traditional Japanese fashion to show respect, enraging many of the Americans who'd suffered in captivity. "I ask you, can you believe that one? If they felt that way, you'd think they would have the common decency to keep it to themselves," wrote Briggs, adding that many of his fellow ex-prisoners wouldn't have minded if those people had boarded the ships too.[6]

Those traveling on the *Asama Maru* enjoy being on a Japanese ship served by their countrymen, many of whom confide that they'd served the foreigners stingily so there'd be more food for their compatriots coming home. The Iguchis are delighted to have the same waiter as when they'd arrived in San Francisco on its sister ship, the *Tatsuta Maru*, two years before. Takeo's also thrilled to learn that the *Asama Maru* has just returned from transporting Japanese troops, a rare honor in this patriotic twelve-year-old's mind. It's a long monotonous journey, sailing into a hotter climate and marked by bored children's screaming and commotion. One day there's a burial at sea for the ship's barber, who died of an illness. On another day rough seas cause Takeo to slip on deck. Knocked unconscious, he awakens to his worried mother hovering over him. A doctor, with no equipment to examine the boy further, diagnoses no fracture and prescribes simple bed rest. His intuition proves correct.

One of the best parts is the abundant Japanese food. "You'd better eat plenty of those cakes, Mari-chan," a steward tells the Terasakis' daughter. "There won't be any when you get back to Japan."[7] On August 9 the ships sail into Singapore, a harbor that only several months before had been a seemingly impregnable bastion of British might in the Far East. Here the passengers get a tumultuous welcome, as the Americans had received in Lourenço Marques: a flotilla of boats large and small, all flying Japanese flags with whistles a-blowing and people waving exuberantly. Gwen Terasaki sequesters herself in her cabin to avoid reporters and photographers eager for a propaganda story or photo. Military and naval officers don their uniforms and get fresh haircuts, making some almost unrecognizable to Terasaki, who'd lived alongside them for the last seven months. Military police hold compulsory lectures to imbue the returnees with patriotic spirit, reiterate the certainty of Japan's inevitable victory, and banish any Western ideas acquired in their long sojourns abroad. She barely understands a word.

Brisk competition to break stories replaces the returning reporters' prior spirit of cooperation, though Kato and his colleagues soon learn that owing to censorship few articles will be published. Back in DC, under no such strictures, his former assistant Clarke Kawakami opines that Nomura will surely speak the truth to his government. "Anyone who knows the blunt-speaking old admiral knows that he will not mince words in telling the militarists of their blunder," opines Kawakami, who's spectacularly wrong.[8] For in his first interview with a Singaporean newspaper, Nomura wastes no time in kowtowing to those who used him as a dupe in their war plans. Their names are lost to history, but his lives on in infamy for eternity. "War was inevitable," says Nomura, "because the United States wished to force Japan to her knees by threats of violence."[9]

"Peace envoy" Kurusu delivers an even more brazen dose of propaganda. "At the port of Shogun [Japan's new name for Singapore], we were happy to observe that in all the Southern Regions under Japanese occupation various constructive works, political, economic and cultural, aiming at the establishment of the Greater East Asia Co-Prosperity Sphere were already being pushed steadily with the cooperation of the inhabitants of these districts."[10] A typical example of "cooperation" is the spacious new headquarters for Domei, confiscated from a Dutch steamship company.

The reporters enjoy a welcome-home luncheon, complete with a Malayan band and snake charmer, at a private suburban home also seized from the same company. Afterward they visit the automobile plant where, five months before, General Sir Arthur Percival gave up: the largest British surrender in history. His victorious adversary, Lieutenant General Tomoyuki Yamashita, had kicked off his boots and pounded the table with this fists. "All I want to know is, are our terms acceptable or not? Do you or do you not surrender unconditionally? Yes or no?" Head bowed, Percival softly replied, "Yes," and uncapped his fountain pen.

Kato and eight other reporters board a plane and arrive in Tokyo well before the other returnees, whose ships steam into Yokohama harbor on August 20 to a thunderous reception. Having been warned not to appear too fashionable or frivolous, the women passengers wear their plainest clothes. Nomura and Kurusu board a car that drives them straight to Tokyo, where they receive gifts "in recognition of their conduct of Japanese-American relations."[11] They enjoy a royal welcome: an audience with the emperor, dinner at the palace, and lunch the next day with the prime minister. Being a loyal servant, just as in Germany, has its privileges. While Nomura and Kurusu continue to unabashedly mouth government talking points, in the other major Axis capital Hans Thomsen displays surprising candor. He acknowledges that U.S. aviation manufacturing has reached full wartime capacity and that other war production is quickly ramping up. Asked what prompted remarks so different than the standard Nazi ridicule of America, he replies that underestimating an enemy can prove fatal. Unprompted he adds praise of President Roosevelt as "super-intelligent" and derides the German press's constant ridicule of Eleanor Roosevelt. "She may not be a beauty queen," said Thomsen, "but she has great charm and purpose of mind and is, therefore, a great asset to her country."[12]

Thomsen's willingness to express such a change of heart in wartime Berlin is remarkable. But back in the United States a contemporaneous report of some prewar activities adds to a mounting realization that his amiable manner masked far more nefarious pursuits. Reporter Helen Lombard links him to assisting in the Nazis' looting of art treasures, especially the vast collection of avaricious Reichsmarschall Hermann Göring.

"The cultured Hans Thomsen was known to Washington auctioneers as one of their most assiduous and discriminating customers," she writes. "When something really fine appeared in a catalogue sale, Thomsen would get it regardless of cost."[13] He bought extensively, for example, at an auction at the Latvian legation after that country's invasion by the Soviets and Nazis. Thomsen's purchases there and elsewhere were quietly shipped out to neutral countries long before war broke out. After the war, when U.S. government agents broke into an ancient massive safe at the German embassy, they discovered considerable cash: none more than an envelope with Thomsen's name that contained $13,000 in hundred-dollar bills, the equivalent seventy-five years later of $225,000.

With the diplomats gone the number of foreign nationals at the hotels has dwindled considerably; by mid-July only around a hundred, overwhelmingly German, remain. Last month the Grove Park Inn switched to hosting Allied diplomats, but it wasn't a detention. Rather, the ambassadors of China, Great Britain, and the government-in-exile of the Netherlands came to address a U.S. governors conference. The event had long been scheduled at the hotel, hence the hurried removal of the remaining detainees to the Greenbrier barely a week before. The three-day conference set a record with more than forty governors and a passel of federal officials gathering to discuss myriad war issues pertinent to the states.

But as soon as it's over, the administration reverses course. It ends the involvement of the Greenbrier after nearly seven months: the longest tenure of any hotel. The Grove Park Inn reopens on July 9 for detainees, and at reduced rates: $6 per day for adults, $4 for children, and $5 for guards. Letters fly between Loren Johnston and the federal agencies, praising the efforts of many hotel and government employees. Roy Morgan asks the bureau to send letters of commendation for "splendid service and cooperation" to Johnston, George O'Brien, Roy Sibold, and several telephone company employees whose clandestine taps produced voluminous information.[14] Johnston returns the favor with a classy farewell to chief immigration inspector E. J. Lincourt. "We have gone through this trying period with your constant and helpful cooperation, with men of the finest caliber I have ever had the privilege of knowing, and who have done a job under your supervision that merits the highest praise," writes Johnston, who invites Lincourt and his wife to visit after things get back to normal.[15] Given the problems Lincourt soon encounters upon transferring back to the Grove Park Inn, that offer may sound even more tempting.

In early July the Greenbrier sends out formal invitations proudly announcing that it "has just completed its first service in war-time! We are now open for regular patronage and ready to welcome our old friends and new."[16] Advertisements fill newspapers and longtime patrons return. Ever vigilant and mindful of the wartime warning "loose lips sink ships," Johnston sends a memo to all department heads that anticipates the questions employees might hear. He suggests they respond as follows: the diplomats were courteous and caused no damage to property or any untoward incidents. Everyone should remain silent about any FBI, State Department, or INS operations. "This is one duty that we must perform 100 percent," Johnston continues. "There must be no exception to this rule, whether the guest be old or new, a friend of someone in the staff or for some other reason intimate. There must be no confidential statements. This is war, and talk is dangerous."[17]

In his typically thorough fashion, Johnston asks Sibold to prepare a comprehensive report of the detainment, and his chief clerk doesn't disappoint. A few relevant numbers contained therein: for the 201 days, the average house count was 575 per day; the total of 1,697 Axis detainees consisted of 1,054 Germans, 408 Japanese, 170 Italians, 53 Hungarians, 11 Bulgarians, and 1 Swiss from South America. In total they carried 8,519 pieces of baggage. Total gratuities paid to Greenbrier employees: $65,002. He concludes with a personal reflection: "Now that it is over after 29 weeks, which seems to be merely a dream and although it was a strain unknown because of its nature to the personnel, no one broke down [and] everyone got along extremely well. Although one cannot determine the inner feeling of each and every person connected with it, it is a complete satisfaction in knowing from expressions of officials of the State Department, as well as letters from J. Edgar Hoover saying how grateful they were at the smoothness and efficient manner in which things were handled here."[18]

The Greenbrier's delayed 1942 season lasts a scant six weeks, undergoing a transformation that mirrors the government's shuttering and reopening of the Grove Park Inn. At the end of August the Greenbrier agrees to sell to the government, which will reopen the property as an army hospital, hearkening back to Civil War days when the hotel-turned-hospital treated both Union and Confederate soldiers. Other hotels in Arkansas, California, and Florida, anticipating reduced wartime patronage, also sell or lease their properties to the army, which under a tight timeframe prefers conversion to new construction. Heavy casualties are expected from the looming invasion of North Africa. The hotel's condemned under the War Powers Act and its owner, the C&O Railroad, receives $3.3 million for its facilities and land.

A mint julep party on August 30 marks the Greenbrier's farewell to the public and drafting into wartime duty. "Tears flowed freely and unashamedly," writes one reporter, "as guests of many seasons here said their last goodbyes to the famous old hotel and the lights blinked out in the upper stories."[19] The *Charleston Daily Mail* calls it "something of a regretful tragedy to all of West Virginia and persons throughout the world who had always looked upon it as the last word in luxury and gracious hospitality."[20] The Greenbrier reopens the next year as the two-thousand-bed Ashford General Hospital, dubbed "Shangri-La for Soldiers." Charles Norelius stays on and oversees water rehabilitation exercises. Other ex-employees like Sibold, Robert Parker, and William Perry enlist and remain on duty. After the war Sibold recalls that the Axis detention "was the roughest work I ever undertook."[21]

Rough also describes the final round at the Grove Park Inn. What seems at first like a minor issue, the hiring of temporary guards, erupts into an imbroglio between INS and State. With the major part of the detainment over, INS hired many local North Carolinians to supplement the few border guards remaining. Local politicians kept badgering Lincourt to hire their friends, with U.S. Marshal Charles Price—a big fish in a small town—the biggest offender. A "bosom" friend of State rep Poole, Price often visits the hotel despite having no official role in the detainment. Once he even brought along his wife, who was refused admittance. One Sunday evening when more Japanese nationals arrived, Price strutted around the railroad station and returned to the hotel during their reg-istration. "An ugly scene could have been created on many occasions by refusing marshal Price admission to the hotel," wrote Lincourt, "but due consideration was given to Mr. Poole's position."

With tempers already on edge, Democratic North Carolina senator Robert Reynolds, undoubtedly at Price's behest, writes a letter alleging discrimination against the local guards for not receiving the same benefits as the border guards, who as permanent employees do receive treatment for which temporary hires don't qualify. Lincourt writes to his boss that Poole's attitude has become "antagonistic," and he's "demonstrated in many picayune ways that he considers himself entirely in charge of all activities concerning the detainees."[22] The bureaucratic pissing contest ends in mid-September when Poole is abruptly relieved of duty. The following month the navy leases the hotel to serve as a center for naval officers recovering from combat missions overseas. And so ends the war-time service of the Homestead, Greenbrier, and Grove Park Inn. But by year's end a fourth luxury hotel will be pressed into service for the final early round of repatriation.

As 1942 draws to a close, the former detainees have scattered to the four corners of the earth. Most will never see any fellow hotel mates from countries other than their own ever again. Each adjusts to a new life in their respective war-torn worlds, where conditions will only grow worse, much worse, in the years ahead. As New Year 1943 dawns Hans and Bébé Thomsen head off to his new assignment as head of the German legation in neutral Sweden, tasked with countering Allied influence in a wary cat-and-mouse game. There they'll enjoy far better lodging and food than anything available in Berlin or Tokyo. "Without question [Bébé] will stage the same song and dance at Stockholm as kept official Washington fooled for a long time," writes columnist Spencer Irwin. "Her role is to be super-critical of the Nazi regime and drop remarks to the effect that Germany will not be happy until it gets rid of Hitler, [a ruse] designed especially to get the diplomatic representatives of the small European neutrals assigned to Washington to commit themselves."[23] Whether the diplomatic set in Stockholm falls for her act remains unknown.

Swapping one luxury hotel for another, Hildy von Boetticher at first lived with her parents at Berlin's famed but faded Hotel Adlon. Her first breakfast there consisted of two slices of black bread with a dab of jam barely enough to cover a Ritz cracker and washed down with a cup of ersatz coffee. At least the Adlon had one of the city's best air raid shelters. Her father got her a job in a letter-censoring office, and they eventually moved into an unfurnished flat after refusing offers of better apartments that had been confiscated from Jews. As the anniversary of Pearl Harbor nears, they're invited to a party at the Japanese embassy. Hildy goes mainly for the plentiful food and drink. Tiring of endless toasts, she cheekily raises her glass and says, "To the United States of America." The crowd goes silent, and her parents anxiously look in her direction and signal it's time to go home.

Half a world away the Terasakis live in similar wartime deprivation. Their rented Tokyo apartment consists of two rooms, a kitchenette and tiny bathroom with hot water two hours a night, and rationed gas and electricity. Gwen spends much time participating in air raid drills or waiting hours in store lines for a few pieces of fish or a bunch of carrots. Her husband's name remains and remains on a waiting list for a job. One day on a train Gwen knows enough Japanese to understand when a mother tells her fussing child to hush or she'll give him to the foreigner. The child immediately stops crying. For New Year's she decides to bake a cake with spices brought from home and sugar conserved from rationing. When she uses the gas stove, a violation of regulations, their gas is cut off. But the cake's delicious.

Masuo Kato lives in Omori, midway between Tokyo and Yokohama, with his wife and elementary school–aged son and daughter. One day Kato realizes the extent of the country's brainwashing when his fifth-grade son blurts out, "Daddy, I will die for our country." Kato gently tries to explain that it's better to live for his country than to die for it. Regimentation takes added prominence, with many families beginning each day at the same hour with radio broadcasts encouraging calisthenics. Every public meeting includes the singing of the national anthem and reading of the war edict, and on the eighth day of every month a ceremony marks the day on which war was declared. On a busy street in downtown Tokyo, someone draws a large American flag and makes pedestrians walk on it. Just before Christmas, Kato prepares a radio broadcast beamed toward the United States that typifies Japanese propaganda: "Franklin Roosevelt for years before December 8, 1941 played a grand game of bluff to the limit, satisfied that the nation was prepared for war with Japan. . . . In both domestic and international affairs Roosevelt has committed grave errors of judgment leading to serious blunders."[24]

On November 8, 1942, unconcerned with such jingoistic drivel, Roosevelt unleashes Operation Torch—the polar opposite of a blunder. Thirty-four thousand troops sail unnoticed across the Atlantic, which is, in itself, an intelligence and logistical feat. Commanded by General Dwight Eisenhower in Gibraltar, 110,000 soldiers, including 20,000 British, storm ashore at dawn at three points in French North Africa. Backed by aerial and naval support the assault, within several days, delivers the smashing success America has hungered for since the Pearl Harbor debacle eleven agonizing months before.

Marking that invasion, plus England's rout of Nazi forces at El Alamein, Egypt, gifted orator Winston Churchill delivered one of his greatest wartime speeches in London. "Now this is not the end. It is not even the beginning of the end. But it is, perhaps, the end of the beginning," he said to the approving guffaws of his audience.[25] In mid-January he and Roosevelt will meet in Casablanca to finalize the Allies' strategic war effort. But first, on New Year's Eve 1942, the Roosevelts and a select group of friends gather at the White House for dinner and a movie.

The film? *Casablanca*, the Humphrey Bogart and Ingrid Bergman vehicle that Warner Brothers rushes into release in late January to capitalize on the success of the invasion—which in turn generates another wave of diplomatic detainment in America.

# 22

## Vichyswap

Six months before Operation Torch, just as the German and Italian diplomats are arriving in Lisbon, the schism widens between the puppet Vichy government and the Free French movement led by General Charles de Gaulle. In Washington DC five French embassy staffers resign in late April, fearful "of the Nazi octopus which is slowly strangling France."[1]

Columnist Helen Lombard likens French ambassador Gaston Henry-Haye to a musician playing to an empty house. And what a house it is, a castle-like Gothic structure with tall leaded glass windows. Inside it's spacious and well-appointed, with lush gardens in back reached by a double stairway winding down from an imposing stone terrace. Chafing at his enforced isolation, the convivial collaborationist expands his invitee list to keep the dinners coming and the wines flowing from his well-stocked cellar. Privately, many potential guests agonize over whether or not to attend but invariably succumb to an old Washington custom: accept and go, if for no other reason than to find out who else was invited. And the food and drink will invariably be *délicieux*. Yet when a reporter rings up to inquire about who attended a recent dinner, Henry-Haye himself comes to the phone: "It is not my habit to give out dinner lists now. This is not because I don't want to satisfy your curiosity . . . but because I don't want to provoke any criticism of my guests."[2]

The limbo ends swiftly with the Allied invasion on November 8. Days later Nazi and Italian troops sweep into previously unoccupied Vichy France, fearful of a purported (that is, imaginary) Allied invasion of the southern French mainland coast. Before communications are severed U.S. diplomats confined to their consulate send cables to Washington describing impromptu, joyous celebrations erupting in Marseille, Lyon, and along the Riviera. After taking years of guff from critics for maintaining diplomatic relations with Vichy, the Roosevelt administration takes a victory lap of sorts by revealing something that more astute, less dogmatic observers always knew: from its outpost in Vichy the United States gleaned and passed along vital intelligence. Now that diplomatic relations are severed the Japanese ambassador, a relatively recent arrival, quickly stakes claim to the highly desirable quarters soon to be vacated by the Americans.

In Washington DC the seasoned Swiss agree to represent Vichy France, just as they had Germany and Italy. In addition to the usual personal and financial problems—post-invasion, funds have been blocked—the Swiss face a most unusual dilemma: what to do with the original copy of the Treaty of Westphalia that had been sent to America for exhibition. To house French detainees from the embassy and eight consulates nationwide, State immediately opens discussions with the Hotel Hershey in Pennsylvania. This time around State will again administer and INS will provide surveillance, but the FBI will have no role.

When Allied troops invaded North Africa, it was another quiet week in sleepy Hershey. The biggest news was the display of a huge topographical map of a soil conservation plan at Hershey Farms. The public library added fourteen new books. The American Legion post held a multidenominational service to observe the twenty-fourth anniversary of the armistice ending World War I. Local papers gave favorable reviews to the road show production at the community theater of a new play starring character comedian ZaSu Pitts. The weekly *Hotel Hershey High-Lights* magazine noted that it was hosting socially prominent guests from eight states, all of whom will be evicted next week to make room for the French.

On November 12, the same day American diplomats and press from Vichy arrive by train in Lourdes, news leaks stateside of the hotel's selection. Soon the demands and petulance of the French ambassador will make his tiresome former Italian counterpart, Prince Colonna, seem like a piker. After complaining to Swiss minister Bruggmann, the Frenchman, out walking with his constant companion, his spotted dalmatian, Pop, barges uninvited into the home of William Bullitt, former U.S. ambassador to France. "Obviously distraught and miserable but by no means belligerent," recalled Bullitt, Henry-Haye grouses about the "indignities heaped upon him by the American Government" regarding his forthcoming Hershey relocation and proposed monthly allowance of a mere five hundred dollars (the equivalent in 2019 of nearly eight thousand dollars).[3] He wants to delay his departure, have his allowance tripled and fumes when told "acceptance of social invitations [are] not considered to be a necessary personal business."[4]

On the morning of November 16, 1942, the ambassador emerges from the embassy's wrought-iron entrance doors into a warm late autumn sun. With Pop by his side, he goes for a last walk through the streets of the capital. A cab brings him back an hour later, and at noontime eighteen staffers and family emerge to take their leisurely leave. Charles Brousse wears his Legion of Honor, France's highest decoration, awarded for his valor in World War I. "In an atmosphere of friendly, unhurried confusion" white-jacketed servants stow luggage into a row of limousines, a scene reminiscent of a fashionable set heading off for a weekend in the country: a far more convivial departure than those of the other Axis powers last winter.[5] At Union Station they board a train for Harrisburg, Pennsylvania. At that station the party's momentarily delayed when Pop makes a break for freedom. A deft railroad employee recaptures the pooch, and it's back into limousines and off to their new temporary home—a majestic 175-room, Mediterranean-style hotel envisioned and bankrolled by chocolate king Milton Snavely Hershey.

Inspired by the world travels of Hershey and his late wife, Kitty, the U-shaped hilltop hotel features a lobby reminiscent of Cuba, a country where he owns sugar plantations and mills. Spacious and welcoming with archways, palm trees galore, elaborate tile and marble flooring, it

**Fig. 48.** Ambassador Gaston Henry-Haye. Coll. Archives communales de Versailles, 5 Z 77-29.

features a huge fountain that "giv[es] a stranger the impression that he's walking under a waterfall."[6] The grand dining room is circular, because the egalitarian Hershey wanted everyone to enjoy a second-to-none seat with a view. "As one sits in the immaculate Dining Room," reads a promotional brochure, "and looks out upon the countryside during the day, the trees and shrubs, with birds flying about, create a quiet, serene atmosphere." Soon after its opening in 1933 came the realization that it unintentionally aped that age-old schoolboy joke: "Tight pants like cheap hotel—no ballroom." So within two years the Castilian Ballroom was added, replete with similar Spanish-style architecture.

Radio broadcaster Lowell Thomas gushingly called the hotel "a palace that out-palaces the palaces of the Maharajahs of India," yet its opulence comes at a very reasonable price: room and board at $7.50 per day for adults and $4.00 for children under twelve and guards. The guests enjoy luxurious room accommodations and fine dining, with daytime access to several acres of the spacious grounds, a freedom they immediately abuse by ignoring boundaries. But comparatively few guests arrive since the majority of French—unlike the previous Axis detainees—are sympathetic to the Allied cause. Of 245 French officials and dependents in America, 151 were released after questioning, leaving only 94 to be sequestered in Hershey. And further questioning in the months ahead diminishes that number considerably.

This round could be called detainment lite, for the French are allowed far greater leeway. Yet with so many countrymen freed, the remaining hardcore Vichyites are immediately contemptuous of their enforced stay. Attempting to fast-forward their exit, State asks the Swiss to convey an offer: the United States will immediately transport them to Portugal if France will do the same for the American diplomats in Lourdes, with both sides staying in Lisbon until details of the repatriation are worked out. But the offer's rejected, complicated by the arrest of German and Italian officials from the governing Armistice Commission during the North African invasion. Antonio Arrivabene, general counsel of Italy, complains to the Swiss minister about the Italians' ill treatment in Algiers. Their transfer by open car to a ship to transport them to England took "an unnecessary, vicious circle through the city where people hurtled insults and objects" while American soldiers "did nothing to protect them and stop the improper tumult."[7] From England the officials will be transported early next year to the United States and housed at the Ingleside Inn in Staunton, Virginia—a parallel detainment that derails chances of any imminent French repatriation.

An early Hotel Hershey advertisement had boasted: "Here you'll find your taste served with that fastidious exactness you demand."[8] But don't tell that to Henry-Haye, who is soon griping about so many indignities: the great "moral" depression of confinement, a ban on horseback riding or playing golf, the fact that they must pay for alcohol. To ease the detainees' discomfort State sends in two representatives but at first most shun them. "The many shades of political opinion among the guests and the consequent suspicion of each other added only that much more static to the already heavily surcharged atmosphere," wrote agent Edwin Plitt. Only after initial private conversations, when the detainees realized that the reps "were treating their confidences with understanding and consideration[,] did the weather inside the hotel change to fair and warmer." Eventually everyone agreed to meet and share their stories, producing what Henry-Haye likened to "a badly needed breath of fresh air from the free world."[9]

On Christmas Eve a mousy young woman—bespectacled, no makeup, in simple black clothes and flat shoes—appears at the gates of the hotel. She's Catherine Waterbury Gordon, whose late husband, a naval officer, was recently reported missing in action in the Pacific. The brokenhearted widow has come to spend the holidays with her only family, her mother, Catherine, and stepfather, Charles.

Such a sad tale, so tragic . . . and such bunk.

It's really ex–embassy intruder Betty Pack, code name Cynthia, posing (as she'd done before) as Catherine Brousse's daughter from an earlier marriage (she'd had *seven* husbands before Charles, who'd been married at least three times himself). A quick call to an in-the-dark Henry-Haye confirms her (fake) identity, and he demands her immediate admittance. But veteran agent Edgar Innes is too savvy to take the story at face value and sends her away. She checks into a local inn while a flurry of calls and telegrams fly among officials, but since it's Christmastime the wheels of bureaucracy barely budge.

Pack returns to Washington DC, and throughout January she, Brousse, Henry-Haye, and the Swiss legation bombard State with missives demanding her admittance. Brousse writes directly to Secretary Hull, citing his longtime support of America and World War I service that won him the Legion of Honor and Croix de Guerre. He drops in famous names, describing how he escorted writers to the front such as Walter Lippmann, Dorothy Thompson, Henry and Clare Boothe Luce. He even takes a swipe at unnamed "Washington members of the French Embassy, who are at large and free, whose wives were not speaking to mine because she is American but who rushed to lick the boots of some minor officials of your Department after the news of November 9."[10]

Even the oft-bickering internees agree that the U.S. government is mistreating a grieving family that only wants to be reunited. OSS chief Bill Donovan pens a personal request to Berle's assistant Fred Lyon, who'd sailed with the Germans on the *Drottningholm*. Though higher-ups at State know her real identity and past work for British and American intelligence, they're hesitant to intercede. And that's not all some people know. The FBI, studiously tracking top French officials for several years, issues a secret memo in late November that quotes a confidential source calling Brousse "a crook and man of little, if any scruples." It adds that "he is very intimate with one Mrs. Arthur Pack. . . . The exact nature of the relationship between Mr. Brousse and Mrs. Pack is unknown."[11] It's not too hard to read between the lines that the bureau knows all but isn't telling. What it probably doesn't know was OSS's initial plan to fly Brousse back to his native France, accompanied by his faux stepdaughter (who speaks flawless, unaccented French), to infiltrate the Vichy community—until Operation Torch torched that idea.

The couple had been informed by superiors that the ciphers they stole from the French embassy last summer had been vital to the success of the Allied invasion, information that won't be divulged publicly for several decades. For now, Brousse's secret agenting is secret, and many reporters are oblivious to his true loyalties. "Brousse is virtually shunned by most of the other members of the Embassy's regular staff," wrote one several months after the embassy break-in, "because he is considered too conspicuously pro-Nazi and anti-American."[12] When young Hearst reporter Howard Kingsbury-Smith privately tells Long that Brousse is decidedly an Allied supporter, a State Department aide adds a handwritten note to the memo: "I do not know Mr. Brousse personally, but I had always been under the impression that he was the reverse of what Mr. Kingsbury-Smith says."[13] Any spy who generates such diametrical opinions is obviously doing a fine job. (After the war Kingsbury-Smith went by Howard K. Smith, becoming a prominent broadcast journalist for CBS and ABC and moderating the first presidential debate between John F. Kennedy and Richard Nixon.)

On February 13, 1943, the pressures prevail, and Catherine Gordon—Betty Pack—gains admittance to the hotel. Yet despite all the hoopla to get her in, there's little intelligence to be found. Upon her arrival around fifty detainees remained, but by May that shrunk to under thirty as Frenchmen supporting the Allies are quietly freed. It lessens the numbers but deepens animosities among the frustrated few left. While the administration has successfully kept a lid on the goings-on, liberal NYC newspaper *PM Daily* gets wind and threatens to publish an exposé. The Office of Censorship gets them to delay, but the paper presses on. "The State Dept. today offered to give this newspaper the entire story," wrote reporter Willard Wiener, "with an explanation of its attitude provided the story wouldn't be printed. The offer was declined."[14] And so on March 12 *PM*'s front-page headline screams, "State Dept Secretly Frees Vichyites Interned in U.S.A."

Meanwhile, the picture brightens somewhat for journalist Paul Scheffer. In early 1943 he's finally paroled from detention and allowed to remain in the United States, but he's now wheelchair bound from the injuries resulting from his desperate bid for freedom. And he's still hounded by a handful of provocateurs. "If he was interned as a dangerous enemy alien," asks columnist Walter Winchell, "what makes him less dangerous now?"[15] Dorothy Thompson writes and offers to meet him privately: "The Scheffer story is far more complicated than anyone knows," but the doubters, like dogs fighting for a bone, won't give up.[16] Still, this

September Scheffer does something no other detainee ever does: write a lead story in the *New York Times Magazine*. It adroitly contrasts Germany in World War I and in World War II, but given his volatility his publishing contacts can only go so far: it's published under a pen name.

Back in Hershey, with so many men enlisting, jobs have opened up for local teenagers like John Vetrulli, who gets hired as a busboy. He recalls Henry-Haye's grand entrance to the dining room, always accompanied by Pop. "One time the dog jumped up on him," said Vetrulli, "and he was almost as tall as he was."[17] He also remembered an older gentleman who'd set up his canvas outside and painted a portrait of Marshal Pétain. He befriends a boy around his age and trades a box of stamps for ten dollars and a small collection of French coins. Vetrulli recalled the adults as elegant, a description confirmed by INS inspector Abner Schreiber. "There were many titled people, generals, counts, dukes, and so on and so forth," he said. "Every time you saw them there was a handshake."[18]

Golf is permitted for one foursome each morning and afternoon. Henry-Haye plays every day, weather permitting, until suffering an attack of severe chest pain in December. Several local doctors diagnose angina and recommend restricted activity in light of the "highly emotional state . . . in one so tense and high-strung who has been carrying a very heavy load and experiencing one psychic shock after another in rapid succession."[19]

Since the hotel has no stores, shopping trips are arranged once a week. One designated member compiles all requests and is accompanied by a guard to Hershey's department store. Every Wednesday detainees can visit a dentist or eye doctor in a nearby town, a privilege they soon abuse by skipping or faking appointments to go shopping instead. A request to use part of the underground parking garage for morning calisthenics is granted and then rescinded when the hotel manager's car is vandalized. When detainees complain that patrol inspectors entering the dining room in uniform make them feel like they're in a military prison, INS prohibits its men from wearing uniforms inside. Outdoors, detainees repeatedly ignore, deface, or remove signs and cross into restricted areas. Some curse out guards and damage furnishings. One time some wore their ice skates inside and ruined carpet. "The Hershey situation will soon be entirely out of hand," writes agent Bannerman. "The French are behaving like spoiled children."[20]

In at least one case they are. Three brothers are caught throwing lighted matches between seat cushions, chalking walls, and forever sneaking into off-limits areas. Instead of disciplining them, their parents blame State for forcing them into the hotel in the first place. "I have had more difficulty with this family, particularly Mrs. [Valentine] Imbault-Huart, than I have had with any of the detainees," writes agent Innes. "She is a chronic complainer and is constantly making unreasonable and petty requests," picking fights with waiters, the assistant manager, and the hotel doctor.[21] When Swiss minister Bruggmann visits the hotel he gets into a heated argument with the equally belligerent father, former head of the Vichy consulate in Chicago who'd quietly added Nazi agents to its ranks last summer, shortly before the German and Italian consulates were closed and their staffs expelled.

Like father, like son, as their eldest son, Roger, ranks as the hotel's top troublemaker. He eggs on his younger brothers, breaks an outside door lock, and is suspected of drawing a swastika in the snow. He's also in the habit of giving the Nazi salute when entering an elevator and crying "Heil Hitler," a practice he stops after an elevator boy punches him. As spring approaches, two other teen brothers go swimming in a nearby reservoir while their mother watches approvingly. Told that the reservoir supplies drinking water for the town as well as the hotel, she replies they'll continue to use it until State provides them a swimming pool. "Our guards keep wailing that we are such 'difficult' people, that the Germans and the Japs, during their internment, were so well-behaved, so well-organized, so calm," she writes to a friend. "And it's quite true, we are not very good at obeying the blowing whistles and curfew bells. . . . With the greatest of pleasure I could drop my training of French culture and diplomacy, take up a good old Irish club and bash somebody's teeth right in!"[22]

Peeved by the constant bad behavior and weekly expense of six thousand to eight thousand dollars, Breckinridge Long again suggests shipping them to Lisbon. That doesn't happen, but his suggestion does trigger another search for a smaller hotel that'll cost the government less. Meanwhile, the administration's leniency emboldens its pampered guests, while Henry-Haye continues to chafe. He's unwilling to accept that the situation is not due to any personal animosity but is based upon the overarching principal of reciprocity to match the treatment of American diplomats in France. Or more accurately, now in Germany. For in January 1943, much to the government's dismay, the Nazis abruptly moved the Americans from Lourdes, in a blinding snowstorm, across the border to Baden Baden. The German spa town's hotel offers deluxe lodging but poor food. Disgusted by the ongoing unpleasantness in Hershey, Long tries tactfully but unsuccessfully to shift responsibility back to Henry-Haye. He asks the Swiss liaison to tell the ambassador that "we look upon him as the principal person in that group and the one through whom responsibility is reflected."[23]

The futility of appealing to Henry-Haye's better nature becomes readily apparent with the resurfacing of an issue that had bedeviled State previously: hoarding. After an inexperienced on-site agent innocently okayed the ambassador's request to buy some food, Henry-Haye had the manager use the hotel's quota to make mega purchases that put all previous German, Italian, and Japanese purchasers to shame: 300 pounds of sugar, 100 pounds apiece of salt, lentils, rice, and navy beans; 12 three-pound cans of Crisco, 1,500 bouillon cubes, 12 gallons of cooking oil, 15 pounds of coffee, 12 pounds of cocoa, 5 pounds of tea, 48 cans of Spam, 6 Virginia hams, "eight pounds of beef tongue in glass jars and quite a bit of chocolate candy."[24] But lest one think he's selfish, his purchases do include 100 pounds of dog food for Pop. He even got a hotel carpenter to build a dozen wooden boxes, 4 feet long by 3 feet wide by 2 feet deep, to transport his bounty.

Wary (and undoubtedly weary) agent Bannerman demands that the food be resold back to its providers. He tells his agents to monitor all transactions henceforth "to be certain that the food products are all sent back as directed and are not otherwise concealed in French baggage." One guard's especially disgusted by the non-Gaullist's gall. "I hate like the devil to see all that stuff leave the country," he writes. "Of course we could always forget to load it on the ship. Some of those longshoremen are pretty careless sometimes."[25] In addition to hoarding there's a bit of poaching too, as State lures away two border guards to become diplomatic couriers. Although INS offers to up their pay the two men opt to depart, prompting Justice to note that it was "regrettable" State went behind their backs to induce their two staffers to leave.

Leaving is also what Betty Pack wants to do as time ticks away slowly at Hershey. Then, in a flash, boredom turns to bedlam when Brousse's wife, Catherine, barges into her "daughter's" room one morning and discovers Betty and Charles *in flagrante*. Catherine had always approved of her husband's pro-Allied undercover work but was ignorant of the affair and explodes, threatening to expose them if she doesn't kill them both first. Their battle royale echoes down the halls as the internees thrill to such a delicious homegrown scandal: an incestuous affair of the heart, *ici!* Trying mightily to maintain his cover Brousse deflects by unleashing an attack on Henry-Haye, accusing him of pro-Americanism and threatening to release evidence that will sink the ambassador upon his return to France. His assault is so convincing that a State agent who overhears their argument believes Brousse is a staunch Nazi, a misconception that the press has often falsely repeated.

To help maintain a valuable agent's career Long immediately okays Pack's release and even approves reimbursement for her train tickets, a quite generous out-of-character offer. He writes a read-between-the-lines memo decrying "a very sordid picture. There were a lot of personal antagonisms and animosities and some rather lurid details . . . in which Mr. Brousse is the aggressor. . . . There are several other rather lurid details which it seems not necessary to record but none of which reflect credit upon any of the participants."[26] Ten days later Catherine Brousse is released too, and the following month Charles departs to be reunited with Betty in DC. An exasperated and perplexed on-site agent writes his boss: "Good heavens! Are we running a hotel for these people?! I give up." Lyon replies, "Try doubling the amount of gin in your next martini and see how much better your feel," while an anonymous staffer pencils in, "If this doesn't work try leaving the vermouth out!"[27]

In late September the remaining eighteen detainees—including the quarrelsome Imbault-Huarts—relocate to the Three Hills Hotel in Warm

Springs, Virginia, a few miles from the Homestead. True to form Henry-Haye calls the move "an insult to his dignity" after learning that this "third class establishment" charges only two dollars a day.[28] Informed that they could possibly be placed instead at the Ingleside along with the Germans and Italians from the North African Armistice Commission, he declines. But then, to no great surprise, his reaction is pitch-perfect pique: "After arriving at Three Hills, Ambassador Henry-Haye refused to allow any baggage to be taken to their rooms or any of their heavy luggage to be put in storage."[29]

Ever accommodating but increasingly exasperated, State restarts its search and unearths a nearby option: the Cascades Inn, owned by the Homestead but in need of a good cleaning and refurbishing before it can accept guests. So that's where the French wind up, though State remains under no delusion that the latest hostelry will prove satisfactory: "Mr. Henry-Haye, regardless of everything that may be done to make the Inn a comfortable place for his sojourn, will probably find sufficient fault with the place to demand greater liberty for himself and his entourage as a compensation."[30]

While the Vichy detainment rankles, an out-of-the-blue bureaucratic battle explodes in November with Breckinridge Long at center stage. A low-level staffer in the Far Eastern Division, Laurence Salisbury, leapfrogs protocol and writes directly to Under Secretary of State Edward Stettinius. He excoriates Long for being personally responsible for delaying the second round of American and Japanese exchanges and for endangering future exchanges. Long immediately marshals his considerable forces, instituting a full-throated attack on a young "understrapper" who wrote "without the knowledge or consent of his superior officers."[31] Several experienced hands riddle the inexperienced writer's cherry-picked attack, dismissing his memo as "a diatribe filled with errors and misrepresentations"[32] whose "reasoning is pure fallacy."[33] The uproar never escapes beyond closed government doors, and Long emerges unscathed.

By year's end negotiations near completion for the repatriation of the remaining Vichy French, twenty-six Armistice Commission officials, and nearly seven hundred German nationals. The armistice group includes an Italian civil attaché, Alessandro Cultrera, the only detainee to be repatriated *twice*. Formerly stationed in Lima, Peru, he and his wife and five children first came to America last March aboard the *Acadia*. They stayed at the Gibson Hotel in Cincinnati before continuing east for the *Drottningholm*'s first voyage to Lisbon. Later assigned to Algiers, Cultrera was captured on November 8 and returned to America, paving the way for his record-setting double detainment and departure.

In early February 1944 departure looms for the eighteen former Vichy diplomats and their families, but Henry-Haye remains obstreperous to the end. Why will there be only one drawing room car on the train to New Jersey? Didn't Ambassador Leahy receive a private car when he left Vichy? "Whatever accommodations have been provided were the best that could be procured in existing circumstances," writes agent Plitt, "and it is well known that Americans when they have to travel today are not traveling in comfort."[34] Henry-Haye's wants extend to the ship too, and he demands dining and recreation accommodations apart from the Germans.

On February 15, 1944—fifteen long months after they were first detained the Vichyites sail out of New York harbor aboard the *Gripsholm*. After arriving in Lisbon several weeks later, Henry-Haye makes worldwide news for a rather tart exchange. He spies diplomat Douglas MacArthur II, nephew of General Douglas MacArthur, and remarks upon his notable weight loss. "You wouldn't be surprised," MacArthur replies, "if you remembered that I am just out of an internment camp in Germany." When Henry-Haye parries that "we diplomats run some risks," MacArthur lambastes the French for having handed them over to the Nazis. "You know France was occupied and there were certain legal points," dissembles the no-longer-smiling Frenchman. The gaunt American replies, "You would have probably lost weight yourself too, sir, if we had handed you over to the Japanese."[35]

With that stinging coup de grace, the curtain closes on diplomatic detainment during World War II. But there's a final postwar installment to come. It includes an ambassador who, thanks to the Allies' proficient code-breaking, unwittingly provided an invaluable window into the Axis's thinking direct from Berlin. Though he went on to live another thirty years, he never knew it.

# 23

## Last Grasp

The sun streams down on teeming New York harbor on the afternoon of July 12, 1945. Ships big and small blare a thunderous welcome, none larger than the multi-decked *Queen Mary* crammed with nearly fifteen thousand men returning from the European theater. Airplanes and a navy blimp sweep the skies as thousands watch and cheer from ferry boats and onshore. The navy carrier *West Point* and the Swedish ship *Kungsholm* carry in an additional 7,500-plus each. Along with four smaller ships that docked this morning, the day's total tallies a record-breaking 34,355 arriving troops. Flags fly; whistles and horns blast. A band on the pier switches from star-spangled favorites to "God Save the Queen" to salute arriving Canadian soldiers, recognizable by their berets. Like the Americans before and after them they pepper the docks with silver and copper coins. One man leans out a porthole waving a tartan plaid kilt of the famed Forty-Eighth Highlanders of Toronto. Fighting men cry and cavort and cheer 'til they're hoarse.

In the midst of the daylong celebration, one small somber group disembarks from the offshore side of the *West Point* along whose portside deck runs a huge banner inscribed "On to Tokyo." Though that's the

**Fig. 49.** An overdressed Ambassador Hiroshi Oshima exits a troopship in New York Harbor. Library of Congress, New York World-Telegram and Sun Newspaper Photograph Collection.

departees' homeland, they're not heading there now. Since war still rages in the Pacific, these thirty-three officials captured in Germany will be used as "blue chips" to bargain for American hostages in Japan.[1] Since they must still exit via the docks, though, the War Department's attempt to avoid attention fails as photographers snap away at the fast-stepping Japanese led by Ambassador Hiroshi Oshima. "Hundreds of GIs," writes the *New York Times*, "who lined the transport's rail hurdled candid Anglo-Saxon invective down upon them."[2] Cries like "Hey, them guys walk like they won the war" and "Dump 'em overboard" to "Shoot the bastards!" rain down. Thousands of miles from war-torn Berlin, this most ungracious reception portends an uneasy stay for these involuntary guests of Uncle Sam.

For America is a far different place than when the first Axis diplomats were rounded up after Pearl Harbor. Back then, with the war barely begun, reaction to their high-end housing was instinctual and harsh. Now Americans have endured three agonizing years of overseas battles and bloodshed. Families everywhere mourn the deaths of more than four hundred thousand GIs, whose average age was twenty-three; hundreds of thousands more lie injured, some never to recover. The heaviest casualties have come in the last year since D-Day. The Nazis have been defeated, and Hitler committed suicide in April, but war grinds on in the Pacific, where kamikaze attacks alone have killed more than five thousand soldiers.

So the hatred of the Japanese now is more venomous, less visceral. More personal and for too many, unremittingly excruciating. Hearts have hardened. When State announces the forthcoming detainment—an "accommodation" reads its press release—at the Bedford Springs Hotel in Bedford, Pennsylvania, of 132 Japanese diplomatic personnel and dependents, the reaction is fierce. (Pennsylvania has lost more than 25,000 citizens, second only to New York in number of soldiers killed.) Protests pour in from organizations and individuals. The American Legion post in McConnellsburg decries the "nip diplomats [being] handled with kid gloves and fed to the Queen's taste."[3] Inundated by constituents, Republican Congressman Harve Tibbott compiles and forwards to State a long list of complaints, including a multipage petition signed by hundreds of local residents. "I do not want to burden you," he writes, "with many hundreds more protests as they are similar in nature to the enclosed."[4] But for public consumption, Tibbott hews to his constituents' hard line: "The ruthless and barbarous Japanese are not entitled to the beauty and comforts of Pennsylvania."[5]

Letter writers flood local newspapers. One Johnstown woman facetiously invites the Nazis: "Let them come with the Japanese and enjoy the fruits of our hospitality. The fact that our children have no meat, butter, oranges, bacon, sugar, shoes and that the few things they do get are horribly inferior to what we give our enemies, should gladden our hearts."[6] Another woman writes, "If they bring them here, why not give us the privilege of entertaining them with our shotguns. I'd love it."[7] When a mother informs her son stationed in Austria, he writes to a local Veterans of Foreign Wars post: "That made my blood boil. I think something should be done about it. Of course I like thousands of other soldiers just sweat it out in some dirty old fox hole, or some distant Island when it isn't the enemy that get you it's some kind of disease," signing off as "just a G.I. in the Infantry."[8]

Newspapers overwhelmingly fan the flames. In an editorial entitled "Aren't We Being Too Nice?" the *Johnstown Tribune* reports, "To house them and dine them as though they were welcome guests come to spend a pleasant vacation seems to us to be piling it on a bit thick."[9] A gutsy competitor, the *Johnstown Observer*, calls out the naysayers, an especially courageous stand given that local papers survive only with local support. "Frankly, We Think They Are Nuts," reads its front-page editorial. "Horny-handed workingmen, embattled Legionnaires and others yammer excitedly because a hundred or so Jap diplomats will be stabled at Bedford Spring for a few weeks. . . . The treatment accorded a few Japs is a fly speck—but the lack of adequate housing for America's working millions is a mighty blot on the national map. Let's get a sense of proportion and become all stirred up about big things instead of becoming hot and bothered about so many little things."[10]

Recently acquired by new owners, the Bedford Springs Hotel boasts an illustrious history. Renowned for the purported curative powers of its mineral springs, it opened in the early 1800s and over the next century and a half attracted a powerful and influential clientele including a half dozen presidents such as Thomas Jefferson, Andrew Jackson, and native son James Buchanan. For a time in the mid-1920s it was managed by Loren Johnston before he joined the Greenbrier. But the Great Depression cut deeply into its wealthy customer base and brought bankruptcy in 1936. In early 1942 the navy bought and converted it into a school for training radio operators, from which six thousand sailors graduated before it closed in late 1944. On June 7 the new owners, which include the manager of Washington's famed Shoreham Hotel, offered to house the Japanese for a minimum of four months at very favorable rates: $3 a day per person for room, government personnel at $1.50, plus meals that adhere to rationing guidelines on a cost-plus basis. Less than three weeks later the government signed on, and renovations began immediately.

Inside and out, workmen and gardeners toil away. Carpenters build sentry boxes and a high-board fence facing well-traveled Route 220. Resentment grows when waters from a local spring, which are guaranteed for public use in perpetuity, are cut off to stop people from parking and loitering in front of the hotel's grounds. Soon access is granted to another spring nearby. Locals fill positions as telephone operators, waitresses, chambermaids, clerks, chefs, busboys, and more, while local men are hired as guards to supplement border patrol agents. Soon the *Bedford Gazette* reports a shipshape result: "The woodwork on the Annex is gleaming, glistening white against the red brick of the structure. Many of the rooms have been freshly papered and spacious lawns which are always kept velvety and beautiful during the summer season are in that condition now."[11]

Three State Department representatives host a meeting in its dining room to address concerns, attracting area Veterans of Foreign Wars and American Legion members, Gold Star Mothers, reporters, civic leaders, and civilians. They stress the diplomats won't be coddled but "treated as prisoners, not guests." The pool and golf course will be off-limits; meals will be cafeteria style. In the following Q&A session many unconvinced attendees vent and carp. When one announces plans for a multicounty radio broadcast opposing the detention, State agent John Peurifoy quickly responds. "I wasn't going to mention this," he says, "but my own brother is a prisoner of the Japanese. We must see this through."[12] He gets support from Brigadier General Leonard Boyd, just back from a long tour of duty in the South Pacific. "I've seen prisoners in camp in the Philippines," he says, "and we should be willing to sacrifice anything to save our people from that. Things that are said and done in the U.S. are carried back to Japan and may result in making mistreatment of prisoners worse than it has been."[13]

Vocal opposition fades as the town uneasily awaits the imminent arrival. The local grapevine hums and on August 3 the *Bedford Gazette* reports that local guards hired more than a month ago have finally received notice to report the following Wednesday. Next week's already shaping up to be a big one as the seventieth annual Bedford Fair opens on Monday for five days of circus and vaudeville acts, stage shows featuring "beautiful girls, dance teams, musical numbers, gorgeous scenery," harness and pony races, livestock exhibitions, and the motorcyclin' Hollywood Hell Drivers: "the most reckless, fearless stuntmen who have ever lived, defying death at every turn."[14] Wow, it sounds like ole Bedford Springs is in for one heck of a razzmatazz spectacular. What could possibly top that? How about the war in the Pacific, which takes an unprecedented, devastatingly deadly turn on the same day the circus comes to town.

At 8:16 a.m. Japanese time on August 6, 1945, the American bomber *Enola Gay* releases the world's first atom bomb over the city of Hiroshima: a five-ton device equivalent to fifteen thousand tons of TNT. It reduces four square miles of city to ruins, killing an estimated 80,000 people immediately and another 40,000 by year's end. Three days later the United States drops another bomb at Nagasaki and kills 75,000. That same day, sequestered Ambassador Oshima and five aides hear the news while being driven from Washington DC to Bedford. "They didn't say anything," said one State agent.[15]

On Tuesday, August 14, at 7 p.m. President Harry Truman delivers the eagerly awaited news of Japan's surrender. The war is over. Celebrations erupt in cities and hamlets nationwide, and Bedford is no exception as thousands pour into town. A cacophony of car and truck horns, factory whistles, loudspeakers blaring patriotic music, and ringing church bells can't drown out the shouts and cheers and cries and tears of men, women, and children. A jubilant crowd celebrates outside the Bedford Springs Hotel, with their noise clearly carrying inside to where the internees, now numbering some 150, gather at 8 p.m. "The Japanese government has accepted the conditions of the Potsdam declaration," Oshima tells the stone-faced assemblage. "We are therefore commanded by the Emperor to lay down our arms. I wish to add that I appreciate all the effort you have made in this struggle and I feel assured that while your efforts have not enabled us to win, you have at least done your utmost for the Emperor." An agent from State later tells a reporter, "They seemed to take it very placidly. There was no more reaction on their faces than if they had been told that Detroit won the American League pennant."[16] (Which they do next month, followed by a 4–3 triumph over the Chicago Cubs in the World Series.)

Joyousness outside, joylessness within. While the outrage of townspeople at their presence gradually dissipates, the captives' sense of helplessness and fear of what lies ahead only deepens. How long will they be held? Are family and friends still alive? For anyone from Hiroshima or Nagasaki, the weight must be excruciating. Yet Oshima and other high-ranking officials face an even more daunting personal dilemma: war crimes trials. The day after arriving in Bedford a *New York Times* headline screamed, "SOVIET DECLARES WAR ON JAPAN," but a below-the-fold story delivered even more devastating news. A new code of international law, announced from London, "extends to the highest level the principle of individual responsibility for crimes against society. . . . Individuals are to be held responsible for 'planning, preparation, initiation or waging of a war of aggression, or a war in violation of international treaties.'"[17]

Though Oshima—a fluent German speaker and longtime confidant of top Nazi leaders including Hitler—doesn't know it, his part has been minutely documented. For more than four years he telegraphed cables from Berlin, not knowing that he each time he was also telegraphing Axis plans to the Allies. His cables were intercepted, decoded, translated, and transmitted to U.S. military leaders often before being received by their intended recipients in Tokyo—despite Thomsen's warning in April 1941 of the Allies' code-breaking, which the Japanese arrogantly ignored. "His reports [were] well-informed, richly detailed and at times surprisingly objective for a Nazi sympathizer," wrote author Charles Fenyvesi after hundreds of documents were declassified in 1998, more than twenty years after Oshima died.[18]

Oshima fled the collapsing capital last April 15 as Soviet artillery and bombers reduced Berlin to rubble. He and his staff joined his wife, Toyoko, at a resort hotel in the Alps south of Salzburg, where they were captured a month later by the U.S. Seventh Army. Major General Maxwell D. Taylor—who had parachuted with his troops onto Normandy Beach on D-Day, becoming the first Allied general to land in France—arrived at the hotel. In a lobby filled with Japanese he asked the duty officer, in English, to summon the ambassador. Oshima never appeared, so he asked again. When another Japanese made a s(n)ide comment, Taylor tore into him in fluent, idiomatic Japanese. The men scattered, and soon Oshima came hurrying down the stairs. Turns out Taylor had served at the U.S. embassy in Tokyo and thus perfectly understood the man's comment that the ambassador was taking a nap and that the American could "cool his heels."

Which is what the 180 interned diplomats, attachés, businessmen, engineers, news correspondents, servants, and families do as summer turns to fall in the picturesque Central Pennsylvania countryside. Three women are pregnant. Dependents include several newborns, two dozen children under ten, and nearly a dozen teenagers. For the first time ever, a detainee dies when the oldest, a sixty-five-year-old cook, collapses while playing cards. Though an American doctor quickly arrives and administers a shot of adrenaline, he dies without regaining consciousness. Two Japanese doctors examine him and concur with his diagnosis of a heart attack. The body is transported to Pittsburgh for cremation, and the ashes are given to Oshima for their eventual return to Japan. Responsibility for writing up the report falls to agent John O'Hanley, who'd served so ably at the Greenbrier and Grove Park Inn and has been resummoned to lend an experienced hand.

To address any remaining public objections to their presence, State suggests its employees tell citizens that "Very fortunately the Government's objectives have now been attained by the complete capitulation of the

Japanese Government without the need of prolonged negotiations."[19] However a shortage of transport at a time when the military still takes precedence, back-and-forth overseas negotiations and standard bureaucratic foot-dragging ensures that the stay won't be ending quickly. Plus the government has committed to pay for a minimum four-month stay, so there's no financial inducement to leave early. Internees are left to grapple with common personal problems. Several European women married to Japanese fear expulsion to a country they've never even seen. A Hungarian woman wants a divorce, a request ultimately nixed due to Pennsylvania residency requirements. Many brought only foreign currencies that are exceedingly difficult to convert into U.S. dollars. In the jumble of leaving Europe many left behind or lost luggage that, despite inquiries by the Swiss, never reappears.

In early September an official from the Office of Price Administration arrives unannounced. Claiming to have proof that State is violating the law by purchasing food at prices above OPA ceilings, he demands admission to the hotel. Since standing policy prohibits any unauthorized visitors, guards rebuff him. The man protests to his bosses in Washington, but a State investigation reveals he was previously "one of the most unreasonable and persistent critics of the Department's policy" and only wants to stir up trouble—which is exactly what a nosy newsman does.[20]

James Young, a Hearst correspondent in Japan for more than a dozen years before the war, was imprisoned there for several months in 1940 for reporting on its use of chemical weapons in China. He's written several anti-Japanese books including *Behind the Rising Sun*, which was adapted into a 1943 potboiler from RKO Pictures that director Edward Dmytryk, an émigré from Nazi Germany, noted, "We bought the book for its title [and] concocted a story based largely on incidents as they had been reported from the Orient before Pearl Harbor."[21] Young visits Bedford and writes a three-part syndicated series whose titles alone—like "Jap War Figures Loll Here in Ease" and "Key Jap Plotters Claim Immunity"—bespeak its yellow journalistic style, a Hearst specialty.

Though denied entry, like all outsiders, he colorfully describes the scene. "The Japs arrived with hundreds of fine leather goods pieces, golf bags, walking sticks, tennis racquets, lap robes, radios, fine tweed suits and overcoats, perambulators and $15,000 in American currency." Young also claims an appreciative Japanese man tipped a bellboy $20 (the equivalent in 2019 dollars of $275) and that a hotel store sells "kimonos, shoes, clothing and drug store items [including] pints of perfumed hair tonic."[22] His fanciful claims bedevil State, which compiles a three-page memo that concludes the article is "inaccurate and misleading."[23] In late December, after the Japanese have departed, Young returns for a victory lap with a speech that the *Bedford Gazette* calls "one of the most informative talks ever given at a Ladies Night of the Bedford Rotary Club."[24]

The war trial worries of the top officials redouble in mid-October when twenty-four Nazis including Joachim von Ribbentrop, Hermann Göring, Wilhelm Keitel, and Albert Speer are indicted in a Nuremberg courtroom. Oshima knew them all well, having dined and plotted and celebrated during his four years as the key link between Imperial Japan and the Third Reich. Another prisoner had been arrested with Oshima at the Alpine hotel: Walther Funk, also known as "The Banker of Gold Teeth" for overseeing the extraction of gold fillings from concentration camp inmates and their melting down into bullion for the Reichsbank. "Chubby Walther Funk, Hitler's purse keeper, broke down in tears today," wrote the *New York Times*, "when he and his cohorts received their copies of the indictment."[25] Funk later receives a life sentence; Oshima knows his time is coming.

Meanwhile, some Nazis who plied their devious trade in America make an odd reappearance in *The House on 92nd Street*, a documentary-style, now-it-can-be-told melodrama about spies out to steal atom bomb secrets. Made with the cooperation of the FBI, the 20th Century Fox film incorporates actual footage of Hans Thomsen, Ulrich von Gienanth, Friedrich von Boetticher and others shot by G-men hidden in a building across the street from the embassy using cameras with telephoto lenses. Mixing this genuine prewar footage into a fictionalized tale makes for a groundbreaking box-office hit that even wins an Oscar for best story.

It's playing in theaters nationwide on November 16, 1945, when the internees depart in seven buses and an ambulance, the latter carrying two ill children. The caravan drives to Cumberland, Maryland, where they board a westbound train. Shortly after their departure a fire starts near the place where they'd boarded the buses. A local sixty-year-old guard dies after suffering a heart attack while fighting the blaze, which authorities later surmise was caused by a carelessly discarded cigarette. That same week local Sergeant John Murphy, a prisoner of war for more than three years, returns to Bedford on leave from his hospitalization in Virginia. "His impression of the Japs was that they were 'nothing but animals,' primitive despite the veneer of Western civilization they acquired," wrote the *Bedford Gazette*. "Murph" recalled talking to a fellow soldier who'd visited Hiroshima. "'It wasn't burned,' he was told. 'It was melted.'"[26]

Immediately upon their departure, workmen begin additional repairs and renovations. Though it closes for the winter, plans call for a grand reopening next spring to reclaim its mantle as one of America's premier resort hotels. The newspaper speculates that the internment netted the area thousands upon thousands of dollars of free publicity with extensive coverage in metropolitan papers and national magazines.

Two days after Thanksgiving the 184 internees arrive in Seattle and board the troop transport SS *General George M. Randall*. Soon they're joined by 1,300 deportees of Japanese descent who renounced their citizenship at relocation centers. On the gray drizzly morning of Sunday, November 25, 1945—the antithesis of their tumultuous entrance into sunny New York harbor last July—the ship sails quietly for Yokohama.

Detainments that began with a bang end in a calm winter.

# Afterword

If I ever write a book about the Greenbrier—and we all want to write novels or short stories about the Greenbrier—then it will be a treatise on the rumor. Everyone knows how rumors arise. But no one who was not interned knows what scale they can assume when eight hundred people are locked together in a small space, and when all external events reach them only through multiple filters.
—Margret Boveri, *Verzweigungen*

From inside a splendid prison, Margret Boveri and her fellow detainees speculated endlessly. When will we leave? How much luggage can we take? Are we really going to be sent down to Georgia for the rest of the war? Did a certain German diplomat sneak off to Washington DC for a day? Why were all those German waiters arrested, anyway?

Rumor upon rumor sparked and spread and faded away, with another always sure to follow. The detainees were no ship of fools, an allegory dating to Plato's *Republic* that Katherine Anne Porter spun into *Ship of Fools*, a book set aboard a luxury German liner crossing the Atlantic in the early thirties. But they were often fooled. One day word spread about a demonstration in the swimming pool of a waterproof, unsink-able trunk that could be converted into an inflatable raft in the event of shipwreck. People rushed to the pool for the nonexistent presentation. Another time word went around that cash-starved German diplomats from a South American country would be auctioning off silver they'd brought along. People poured into the Virginia Room, eager not just for the diversion but to perhaps snap up a bargain. But as time passed the realization dawned that they'd been had by an unknown prankster.

Running even deeper than rumor was rancor. For this detainment represented the only time in history that Axis country representatives of all stripes were forced to live side by side. With the prewar veneer of false diplomatic bonhomie stripped away, antagonism emerged quickly between the Germans and Italians and later even more vigorously between the Germans and Japanese—distrust that presaged tensions that were to persist throughout the war.

"The German and Italian children began to fight and beat each other up," recalled Swiss liaison Frederick Stocker, one of a bare handful of outsiders allowed to live among the detainees. "Also from other symptoms one could easily detect that the two nationalities, although brothers in the war, in reality did not like each other at all." After Gwen Terasaki and the Japanese stopped in east Africa en route to Japan, the Axis delegation stationed there hosted a party. "It should have been most pleasant. Surely we had been pent up long enough to be gay if given the chance [yet] I had the distinct feeling that our hosts did not really like us, that their hospitality was insincere and somewhat forced. . . . As for the Italians, my husband remarked that they could only be described as 'among those present.'"

That's a pretty fair encapsulation of the makeup of the Axis triumvirate. The discomfort Terasaki felt that night didn't dissipate upon her return to Japan; it increased. "All during the war I was to see how unnatural and even hostile the Germans and Japanese were to each other in all their relationships. The hostility I was to experience toward myself throughout the war occurred almost without exception because I was mistaken for a German. There was none of that respect and hearty admiration for the Germans that I had always seen shown between the British and Americans."

While Terasaki's personal recollections cannot be discounted, she unconsciously plays up a common refrain associated with the Allies during World War II: "one for all and all for one." While this made for a great gung-ho slogan, it wasn't true. During the war the Brits and the Russians fielded far more—and more effective—spies in America than the Nazis, Italians, or Japanese ever did. The Allies fought together but, eyeing postwar dominance, often deceived each other in pursuit of widely different agendas.

As the Axis envoys departed their splendid prisons, they crossed paths with American counterparts gratefully returning home. In Lourenço Marques, Masuo Kato met up with an old acquaintance, newsman Max Hill. Over drinks they compared their respective confinements: Hill's mistreatment versus Kato's luxurious life.

When they finished, Hill simply said, "I am proud of my country."

Hill soon published his account of his barbaric treatment—incarceration, solitary confinement, freezing cells, meager food, harsh interrogations and a sham trial—in the *New York Times*. Shortly thereafter, even Japanese American newsman and ex-Domei reporter Clarke Kawakami slammed Japan's outrageous actions while lauding America's high-mindedness: "The magnanimous treatment of Japanese newsmen in this country was a shining example of fairness and justice possible only in a land of free, democratic ideals."

Who made it all possible? Unsung Americans who worked long and hard. Those at the Greenbrier received encouragement and thanks from their boss, Loren Johnston:

You may all rest assured that our Government has a very good reason for everything they request us to do, and it is not our privilege to question. It is our duty to serve these people for the duration of their stay in the best possible manner. A great many millions of people are serving their governments under greater hardships than any of us have known up to this time, so I bespeak your continued loyalty and assure you of my keen appreciation. It must be remembered that this country is in a grievous war which will affect each and every one of us no matter what our work may be, and in order that we may properly perform our service we must be polite and patient, helpful to each other, and do our full duty.

Duty is a word most often applied to soldiers and, indeed, Johnston's words reminded me of a letter that my father, one of millions of World War II veterans, received in 1945 from Secretary of the Navy James Forrestal. It read, in part: "You have served in the greatest navy in the world. It crushed two enemy fleets at once, receiving their surrenders only four months apart. It set our ground armies on the beachheads of final victory. The nation which you served at a time of crisis will remember you with gratitude. For your part in these achievements you deserve to be proud as long as you live."

My dad ran a men's clothing store on Main Street started by his grandfather out of a covered wagon in 1878. He would have empathized with the hotel employees who faithfully served their customers day in and day out, and to whom I dedicated this book. But hey, Dad, this book's for you and Mom too.

# Epilogue

After the war . . .

**Masuo Kato** was one of four Japanese journalists to cover Japan's surrender to General Douglas MacArthur aboard the battleship USS *Missouri* on September 2, 1945. The next year he published his memoir, *The Lost War*, to worldwide acclaim. Kato served as managing editor and executive editor at Kyodo News Agency, which was created in 1945 after Domei was disbanded, and hosted annual gatherings in Tokyo for fellow University of Chicago alumni for many years. He died in 1986 at age eighty-seven.

**Paul Scheffer** eked out a living as a freelance writer and editor in Chicago. He later moved to a farm in White River Junction, Vermont, where he continued to write and remained close to Dorothy Thompson. He passed away in 1963 at age seventy-nine. Publisher Henry Regnery wrote about him, "Paul Scheffer was a rare person: he experienced the winds of his time at their cruelest and bent with them when he had to, but never surrendered his integrity as a person."

**Gwen Terasaki** returned to America in 1949 with her daughter, **Mariko**. In 1957 her memoir *Bridge to the Sun* became a surprise best seller that was made into a movie starring Carroll Baker. She passed away in 1990 at age eighty-four. Her husband, **Hidenari Terasaki**, assisted at the International Military Tribunal for the Far East in Tokyo in 1946. Afterward, in increasingly poor health, he suffered a stroke and heart attack and died in Japan in 1951 at age fifty.

**Hans Thomsen** returned to his hometown of Hamburg, where he headed its Red Cross office. He remained quite active after his retirement in 1963 and stayed in touch with many friends worldwide. He served on the boards of numerous charitable organizations and was board chair of the Anglo-German Club. When he passed away in 1968 at age seventy-seven, his death notice read, in part: "His great tact and his kind and obliging manner will always be a role model." He and his wife, **Bébé Thomsen**, separated after the war but remained close. She spent her summers in Oberstdorf in the Bavarian Alps, her winters in Munich. She passed away in Neustadt in Holstein, on the Baltic Sea, in 1973 at age eighty-one, her oft-repeated promise to return to America unfulfilled.

Working in a mayor's office in Germany, **Hildegard von Boetticher** met British officer Horace Marsden. They married and had three children before immigrating to Canada. In 1959 they drove from their home in Kitchener, Ontario, to Lynchburg, Virginia, where she finally received her BA degree from Randolph-Macon Woman's College. She received her MA from the University of Waterloo, where she later taught and served as dean of women. She died in 1988 at age sixty-eight.

**Else Arnecke** returned to America in 1952, working in New York for twenty more years before returning to Germany. She died in her hometown of Bremerhaven in 2011 at age ninety-nine, three months shy of her hundredth birthday.

**Margret Boveri** wrote movingly of the destruction of Berlin she witnessed in 1945. Despite her prickly disposition, this passionate nationalist became one of Germany's most influential postwar writers but always wrestled with her life under Nazism. She died in 1975 at age seventy-five.

**Charles Brousse** and **Betty Pack** journeyed to liberated Paris in 1944. In the spring of 1945 they bought and refurbished an ancient chateau in a small village in the Pyrenees. They married and lived happily for nearly twenty years, until she was diagnosed with cancer. She died in December 1963, one week after her fifty-third birthday. Disconsolate and ailing, Charles died ten years later.

Retiring from the Italian Foreign Service in 1947, **Prince Ascanio dei Principi Colonna** lived with his wife in accustomed luxury at his palatial spread in Rome, which included many stately buildings and gardens. He died in 1971 at age eighty-eight.

Lifelong unapologetic Pétainist **Gaston Henry-Haye** fled to South America shortly after the war to escape death threats from the resistance. He returned to France in 1950, wrote a bitter autobiography, and in 1996 won a libel lawsuit against British journalist H. Montgomery Hyde for his claim that Henry-Haye had collaborated with the Germans. He died in 1983 at age ninety-three.

While **Laura Ingalls** was in prison, her spewing of racist, pro-Nazi rhetoric got her beaten up by fellow inmates. After her release in 1943, she moved to Burbank, California, and faded into obscurity. She lobbied continuously, and unsuccessfully, for a presidential pardon. She died in 1967 at age seventy-four.

After retiring in 1942 when the Greenbrier became an army hospital, **Loren Johnston** moved back to his home in Clearwater, Florida. He died in 1955 at age seventy-eight. A stained-glass window in his memory still stands at Saint Thomas Episcopal Church in White Sulphur Springs: "To the Glory of God and in Loving Memory of Loren Robert Johnston 1877–1955."

In February 1945 **Saburo Kurusu**'s son, Ryo, a pilot, was killed when struck by a plane's propeller. Although unindicted by the International Military Tribunal for the Far East, Kurusu himself was barred from holding postwar public office. His home in Tokyo was destroyed during the war, so he and his wife, Alice, moved to a countryside estate. He became a visiting professor at Tokyo University and died in 1954 at age sixty-eight, forever insisting that he had no prior knowledge of the attack on Pearl Harbor. The author is unconvinced.

**John Lawler** worked at the FBI field office in Richmond until retiring in 1950. He later worked for the CIA and an insurance company and served on the Richmond City Council. He was bludgeoned to death in 1982 during a robbery by the teenage brother of an underage prostitute, a young woman the divorced Lawler had met several times before.

In November 1943 **Breckinridge Long** gave misleading testimony before a House committee that inflated the number of refugees admitted to the United States. This led to the revelation of his persistent behind-the-scenes efforts to limit Jewish immigration and suppress information about the Holocaust. Demoted, he resigned in 1944 and spent his later years far from the spotlight, focusing on breeding and racing horses. He died in 1958 at age seventy-seven.

**Roy Morgan** served as associate counsel and investigator in Tokyo at the International Military Tribunal for the Far East. Later he held a number of positions for the U.S. and Japanese governments, including special assistant to the secretary of commerce, U.S. advisor to Japan's prime minister, and head of U.S. trade missions to Japan. He died in Florida in 1985 at age seventy-six.

Unindicted by the International Military Tribunal for the Far East, **Kichisaburo Nomura** began a new career managing the electronics and consumer goods giant JVC. He also served on a prestigious committee studying Japan's rearmament and was elected to the upper house of the National Diet (parliament) of Japan. He died in 1964 at age eighty-six, and, like his colleague Saburo Kurusu, forever insisted that he had no prior knowledge of the attack on Pearl Harbor.

**John O'Hanley** traveled worldwide as security officer for Secretary of State John Foster Dulles. On a trip to Rome he was thrilled to meet the pope and also reconnect with one of the Italian detainees, Alberto Rossi Longhi. He later escorted many notable world leaders visiting the United States, including the shah of Iran, the Duke and Duchess of Windsor, Israeli prime minister Ben Gurian, and Sean O'Kelly, president of Ireland. He died in 1959 at age sixty.

At the International Military Tribunal for the Far East trials in Tokyo in 1946, **Hiroshi Oshima** unsuccessfully argued that his wartime activities were shielded by diplomatic immunity. Found guilty of conspiracy to wage wars of aggression in violation of international law, he was sentenced to life imprisonment. Paroled in 1955, he was granted clemency in 1958. He died in 1975 at age eighty-nine, unaware that his decrypted telegrams from Berlin offered unprecedented insight into Axis diplomacy during World War II.

During the war, **Dr. Carl Sennhenn** supervised the starvation, murder, and poisoning of thousands of children, whose brains were supplied to Nazi researchers. He received a seven-year sentence at Nuremberg. Sennhenn is the only known German detainee at the Greenbrier to be convicted of war crimes.

In 1943 **Charlie Spruks** moved to Miami, where he oversaw the visits of foreign dignitaries and worked for Nelson Rockefeller's Office of Coordinator of Inter-American Affairs. He later returned to Washington DC and worked as assistant protocol chief. He died in 1966 at age seventy.

In 1942 **Dr. Frederick Stocker** joined the staff of McPherson Hospital in Durham, North Carolina, where he worked as a surgeon for more than thirty years. He also served as a professor of ophthalmology at Duke University and the University of North Carolina and was a member of many medical organizations. He passed away in 1974 at age eighty-one. His wish for his eightieth birthday was to have breakfast—caviar and champagne—in bed. And he did.

After being released from the mental hospital in 1944, the younger **Friedrich von Boetticher** enlisted in the U.S. Army and served in the Pacific. He became a U.S. citizen, married, worked on the railroads, and died in Illinois in 1997 at age eighty-six.

# ACKNOWLEDGMENTS

Early on I realized that writing about events that took place more than seventy-five years ago would make finding living participants with memories of the era problematic. So while most of my research focused on materials in archives and libraries—more on that shortly—I unearthed some leads, reached out, and was immeasurably rewarded by connecting with four hearty folks. Dietrich von Knoop, once a young lad interned with his parents, phoned from Germany and not only shared his recollections but led me to his older brother, George, who generously did the same. I corresponded with Takeo Iguchi, whose memories of his life as a mature-beyond-his-years eleven-year-old in 1942 were invaluable. Finally I spoke with delightful Lucy Cornett, whose father ran the men's clothing stores at the Greenbrier and Homestead. I can't thank each of them enough for answering my call and providing vivid firsthand recollections that help bring history alive.

I also tracked down some descendants. Sprightly Jean Russell shared stories and memorabilia of her father Charlie Spruks, as Don O'Hanley did for John, his dad. V. Elizabeth Powell not only shared her grandfather Frederick Stocker's wonderful unpublished memoir but gave me an impromptu lesson in high German. My deepest thanks to all, and to Shelly Craft, Sondra Lincourt, and Malcolm and Celia Lovell. To those descendants who never answered my entreaties, I'd have been delighted to include memories of your forebears too.

Unquestionably my richest source of information was the inestimable Robert Conte, historian at the Greenbrier for four decades and counting. I mean, really, how many hotels do you know that have a full-time historian on staff? I know of only one, and he opened up his unique trove of materials and shared one-of-a-kind stories of hotel lore. Time and time again he'd delve into one of those battered metal file cabinets lining his overflowing office and unearth some nugget. Bob, your gentlemanly erudition runs as deep as the legendary White Sulphur Springs, and any book I might have produced without your input would be poorer still.

My cold inquiries, often with the help of Google Translate, brought many kind replies from people overseas. From Japan, my thanks to Professor Haruo Iguchi, Takeo's son; Yoichi Kosukegawa at Kyodo News; the late Fumio Matsuo; and especially author Hideharu Torii, who generously mailed me an autobiographical article by Masuo Kato that was unobtainable in America. Thanks to Yukiyo Moorman, stateside, for translating said article. Great thanks to Takuya Arai, head of the Kyodo branch in Washington DC, for obtaining and translating invaluable documentation from Tokyo.

From Germany, my thanks to Meike Borgert, Anna Maria Boß, Claudia Bourcevet, Dr. Norman Domeier, Helga Mügge, Harriet Scharnberg, and Ines Schröder-Heberle. My especial thanks to Sabina von Thuemmler, who masterfully negotiated the German genealogical system, impenetrable to this outsider; if you ever need a genealogist in Germany, look her up.

Archivists and librarians are an overwhelmingly welcoming lot who freely unlock their vaults for us interlopers to explore. Thanks so much to Rick Armstrong of the Bath County Historical Society, with its unparalleled collection of materials related to the Homestead and Hot Springs, Virginia; Jessica Smith and David Wood at the Historical Society of Washington DC; Mat Darby of Georgetown University; Cecilia Brown of the University of Virginia; Jackie Hoyt of Syracuse University; Laurel Howard of Catholic University; Violaine Levavasseur at the Archives communales in Versailles; Cameron Penwell at the Asian Division of the Library of Congress; and William Baehr of the FDR Presidential Library. To the staff members at the National Archives and Library of Congress: though you toil largely anonymously, your daily efforts to address countless researchers' requests are much appreciated and make all the difference between a finding uncovered or something remaining buried in the stacks.

Years ago Dr. Alfred Beck trod ground similar to mine for his dissertation and later superb biography of General Friedrich von Boetticher.

He graciously shared both his prodigious knowledge of this swathe of history and the considerable materials he amassed for his book. Thanks, Fred, for your insight and advice. Thanks to raconteur extraordinaire George Borden for sharing your knowledge and vast collection of World War II memorabilia, some of which is reproduced herein. Thanks also to Tiffany Cabrera at the Office of the Historian at the Department of State for answering an especially thorny question or two.

In the newspaper world—and yes, there are thankfully still some newspaper readers out there in this digital age—I'd like to thank (Queen) Margo Oxendine at *The Recorder* and John Kelly at the *Washington Post.* Their interviews and stories about the book elicited, in turn, some extraordinary contacts who provided me yet more unique material. One paper big, one paper small: two dedicated reporters whose legwork goes the extra mile to deliver for their readers. And for this author.

Thanks to new friends down in Hot Springs and Warm Springs and White Sulphur Springs who made this small-town New England boy feel right at home: Lynn Swann and Eileen Judah at the Homestead, Frank Collins, Opal Gazzola, and Nancy and Robin Vance. Thanks also for the assistance and advice of Benton Arnovitz, Jen Grieve, Aviva Kempner, Scott Seligman, Peter Spalding, Yui Suzuki, and Carol Briggs Waite. Thanks to Jane and Drew Spalding for translation and research help, but most of all for your irreplaceable friendship. And step right up, artist extraordinaire Stephen Fischer, for your masterful—or as they say in Boston, wicked pissa—cover design. Thanks, pal.

My thanks to several fine publishing professionals. Agent Ike Williams at Kneerim & Williams, who not only knows all but shares all about the vagaries of publishing. Thanks to editors Tom Swanson and Elizabeth Zaleski at Potomac and to painstaking copyeditor Sarah C. Smith of Arbuckle Editorial.

Finally, a fiercely debated adage among historians says history is written by the victors. For this book I'd say history was written by the contemporaneous letter and memo writers, especially Greenbrier manager Loren Johnston and State Department men John O'Hanley and Charlie Spruks. Reading their writing—sometimes witty, sometimes eloquent, always candid—more than three-quarters of a century later felt a bit like eavesdropping. O'Hanley wrote to his boss that Johnston "is a nice old gentleman who's almost as prolific as I am on this letter writing." Thanks to my hat trick of yeomen wordsmiths—Loren, John, and Charlie—for illuminating your worlds and making my job that much easier.

# NOTES

ABBREVIATIONS

BLP     Breckinridge Long Papers

*DGFP*    *Documents on German Foreign Policy*

DTC     Dorothy Thompson Collection

*FRUS*    *Foreign Relations of the United States*

GB      Historical Collection, Greenbrier Hotel, White Sulphur Springs, West Virginia

LOC     Library of Congress

MBPH    The "Magic" Background of Pearl Harbor

NARA    National Archives and Records Administration, Washington DC

NACP    National Archives and Records Administration, College Park, Maryland

RMC     Roy Morgan Collection

RG      Record Group

SUSC    Syracuse University Special Collections

SWPD    Special War Problems Division

UVAL    University of Virginia Law Library

PROLOGUE

1. "Roosevelt Sends Note to Hirohito," *Sunday Star*, December 7, 1941, 1.

2. Franklin Delano Roosevelt, campaign address at Boston, Massachusetts, October 30, 1940, American Presidency Project, http://www.presidency.ucsb.edu/ws/ ?pid=15887.

3. *The American*, January 1942, 14.

4. Doherty, "Hawaii Looks Ahead," 662.

5. Kato, *Lost War*, 58.

6. Hotta, *Japan 1941*, 280.

7. Kato, *Lost War*, 59.

8. Paul W. Ward, "Japanese Embassy Guarded by Washington Police Squad," *Baltimore Sun*, December 8, 1941, 4.

9. Ralph Blumenthal, "Chronicler of War Nears 100, and Counting," *New York Times*, October 28, 2013, https://lens.BLPogs.nytimes.com/2013/10/28/chronicler-of -war-nears-100-and-counting/.

10. Mike Richman, "Flashback: Forgotten Redskins-Eagles Game," Redskins.com, December 30, 2011, www.redskins.com.

11. Terasaki, *Bridge to the Sun*, 3.

12. Letter, FBI Director J. Edgar Hoover to Adolf A. Berle Jr., December 9, 1941, Sorge: A Chronology, http://www.richardsorge.com/appendices/schuleraffidavit /japansspy/hoover.pdf.

13. Von Boetticher, *Waiting for Letters*.

14. Von Boetticher, *Waiting for Letters*.

15. Hans Thomsen, *Documents on German Foreign Policy (DGFP)* (Washington DC: Government Printing Office), series D, vol. XIII, no. 553, December 7, 1941, 968–69.

16. Kato, *Lost War*, 64.


1. ON THE DIPLOMATIC FRONT LINES

1. Lombard, *Washington Waltz*, 48.

2. Fromm, *Blood and Banquets*, 139.

3. Fromm, *Blood and Banquets*, 98.

4. Ybarra, *Young Man*, 192.

5. Beth Blaine, "By the Way," *Evening Star*, June 9, 1937, B-3.

6. "Germany Protests 'Insult' by Mayor; Hull Voices Regret," *New York Times*, March 5, 1937, 9.

7. "800 Refugees Are Massacred as Insurgents Destroy Town," *Washington Post*, April 28, 1937, 1.

8. Beth Blain, "By the Way," *Evening Star*, March 1, 1937, B-3.

9. Fromm, *Blood and Banquets*, 139.

10. Kiplinger, *Washington Is Like That*, 398.

11. Jessie Ash Arndt, "Frau Hans Thomsen Attends First Party in Capital," *Washington Post*, January 13, 1937, 11.

12. Brinkley, *Washington Goes to War*, 34.

13. Beck, *Hitler's Ambivalent Attaché*, 71.

14. Hildegard von Boetticher, "So This Is America," *The Quarterly* (1938): 16.

15. Von Boetticher, *Waiting for Letters*.

16. "Yuletide Dance of Navy Lures Many 'Juniors,'" *Washington Post*, December 29, 1937, 12.


2. RIVALS AND ARRIVALS

1. "Hirosi Saito, Former Envoy from Japan, Succumbs at 51," *Washington Post*, February 27, 1939, 1.

2. Katherine Brooks, "Japanese Fete," *Evening Star*, April 30, 1937, 23.

3. *Washington City and Capital*, 689.

4. Lombard, *Washington Waltz*, 178, 23.

5. Clark, *Washington Dateline*, 222, 226.

6. H. R. Baukhage, "What's Back of It All," *Evening Star*, October 14, 1937, 13.

7. Drew Pearson and Robert Allen, "Washington Merry-Go-Round," *Clarion-Ledger* (Jackson MS), April 10, 1938, 22.

8. Sam Tucker, "As I View the Thing," *Decatur (IL) Daily Review*, January 30, 1938, 16.

9. Regnery, "At the Eye of the Storm," 24.

10. Frederick T. Birchall, "Paul Scheffer Out as Editor in Reich," *New York Times*, January 3, 1937, 26.

11. Birchall, "Paul Scheffer Out," 26.

12. Maurine Beasley, "The Press Conferences of Eleanor Roosevelt," paper presented at the Annual Meeting of the Association for Education in Journalism and Mass Communication, August 1983, https://archive.org

13. "Faces of the Month," *Texas Parade*, June 7, 1938, 28.

14. Sigrid Arne, "Three Washington 'Fates' Stir Pot And Dictate 'Who's Who' Socially," *Columbia Record*, December 4, 1934, 6.

15. Lynda Reeve, "Colorful Diplomatic Ride at Fort Meyer Is Occasion for Luncheons and Tea Dance," *Washington Post*, February 27, 1937, 10.

16. Jessie Ash Arndt, "Dr. Hans Luther is Host at Dinner and Musicale," *Washington Post*, March 20, 1937, 11.

17. Lynda Reeve, "Polish Counselor, Wife Entertain Informally," *Washington Post*, April 30, 1937, 14.

18. "Hirosi Saito, Former Envoy from Japan," 4.

19. Preston Grover, "Watching Trends," *News-Journal* (Mansfield OH), March 15, 1939, 14.

20. Hope Ridings Miller, "Hundreds Pay Tribute to Saito at Embassy," *Washington Post*, March 1, 1939, 14.

21. Grover, "Watching Trends," 14.

22. Franklin Delano Roosevelt, Quarantine Speech, October 5, 1937, http://teachingamericanhistory.org/library/document/quarantine-speech.

23. Editorial, *Boston Herald*, October 6, 1937, 22.

24. "Mussolini Foes Picket Embassy," *Evening Star*, October 11, 1937, 1.

25. Franklyn Waltman, "The President's Protest," *Washington Post*, December 14, 1937, 1.

26. Davis, *FDR*, 135.

## 3. SOIREES TO SPIES

1. Fromm, *Blood and Banquets*, 211.

2. Lombard, *Washington Waltz*, 62.

3. Carolyn Bell, "Spills and Thrills Keep Crowd on Toes as Washington Horse Show Opens," *Washington Post*, May 18, 1940, 10.

4. Eva Hinton, "Town Talk," *Washington Post*, November 17, 1946, S1.

5. Bloom, *There's No Place like Washington*, 227.

6. Harlan Miller, "Over the Coffee," *Washington Post*, May 10, 1938, X-13.

7. Miller, *Embassy Row*, 236.

8. Abell and Gordon, *Let Them Eat Caviar*, 135.

9. Baxa, "Capturing the Fascist Moment," 241.

10. Beale, *Power at Play*, 16.

11. Fromm, *Blood and Banquets*, 233.

12. "Dieckhoff Denies Any Link to Bund," *New York Times*, October 1, 1938, 36.

13. Hans Dieckhoff, *DGFP 1918–1945*, series D, vol. IV, no. 218, November 11, 1938, 639.

14. "Dieckhoff Sails Quietly for Home," *New York Times*, November 24, 1938, 5.

15. "Envoy May Leave 'To Be with Son,'" *Washington Post*, October 27, 1938, p. X-16.

16. Clark, *Washington Dateline*, 233.

17. Hope Ridings Miller, "Uneasy World Is Reflected at the White House Diplomatic Reception," *Washington Post*, December 16, 1938, 24.

18. Nancy Archibald, "Year of Change Marked in Diplomatic Corps," *Washington Post*, December 18, 1938, s-6.

19. Lombard, *Washington Waltz*, 198.

20. Advertisement, *American Foreign Service Journal* 17, no. 12 (December 1940): 707.

4. INACTIVE VIGILANCE

1. Terasaki, *Bridge to the Sun*, 5.

2. Thomas Ewing Dabney, "Japanese News Gatherer Looks New Orleans Over, and Likes It," *New Orleans States*, May 25, 1939, 15.

3. Drew Pearson and Robert Allen, "Washington Merry-Go-Round," *The Tennessean* (Nashville), April 24, 1939, 18.

4. Phineas J. Biron, "Strictly Confidential," *The Sentinel*, November 16, 1939, 4.

5. "Welles Tells Attache Berlin Must Expect Verbal Darts as Long as Press Attacks Us," *Washington Post*, December 23, 1938, 1.

6. Thomsen, *DGFP 1918–1945*, series D, vol. VI, no. 107, March 27, 1939, 129.

7. Lombard, *Washington Waltz*, 19.

8. Sigrid Arne, "Little Known Persons Have Big Hand in Royal Visit," *The Canton Repository*, June 1, 1939, 8.

9. Jean Spruks Russell, interview with author, October 29, 2017, Arlington, Virginia.

10. Childs, *I Write from Washington*, 141.

11. "Sunburned Queen, Cutawayed King Spend Hour at Socially-Explosive Garden Party," *Morning World Herald*, June 9, 1939, 1.

12. "3 Who Tarred Igor Cassini Fined $500," *Washington Post*, December 2, 1939, 3.

13. Myrna Oliver, "Igor Cassini, 86; Wrote N.Y. Society Column," *Los Angeles Times*, January 10, 2002, 46.

14. Bertram Hulen, "U.S. Denounces Japanese Trade Treaty," *New York Times*, July 27, 1939, 8.

15. Masuo Kato, *Japan Times and Mail*, August 3, 1939, 1.

16. Thomsen, *DGFP 1918–1945*, Series D, Vol. VII, no. 171, August 22, 1939, 180.

17. Edward Folliard, "Black Cat Looks at King's Ambassador," *Washington Post*, August 31, 1939, 2.

18. "Four Roosevelts Have Reunion as Liner from Europe Docks," *Evening Star*, August 31, 1939, 14.

5. REVERBERATIONS OF WAR

1. Mark Sullivan, "Washington on Sept. 1," *Washington Post*, September 2, 1939, 9.

2. Thomsen, *DGFP 1918–1945*, Series D, Vol. VII, no. 549, September 2, 1939, 520.

3. William V. Nessly, "U.S. Will Cling Hard to Peace, Roosevelt Tells Nation on Radio," *Washington Post*, September 4, 1939, 1.

4. Thomsen, *DGFP 1918–1945*, Series D, Vol. VIII, no. 289, October 21, 1939, 331.

5. Helen Stoddert, "Hull's Wife Prescribes Bicarbonate," *Oakland Tribune*, November 20, 1939, 2.

6. "Some Parties to Dispel Gloom for Diplomats," *Washington Post*, September 9, 1939, 12.

7. Evelyn Peyton Gordon, "R.S.V.P.—Meaning Reds Snubbed Very Politely," *El Paso Herald-Post*, November 7, 1939, 12.

8. Acheson, *Present at the Creation*, 34.

9. Charles Stewart, "Washington at a Glance," *Washington Court House Record-Herald* (OH), December 13, 1939, 15.

10. Dorothy Thompson, "On the Record," *Washington Post*, December 6, 1939, 11.

11. Helen Essary, "Dear Washington," *Washington Times-Herald*, December 3, 1939, 16.

12. Letter, Lord Lothian, British Embassy to the Viscount Halifax, December 14, 1939.

13. "Changing Scene," *Palestine Post*, December 14, 1939, 8.

14. Helen Stoddert, "Trepidation of Diplomats," *Oakland Tribune*, December 1, 1939, 57.

15. "Diplomats Conceal Feelings at White House Reception," *Evening Star*, December 15, 1939, 2.

16. Hope Ridings Miller, "Envoys Trade Nods Like Ice at White House," *Washington Post*, December 15, 1939, 18.

17. Drew Pearson and Robert Allen, "Washington Merry-Go-Round," *San Bernardino Sun*, November 9, 1939, 13.

18. Harlan Miller, "Washington," *Washington Post*, November 29, 1939, 16.

19. Russell, *Berlin Embassy*, 148.

20. Lombard, *Washington Waltz*, 75.

21. Thomsen, *DGFP 1918–1945*, Series D, Vol. VIII, no. 683, March 18, 1940, 934.

22. Von Boetticher, *Waiting for Letters.*

23. "Blames War on Oppression of Germany," *Baltimore Sun*, April 4, 1940, 4.

24. "Crow Caws Greet Visitors to Hull," *New York Times*, April 11, 1940, 14.

25. "Hurban, 'Sitting Tight,' Still Calls Self Czech Minister after Visit to Benes," *Washington Post*, March 21, 1939, 4.

26. Helen Stoddert, "Senator's Daughter," *Bradford Evening Star* (Bradford, Pennsylvania), June 8, 1940, 17.

6. ISOLATION VERSUS INTERVENTION

1. "Editor's Column," 438.

2. Simonds, "Mechanized Force in Warfare," 305.

3. Harmon, 567.

4. Harlan Miller, "Over the Coffee," *Washington Post*, May 21, 1940, 2.

5. Helen Essary, "Dear Washington," *Washington Times-Herald*, May 23, 1940, 23.

6. Thomsen and von Boetticher, *DGFP 1918–1945*, Series D, vol. IX, August 6, 1940, 132.

7. "Aviatrix Bombards Capital with Leaflets for American Peace," *Washington Post*, September 27, 1939, 1.

8. "Suspends Air License of Laura Ingalls," *New York Times*, December 23, 1939, 6.

9. Dillard Stokes, "Laura Ingalls to Take Stand at Trial Today," *Washington Post*, February 12, 1942, 26.

10. "George Sylvester Viereck, 77, Pro-German Propagandist Dies," *New York Times*, March 20, 1962, 37.

11. "Viereck, Nazi Agent, Quits Overseas Club," *New York Times*, December 24, 1940, 5.

12. Thomsen, *DGFP 1918–1945*, Series D, Vol. VIII, no. 129, September 24, 1939, 129.

13. Parmet and Hecht, *Never Again*, 139.

14. Advertisement, *New York Times*, June 25, 1940, 19.

15. Thomsen, *DGFP 1918–1945*, Series D, vol. XIII, no. 81, July 7, 1941, 99.

16. Albin Krebs, "William Stephenson, British Spy Known as Intrepid, Is Dead at 93," *New York Times*, February 3, 1989, D17.

17. "Colonna Protests on Italian Charges," *New York Times*, June 15, 1940, 9.

18. Lombard, *Washington Waltz*, 232.

19. Carolyn Bell, "Leaders of Society, Diplomatic Circles Attend Party," *Washington Post*, September 24, 1940, 14.

20. Phineas J. Biron, *The Sentinel*, November 28, 1940, 4.

21. Hugh Byas, "Warning to U.S. Is Seen in Tokyo," *New York Times*, September 28, 1940, 1.

22. Reed, *Admiral Leahy at Vichy France*, 26.

23. Gaston Henry-Haye, statement of the embassy of the French Republic, September 12, 1940, NACP, RG59, box 1841.

24. Kathleen Cannell, "France Puts Faith in New Envoy Here," *New York Times*, August 11, 1940, 18.

25. Kato, *Lost War*, 19.

26. Jeans, *Terasaki Hidenari*, 26.

27. Letter, Adolf Berle Jr. to Breckinridge Long, December 16, 1941, NACP, RG59, box 1866.

28. *MBPH*, Department of Defense, November 15, 1941, vol. IV, no. 192.

29. "Defers Japanese Inquiry," *New York Times*, September 22, 1941, 4.

30. Kato, *Lost War*, 80.

## 7. WAR WARY

1. Brown, *Last Hero*, 188–89.

2. Thomsen, *DGFP 1918–1945*, Series D, Vol. XII, no. 418, April 28, 1941, 661.

3. "Bushnell Sees Action against Nazi Agents," *Boston Daily Globe*, May 15, 1941, 6.

4. "Text of the Roosevelt Message," *New York Times*, June 22, 1941, 6.

5. Letter, Robert Phalen to Cordell Hull, June 16, 1941, NACP, RG59, SWPD, box 1938.

6. Arthur Krock, "In the Nation," *New York Times*, June 17, 1941, 20.

7. Arnecke, *Mein Traum*, 22.

8. Arnecke, *Mein Traum*, 23.

9. "Dr. Sennhenn Morally Unfit, Roosevelt Says," *Washington Post*, August 2, 1941, 7.

10. Letter, Rep. Emanuel Celler to the Honorable Franklin Delano Roosevelt, June 20, 1941, NACP, RG59, box 1866.

11. Martha Ellyn, "Men Like Salads—If They're Not Too Frilly," *Washington Post*, August 22, 1941, 10.

12. "Pro-Nazi Reports Stir Henry-Haye," *New York Times*, September 3, 1941, 5.

13. FBI memo, unsigned, September 24, 1941, NACP, RG59, box 1866.

14. "She'll Stay Here If Envoy Leaves," *Los Angeles Times*, June 21, 1941, 6.

15. "Dr. Thomsen Denies Report Wife Would Stay in U.S.," *Evening Star*, June 21, 1941, 3.

16. FBI memo, November 7, 1941, NACP, RG59, box 1866.

17. Drew Pearson and Robert Allen, "Washington Merry-Go-Round," *Coshocton Tribune*, April 6, 1941.

18. Lombard, *Washington Waltz*, 72.

19. Blair Bolles, "Capital Is Thrown in Turmoil by Book Dissecting Diplomats," *Evening Star*, November 9, 1941, 71.

20. Lombard, *Washington Waltz*, 149.

21. Lombard, *Washington Waltz*, 192.

22. Reiss, *Total Espionage*, 291.

23. "Text of Lindbergh's Address at America First Rally in Madison Square Garden," *New York Times*, October 30, 1941, 4.

24. "Russian Embassy Responds Handsomely for Billion-Dollar Loan To Soviet Cause; Throws Gosh-Darndest Party Washington Has Seen Since 'Recognition' Blow-Out," *Lexington Herald*, November 8, 1941, 1.

25. "Kurusu, Arriving Here, Sees 'Fighting Chance' of Accord on Far East," *Washington Post*, 1.

26. Hull, *Memoirs of Cordell Hull*, 1062.

27. Childs, *I Write from Washington*, 240.

28. Arthur Krock, "In the Nation," *New York Times*, December 4, 1941, 24.

29. Olson, *Those Angry Days*, 412.

30. Thomsen, *DGFP*, Series D, vol. XIII, no. 541, December 4, 1941, 951.

31. Michael Peck, "The Battle for Moscow: How Russia Stopped Hitler's Military during World War II," *National Interest*, September 9, 2016, http://nationalinterest.org/blog/the-buzz/the-battle-moscow-how-russia-stopped-hitlers-nazi-germany-17641.

32. Baukhage, "Washington Digest," *Cassville (MO) Republican*, January 1, 1942, 2.

33. Ed Lockett to David Hulburd, *War Comes to the U.S.*, December 7, 1941, 1.

34. Thomsen, *DGFP*, Series D, vol. XIII, no. 539, December 4, 1941, 948.

35. Beth Blaine, "By the Way," *Evening Star*, March 20, 1937, 15.

## 8. FULL SPEED AHEAD

1. "War Brings a Tense Day to White House Press Room," *Washington Post*, December 8, 1941, 4.

2. *FRUS*, The British Commonwealth, Eastern Europe, The Far East, vol. III, December 24, 1942.

3. Memo, G. V. Hennett to Mr. Fitch, December 8, 1941, NACP, RG59, box 1866.

4. Persico, *Edward R. Murrow*, 193.

5. Persico, *Edward R. Murrow*, 194.

6. Jerry Greene, *War Comes to the U.S.*, December 7, 1941.

7. Childs, *I Write from Washington*, 244.

8. Thomsen, *DGFP*, Series D, vol. XIII, no. 553, December 7, 1941, 968–69.

9. "Fluttering Attaches Lend Air of Mystery to Axis Embassies," *Washington Post*, December 9, 1941, 8.

10. "Smoke at Germany Embassy Indicates Burning of Papers," *Evening Star*, December 9, 1941, 1.

11. Iguchi, *Demystifying Pearl Harbor*, 6.

12. Terasaki, *Bridge to the Sun*, 71.

13. Von Boetticher, *Waiting for Letters*.

14. Von Boetticher, *Waiting for Letters*.

15. Von Boetticher, *Waiting for Letters*.

16. "Japanese Embassy Short of Food, Cash," *Washington Daily News*, December 9, 1941, 13.

17. Letter, Leonardo Sanchez to Cordell Hull, December 10, 1941, NACP, RG59, box 1887.

18. Letter, W. R. Frank Hines to Cordell Hull, December 15, 1941, NACP, RG59, box 1887.

19. Memo, Stanley Woodward to Head of the Japanese Embassy Representative, December 12, 1941, NACP, RG59, box 1887.

20. Letter, State Department to Attorney General Francis Biddle, December 11, 1941, LOC, BLP, box 206.

21. Terasaki, *Bridge to the Sun*, 72.

22. Letter, George Atcheson to Stanley Woodward, December 19, 1941, NACP, RG59, box 1887.

23. Letter, J. Edgar Hoover to Adolf Berle, December 23, 1941, NACP, RG59, box 1887.

24. Letter, George Atcheson to Breckinridge Long, January 24, 1942, LOC, BLP, box 206.

25. Downes, *The Scarlet Thread*, 96.

### 9. EXECUTING AN EXODUS

1. Clarke Kawakami, letter from former correspondent of Japanese news service, Department of State Bulletin, December 27, 1941, 562.

2. Tully, *F.D.R.*, 293.

3. Evelyn Peyton Gordon, "That War Report Is 'Premature,' Says Nazi Envoy; But They're Burning Stuff at the Embassy," *Washington Daily News*, December 10, 1941, 14.

4. "Embassy Japs Allowed Food; Blockade Opens for Servants," *Washington Times-Herald*, December 9, 1941, 6.

5. Carroll Peeke, "FBI Tightens Blockade of Jap Embassy," *Washington Times-Herald*, December 10, 1941, 4.

6. Berle and Jacobs, *Navigating the Rapids*, 385.

7. Robert Vanderpoel, "Hull's Economic Proposals Follow American Ideals," *Chicago Herald-American*, December 10, 1941, 27.

8. Raymond Clapper, "Suicide for Japan," *Washington Daily News*, December 8, 1941, 34.

9. "Our Nationals and Japan's," *New York Times*, December 10, 1941, 24.

10. Goldstein and Dillon, *Pacific War Papers*, 216.

11. "Axis Envoys Notifying U.S. of War Received by Under-Officials," *Evening Star*, December 11, A2.

12. Press release, Department of State, December 11, 1941, no. 610.

13. "Italian and German Embassies Are Calm at War Declaration," *Evening Star*, December 11, 1941, 3.

14. Dillard Stokes, "Italian and German Embassies Close," *Washington Post*, December 12, 1941, 8.

15. N. E. F. Meekins, "There Is No Alternative . . . but I Shall Come Back Again after the War," *Washington Post*, December 12, 1941, 8.

16. Terasaki, *Bridge to the Sun*, 73.

17. Ulrich von Gienanth, *Wedding and Internment* (unpublished memoir), GB.

18. Carolyn Bell, "Diplomatic Circling," *Washington Post*, November 1, 1942, S3.

19. Mildred Adams, "Echoes of War on the Diplomatic Front," *New York Times*, May 5, 1940, 120.

20. Letter, Adolf Berle to Breckinridge Long, December 16, 1941, NACP, RG59, box 1866.

21. Letter, R. L. Bannerman to Thomas Fitch, December 16, 1941, NACP, RG59, box 1867.

22. W. M. Franklin, memo, "Treatment of Enemy Official Personnel by the United States, December 1941–April 1942," NACP, RG59, Historical Studies Division, Research Projects, 1945–1954, box 4, 16.

23. Letter, R. H. Patterson to Loren Johnston, December 16, 1941, GB.

24. Letter, A. N. Carlblom to D. M. Ladd, December 29, 1941, UVAL, RMC, box 10.

25. Roy Sibold, "Report of the Axis Diplomats and Nationals at the Greenbrier," GB, 1.

26. Ingalls, *Journal of the Sojourn*, 2.

27. Letter, Loren Johnston to Carl Stanley, January 14, 1942, GB.

## 10. FENCED INN

1. Virginia Pasley, "Nazi Diplomat, Aides Removed to West Va. Spa," *Washington Times-Herald*, Dec. 20, 1941, 5.

2. Beth Blaine, "By the Way," *Evening Star*, June 6, 1937, 16.

3. "Laura Ingalls Held as Reich Agent," *New York Times*, December 19, 1941, 1.

4. Letter, Francis Biddle, December 19, 1941, Franklin D. Roosevelt Presidential Library, Francis Biddle papers.

5. Arnecke, *Mein Traum*, 23.

6. Von Boetticher, *Waiting for Letters*.

7. Memo, Thomas Fitch, December 19, 1941, NARA, RG85, box 2412.

8. Letter, W. F. Kelly to Chester Courtney, December 23, 1941, NARA, RG85, box 2412.

9. Letter, R. H. Patterson to Loren Johnston, December 16, 1941, GB.

10. Letter, Loren Johnston to R. H. Patterson, December 19, 1941, GB.

11. "Japanese Officials to Be Interned Here," *Bath County Enterprise*, December 18, 1941, 1.

12. Jack Stinnett, "A Washington Daybook," *Warren (PA) Times-Mirror*, December 24, 1941, 4.

13. Letter, Masuo Kato to H. R. Zaepfel, December 20, 1941, NARA, RG85, box 18461.

14. Letter, Hilary Zaepfel to Joseph Savoretti, December 27, 1941, NARA, RG85, box 18461.

15. Terasaki, *Bridge to the Sun*, 74, 75.

16. Bosworth, *America's Concentration Camps*, 110.

17. William Russell, *Berlin Embassy*, 141.

18. "Greenbrier Denies Alien Objection," *The Sentinel*, December 26, 1941, 1.

19. "Diplomatic 'Courtesy,'" *Charleston Gazette*, December 31, 1941, 9.

20. Letter, John O'Hanley to Charlie Spruks, February 1, 1942, NACP, RG59, box 1868.

21. Iguchi, *Demystifying Pearl Harbor*, 20.

22. Letter, R. L. Morgan, n.d., UVAL, RMC, box 10.

11. MOVING DAZE

1. Telegram, Joseph Savoretti to Rudolph Johnson, December 26, 1941, NARA, RG85, box 2412.

2. Unsigned letter to all Patrol Inspectors on duty at the Greenbrier Hotel, December 24, 1941, NARA, RG85, box 1888.

3. Letter, C. C. Courtney to All Patrol Officers, Immigration Guards and Employees on duty at the Greenbrier Hotel, January 27, 1942, NARA, RG85, box 1888.

4. Stocker, *Eye Surgeon Turns Diplomat*, 27.

5. Stocker, *Eye Surgeon Turns Diplomat*, 18.

6. Letter, John O'Hanley to Fitch, January 3, 1942, NACP, RG59, box 109.

7. Letter, Breckinridge Long to George Summerlin, January 14, 1942, LOC, BLP, box 207.

8. Israel, *War Diary*, 261.

9. Letter, Mires Jackson to Adolf Berle Jr., December 21, 1941, NACP, RG59, box 1866.

10. Stocker, *Eye Surgeon Turns Diplomat*, 40.

11. Hope Ridings Miller, "Capital Whirl," *Washington Post*, December 14, 1941, S1.

12. Weintraub, *Pearl Harbor Christmas*, 114.

13. Fred Pasley, "Jap Diplomats Leave Capital as Crowd Boos," *Washington Times-Herald*, December 30, 1941, 5.

14. Goldstein and Dillon, *Pacific War Papers*, 220–21.

15. Terasaki, *Bridge to the Sun*, 67.

16. Iguchi, *Demystifying Pearl Harbor*, 9.

17. Terasaki, *Bridge to the Sun*, 36–37.

18. Iguchi, *Demystifying Pearl Harbor*, 9.

19. Masterson, *The Japanese in Latin America*, 94.

20. Letter, R. L. Morgan to Mr. Ladd, December 28, 1941, UVAL, RMC, box 10.

21. Kato, *Lost War*, 69.

22. Letter, Fay Ingalls to Raymond Douglas Muir, December 30, 1941, NACP, RG59, box 1888.

23. Letter, A. A. Auers to Mons C. Wallgren, January 5, 1942, NACP, RG59, 1867.

24. Letter, Edward Poole to Thomas Fitch, December 31, 1941, NACP, RG59, box 1867.

25. Letter, Susie to Lohr Vance, December 31, 1941, private collection.

26. Sanders, *Dorothy Thompson*, 290.

27. Letter, Rev. Frank A. Settle to Manager, Hotel Greenbrier, n.d., GB.


12. (NOT SO) HAPPY NEW YEAR

1. Letter, Rev. Frank A. Settle to Manager, Hotel Greenbrier, n.d., GB.

2. Von Boetticher, *Waiting for Letters*.

3. Letter, Robert Parker to Jack Warfel, January 6, 1942, GB.

4. Letter, Royal Ryan to Loren Johnston, January 13, 1942, GB.

5. Letter, Robert Parker to Royal Ryan, January 14, 1942, GB.

6. Letter, Royal Ryan to R. B. Parker, January 19, 1942, GB.

7. "War Spirit Prevails in Every Festivity," *Washington Post*, April 8, 1917, E6.

8. Marshall Sprague, "Season at De Luxe Spas," *New York Times*, March 30, 1941, 3.

9. Lucy Cornett, interview with author, January 2018.

10. Letter, Gladys Childs to Loren Johnston, January 11, 1942, GB.

11. Stocker, *Eye Surgeon Turns Diplomat*, 19.

12. Cordell Hull to Mr. Huddle, *FRUS*, vol. I, 1942, 302.

13. Radiogram, Prince Colonna to Foreign Ministry, Rome, February 2, 1942, NACP, RG59, box 1875.

14. "Roosevelt Lauds Carole Lombard," *New York Times*, January 20, 1942, 15.

15. Kato, *Lost War*, 70.

16. Iguchi, *Demystifying Pearl Harbor*, 15.

17. Memo, R. L. Morgan to Mr. Ladd, January 28, 1942, UVAL, RMC, box 10.

18. Memo, R. L. Morgan to Mr. Ladd, January 15, 1942, UVAL, RMC, box 10.

19. Memo, Interrogation of Masuo Kato, February 6, 1946, UVAL, RMC, box 10.

20. Letter, Carroll Reece to Stanley Woodward, January 15, 1942, NACP, RG59, box 1888.

21. Memo, A. N. Carlblom to Mr. Ladd, January 7, 1942, UVAL, RMC, box 10.

22. Memo, R. L. Morgan to Mr. Ladd, January 20, 1942, UVAL, RMC, box 10.

23. Letter, John O'Hanley to T. F. Fitch, January 29, 1942, NACP, RG59, box 1867.

24. Boveri, *Verzweigungen*, 398.

13. WATCHED WHILE WAITING

1. Memo, R. L. Morgan to Mr. Ladd, January 29, 1942, UVAL, RMC, box 10.
2. Iguchi, *Demystifying Pearl Harbor*, 11.
3. Memo, R. L. Morgan to Mr. Ladd, January 22, 1942, UVAL, RMC, box 10.
4. Memo, Clarence Corkran to Mr. Ladd, January 15, 1942, UVAL, RMC, box 9.
5. Memo, A. N. Carlblom to Mr. Ladd, January 14, 1942, UVAL, RMC, box 9.
6. Letter, Loren Johnston to R. L. Patterson, December 30, 1941, GB.
7. Memo, Clarence Corkran to Mr. Ladd, January 15, 1942, UVAL, RMC, box 9.
8. Letter, Larry Bolton to Mr. Keeley, February 8, 1942, NACP, RG59, box 1866.
9. Letter, John O'Hanley to T. F. Fitch, December 24, 1941, NACP, RG59, box 1867.
10. Memo, Japanese Embassy, January 17, 1942, NACP, RG59, box 1867.
11. Letter, Edward Poole to T. F. Fitch, January 29, 1942, NACP, RG59, box 1867.
12. Kennan, "Report," 473.
13. Memo, J. E. Lawler to Mr. Ladd, January 30, 1942, UVAL, RMC, box 10.
14. Letter, J. Edgar Hoover to Adolf Berle, February 2, 1942, NACP, RG59, box 1868.
15. Letter, J. Edgar Hoover to Adolf Berle, March 9, 1942, NACP, RG59, box 1867.
16. Letter, Paul Scheffer to Dorothy Thomson, June 24, 1942, SUSC, DTC.
17. Memo, A. N. Carlblom to Mr. Ladd, January 20, 1942, UVAL, RMC, box 10.
18. Letter, Richard Baron to the Department of State, February 16, 1942, NACP, RG59, box 1867.
19. Letter, George Summerlin to Richard Baron, February 26, 1942, NACP, RG59, box 1867.
20. Stocker, *Eye Surgeon Turns Diplomat*, 26.
21. Letter, George O'Brien to Charlie Spruks, January 18, 1942, NACP, RG59, box 1867.

14. QUIET DESPERATION

1. Arnecke, *Mein Traum*, 27.
2. Von Boetticher, *Waiting for Letters*.
3. Hill, *Senator's Wife Remembers*, 113.
4. Letter, Breckinridge Long to George Summerlin, January 15, 1942, LOC, BLP, box 208.
5. Letter, John O'Hanley to Charlie Spruks, February 1, 1942, NACP, RG59, box 1866.
6. Letter, John O'Hanley to T. F. Fitch, February 1, 1942, NACP, RG59, box 1866.
7. Letter, Harry Helmke to Chief Patrol Inspector, February 1, 1942, NARA RG85, box 2412.
8. Memo, J. E. Lawler to Mr. Ladd, February 1, 1942, UVAL, RMC, box 9.

9. Memo, E. J. Lincourt to Chief Supervisor of Border Patrol, February 2, 1942, NARA, RG85, box 2412.

10. Letter, Paul Scheffer to John O'Hanley, February 2, 1942, NACP, RG59, box 1867.

11. Memo, W. F. Miller to Lemuel Schofield, February 3, 1942, NARA, RG85, box 2440.

12. Letters, Paul Scheffer to Hans Thomsen, n.d., UVAL, RMC, box 9.

13. Stocker, *Eye Surgeon Turns Diplomat*, 44.

14. Boveri, *Verzweigungen*, 398.


15. *LIFE* AT THE HOMESTEAD

1. Letter, George Slosson Jr. to Raymond D. Muir, January 8, 1942, NACP, RG59, box 1867.

2. Letter, G. W. Mingus to Sumner Welles, February 13, 1942, NACP, RG59, box 1867.

3. "The Homestead: A Great Hotel Entertains Jap Diplomats as Patriotic Duty," *Life*, February 16, 1942, 69.

4. Memo, R. L. Morgan to Mr. Ladd, February 25, 1942, UVAL, RMC, box 10.

5. Ben Beagle, "During a Troubled Era, the Homestead Kept Its Stature," *Roanoke Times and World Review*, September 19, 1976, 1.

6. Bosworth, *America's Concentration Camps*, 110.

7. Letters, anonymous, NACP, RG59, box 1867.

8. Letter, William R. Langdon to Breckinridge Long, January 27, 1942, NACP, RG59, box 1888.

9. Letter, Loren Johnston to R. H. Patterson, December 19, 1941, GB.

10. Letter, Max Hamilton to Breckinridge Long, January 27, 1942, NACP, RG59, 1867.

11. Mrs. Roland A. (Lettie) Fleagle, interview by University of Texas El Paso Institute of Oral History, 1987, Border Patrol Museum, https://www.borderpatrolmuseum.com/history/.

12. Letter, A. A. Berle to J. Edgar Hoover, June 5, 1942, NACP, RG59, SWPD, 110.

13. Eppinga, "Pearl Harbor," 50.

14. Ingalls, *Journal of the Sojourn*, 8.

15. Letter, G. Howland Shaw to Fay Ingalls, February 10, 1942, NARA, RG85, box 18461.

16. Terasaki, *Bridge to the Sun*, 79.

17. Iguchi, *Demystifying Pearl Harbor*, 16.

18. Kato, *Lost War*, 71.

19. Sam Tucker, "As I View the Thing," *Decatur (IL) Daily Review*, February 1, 1942, 19.

20. Kato, *Lost War*, 71.

21. James Reston, "Are We Awake?," *New York Times*, March 1, 1942, 1.

22. Hope Ridings Miller, "Capital Whirl: Grinding the Axis—Not Axes—Chief Reason for Record Party Round in Wartime Washington," *Washington Post*, March 18, 1942, 16.

23. Helen Lombard, "Enemies Seeking Information Have Easy Time in Washington," *Evening Star*, February 16, 1942, 2X.

24. Letter, L. L. Laughlin to Mr. H. M. Kimball, February 10, 1942, UVAL, RMC, box 10.

25. Kato, *Lost War*, 74.

26. Iguchi, *Demystifying Pearl Harbor*, 11.

27. Iguchi, *Demystifying Pearl Harbor*, 12.

28. Ingalls, *Journal of the Sojourn*, 2.

29. Memo, R. L. Morgan to Mr. Ladd, March 30, 1942, UVAL, RMC, box 10.

30. "Cherry Fete is Canceled Due to War," *Washington Post*, March 4, 1942, 17.

31. Kato, *Lost War*, 76.

32. Clifford and Okura, *Desperate Diplomat*, 125.

33. B. T. Gillespie, "Scrap Book," *The African-American* (Baltimore), January 17, 1942, 4.

34. Advertisement, D. L. Bromwell, *Evening Star*, December 11, 1941, 3.

35. Letter, J. E. Lawler to Mr. Ladd, February 25, 1942, UVAL, RMC, box 10.

36. Letter, Richard O. Boyer to Protocol Division, March 10, 1942, NACP, RG59, box 1888.

16. "BUT STILL THEY COMPLAIN . . ."

1. Letter, M. F. Harrington to Loren Johnston, March 3, 1942, GB.

2. Letter, John O'Hanley to T. F. Fitch, February 27, 1942, NACP, RG59, box 1866.

3. Letter, Nancy White to Thomas Deegan Jr., Greenbrier, n.d., GB.

4. Letter, Charlie Spruks to T. F. Fitch, February 27, 1942, NACP, RG59, box 1866.

5. Letter, John O'Hanley to T. F. Fitch, February 27, 1942, NACP, RG59, box 1866.

6. Memo, J. E. Lawler to Mr. Ladd, March 8, 1942, UVAL, RMC, box 10.

7. Memo, "Italian Espionage System in United States," ONI, NCISA History Project, February 17, 1942, www.ncisahistory.org.

8. Indictment, "United States of America, Plaintiff v. Laura Ingalls, Defendant," December 23, 1941, NARA, RG21, box 195.

9. Stokes, "Laura Ingalls to Take Stand," 18.

10. "Laura Ingalls Nazi Agent, Jury Decides," *Washington Post*, February 12, 1942, 1.

11. "Jury Act Today on Miss Ingalls, Who Styles Self a 'Mata Hari,'" *Washington Post*, February 13, 1942, 1.

12. "Miss Ingalls Gets Prison Sentence," *New York Times*, February 21, 1942, 21.

13. Memo, Breckinridge Long, February 23, 1942, NACP, RG59, box 1867.

14. Downes, *The Scarlet Thread*, 93.

15. "Viereck Convicted of False Registry," *New York Times*, March 6, 1942, 1.

16. "Fish Denies He Helped Nazi Agent Knowingly," *Washington Post*, February 21, 1942, 1.

17. Memo, Stanley Woodward, March 17, 1942, LOC, BLP, box 206.

18. Von Boetticher, *Waiting for Letters*.

19. Letter, John O'Hanley to T. F. Fitch, February 23, 1942, NACP, RG59, box 1867.

20. Memo, J. E. Lawler to Mr. Ladd, January 31, 1942, UVAL, RMC, box 9.

21. Memo, J. E. Lawler to Mr. Ladd, March 9, 1942, UVAL, RMC, box 10.

22. Letter, Allan Dawson to Charlie Spruks, March 9, 1942, private collection.

23. Contag and Grabowska, *Where the Clouds*, 99.

24. Letter, Breckinridge Long to Sumner Welles, February 12, 1942, LOC, BLP, box 206.

25. Friedman, *Nazis and Good Neighbors*, 200.

26. Memo, Lemuel Schofield to Mr. Kelly, February 6, 1942, NARA, RG85, box 2412.

27. Memo, J. E. Lawler to Mr. Ladd, March 23, 1942, UVAL, RMC, box 10.

28. Memo, J. E. Lawler to Mr. Ladd, March 19, 1942, UVAL, RMC, box 10.

29. Memo, J. E. Lawler to Mr. Ladd, March 14, 1942, UVAL, RMC, box 10.

30. Memo, Lemuel Schofield to Mr. Kelly, March 16, 1942, NARA, RG85, box 2412.

17. TWICE REMOVED

1. Letter, John O'Hanley to T. F. Fitch, February 23, 1942, NACP, RG59, box 1867.

2. Max Fullerton, "Oh, for Life of an Interned Diplomat," *Rhinelander (WI) Daily News*, March 3, 1942, 17.

3. Advertisement, "Springtime at the Homestead," *Richmond Times-Dispatch*, March 11, 1942, 14.

4. Resolution issued by B. F. Dixon, Acting Mayor, Town of White Sulphur Springs, March 28, 1942, NACP, RG59, box 1867.

5. Letter, F. E. Finks to Hon. H. M. Kilgore, March 29, 1942, NACP, RG59.

6. Letter, Sumner Welles to Senator Harley Kilgore, April 2, 1942, NACP, RG59, box 1888.

7. Memo, J. E. Lawler to Mr. Ladd, April 1, 1942, UVAL, RMC, box 10.

8. "Diplomats Arrive Here for Internment," *Asheville Citizen-Times*, April 4, 1942, 1.

9. Mauch, *Sailor Diplomat*, 215.

10. "A Questionable Diplomatic Maneuver," *Montana Standard*, April 22, 1942, 17.

11. Memo, Italian, Bulgarian and Hungarian Groups to Colonel Gossweiler, April 5, 1942, NACP, RG59, box 1875.

12. Letter, John O'Hanley to T. F. Fitch, April 8, 1942, NACP, RG59, box 1867.

13. Mike Maffeo, interview by Terrie Cornell, September 4, 1986, Border Patrol Museum, El Paso TX, https://www.borderpatrolmuseum.com/history/.

14. Letter, J. Edgar Hoover to Adolf Berle, April 4, 1942, NACP, RG59, box 1875.

15. Letter, R. L. Bannerman to T. F. Fitch, April 6, 1942, NACP, RG59, box 1875.

16. Don O'Hanley, interview with author, October 2017.

17. Letter, John O'Hanley to T. F. Fitch, April 20, 1942, NACP, RG59, box 1867.

18. Letter, Breckinridge Long to George Summerlin, April 23, 1941, NACP, RG59, box 1867.

19. Letter, John O'Hanley to T. F. Fitch, April 23, 1942, NACP, RG59, box 1867.

20. Letter, J. Edgar Hoover to Adolf Berle, April 8, 1942, NACP, RG59, box 1875.

21. Letter, Breckinridge Long to Mr. Acheson and Mr. Reinstein, May 6, 1942, LOC, BLP, box 206.

22. Memo, the Swiss Legation to the Honorable Secretary of State, April 25, 1942, NACP, RG59, box 1875.

23. Letter, Joseph C. Green to Breckinridge Long, April 29, 1942, LOC, BLP, box 206.

24. Letter, Joseph C. Green to Breckinridge Long, May 1, 1942, NACP, RG59, box 1875.

18. A FEUD RENEWED

1. Hill, *Senator's Wife Remembers*, 149.

2. Memo, R. L. Morgan to Mr. Ladd, April 6, 1942, UVAL, RMC, box 9.

3. Memo, R. L. Morgan to Mr. Ladd, April 15, 1942, UVAL, RMC, box 9.

4. Terasaki, *Bridge to the Sun*, 85.

5. Memo, R. L. Morgan to Mr. Ladd, April 24, 1942, UVAL, RMC, box 9.

6. Letter, Loren Johnston to Dr. Hinsdale, February 18, 1942, GB.

7. Boveri, *Verzweigungen*, 400.

8. Lucy Buran, interview with author, January 2018.

9. Letter, T. F. Fitch to Mr. Poole, April 13, 1942, NACP, RG59, box 1867.

10. "Slide, Togo, Slide," 50.

11. Letter, J. Edgar Hoover to Adolf Berle, January 24, 1942, NACP, RG59, box 1875.

12. Letter, Ulrich von Gienanth to Mr. Conte, January 30, 1995, GB.

13. G. D. Horner, book review, "The Japanese Enemy: His Power and His Vulnerability," *Evening Star*, March 8, 1942, 67.

14. Letter, Guy Hinsdale to Loren Johnston, March 18, 1942, GB.

15. Letter, Irene Fritzsching to Mr. Conte, January 1, 1991, GB.

16. Robert Conte, notes of a conversation with Rolf and Alfons Kleindienst, October 2, 1997, GB.

17. Memo, R. L. Morgan to Mr. Ladd, March 23, 1942, UVAL, RMC, box 10.

18. Arnecke, *Mein Traum*, 28.

19. Von Boetticher, *Waiting for Letters*.

20. Sibold, "Report of the Axis Diplomats," 5.

21. Letter, T. F. Fitch to Edward Poole, April 17, 1942, NACP, RG59, box 1875.

22. Memo, R. L. Morgan to Mr. Ladd, April 23, 1942, UVAL, RMC, box 9.

23. Conte, *History of the Greenbrier*, 133.

24. Memo, R. L. Morgan to Mr. Ladd, May 1, 1942, UVAL, RMC, box 9.

25. Memo, E. J. Lincourt to all Patrol Inspectors, employees and guards on duty at the Greenbrier Hotel, April 16, 1942, NARA, RG85, box 18461.

26. Telegram, George Summerlin to Charlie Spruks, April 15, 1942, private collection.

27. Memo, U.S. Department of Justice, Immigration and Naturalization Service to Employees, Gibson Hotel, April 23, 1942, NARA, RG85, box 2427.

28. Hill, *Senator's Wife Remembers*, 149.

29. Kato, *Lost War*, 72.

### 19. HOMEWARD, UNBOUND

1. Hoge, *Cissy Patterson*, 11.

2. David Charnay and William Wallace, "The Axis at Home: Inside Story of Interned Diplomats—Riots, Stabbings, Race Wars," *San Francisco Chronicle*, May 4, 1942, 1.

3. Memo, R. L. Morgan to Mr. Ladd, May 8, 1942, UVAL, RMC, box 10.

4. Letter, Irene Fritzsching to Mr. Conte, January 1, 1991, GB.

5. Memo, R. L. Morgan to Mr. Ladd, May 6, 1942, UVAL, RMC, box 9.

6. Von Boetticher, *Waiting for Letters*.

7. Memo, R. L. Morgan to Mr. Ladd, May 8, 1942, UVAL, RMC, box 10.

8. Israel, *War Diary*, 265.

9. George von Knoop, personal correspondence with author, August 2017.

10. Contag and Grabowska, *Where the Clouds*, 121.

11. Miller, "Sforza in America," 685.

12. Boveri, *Verzweigungen*, 401.

13. Lochery, *Lisbon*, 11.

14. Lochner, *The Goebbels Diaries*, 223.

15. Israel, *War Diary*, 267.

16. "Thomsen Tells Nazis Our Arms Are Bluff," *New York Times*, May 18, 1942, 6.

17. Compton, *The Swastika*, 14.

18. Cameron and Stevens, *Hitler's Table Talk*, 489.

19. Letter, Fred H. Boetticher to Alfred Beck, July 30, 1973, private collection.

20. Von Boetticher, *Waiting for Letters*.

21. "Hitler Decorates Thomsen," *New York Times*, May 27, 1942, 6.

22. Helen Lombard, "Honor for Gen. Von Boetticher Surprises Service Circles Here," *Evening Star*, June 3, 1942, 23.

23. Seabury, *The Wilhelmstrasse*, 121.

24. Memo, R. L. Morgan to Mr. Ladd, May 15, 1942, UVAL, RMC, box 9.

### 20. PERPLEXING PASSAGE EAST

1. Letter, Fred I. Rowe to the Greenbrier Hotel, June 1, 1942, GB.

2. Letter, Loren Johnston to Fred I. Rowe, June 2, 1942, GB.

3. "Diplomatic Exchange Liner Reaches Port with 908 From Europe," *Baltimore Sun*, June 2, 1942, 2.

4. Israel, *War Diary*, 268.

5. Israel, *War Diary*, 270.

6. Letter, Breckinridge Long to Mr. Green, May 25, 1942, LOC, BLP, box 206.

7. Letter, R. L. Morgan to Mr. Ladd, June 7, 1942, UVAL, RMC, box 9.

8. Israel, *War Diary*, 270.

9. Israel, *War Diary*, 272.

10. Terasaki, *Bridge to the Sun*, 87.

11. Memo, Breckinridge Long to Joseph Green, June 13, 1942, LOC, BLP, box 206.

12. Iguchi, *Demystifying Pearl Harbor*, 19–20.

13. Memo, R. L. Morgan to Mr. Ladd, June 12, 1942, UVAL, RMC, box 9.

14. Iguchi, *Demystifying Pearl Harbor*, 20.

15. Kato, *Lost War*, 79.

16. Israel, *War Diary*, 274.

17. Paul Scheffer, letter, n.d. (circa fall 1942), DTC, SUSC.

18. Terasaki, *Bridge to the Sun*, 92.

19. Masuo Kato, "Envoys Nomura, Kurusu, Ishii Feted by Axis Consulates at Party," *Japan Times and Mail*, July 22, 1942, 1.

20. Briggs, *Taken in Hong Kong*, 219.

21. Argall, *My Life*, 279.

22. Hill, *Exchange Ship*, 238.

23. Briggs, *Taken in Hong Kong*, 222.

## 21. HOME AGHAST

1. Terasaki, *Bridge to the Sun*, 94.

2. Terasaki, *Bridge to the Sun*, 95.

3. Clifford and Okura, *Desperate Diplomat*, 191.

4. Blair Bolles, "Grew Acted on Own in Snubbing Nomura at Exchange Port," *Evening Star*, August 1, 1942, 3.

5. Mauch, *Sailor Diplomat*, 215.

6. Briggs, *Taken in Hong Kong*, 231.

7. Terasaki, *Bridge to the Sun*, 96.

8. C. H. Kawakami, "Nomura Returns," *Washington Post*, June 11, 1942, 15.

9. "Nomura Lays War to US," *New York Times*, August 12, 1942, 6.

10. Kurusu, *Treacherous America*, 2–3.

11. "Hirohito's Gifts Welcome Returning 'Peace' Envoys," *New York Times*, August 21, 1942, 6.

12. George Axelsson, "Opposition Seen within Germany," *New York Times*, June 18, 1942, 4.

13. Helen Lombard, "Goering Reported Looting Europe of Its Works of Art," *Evening Star*, August 4, 1942, 22.

14. Memo, R. L. Morgan to Mr. Ladd, June 23, 1942, UVAL, RMC, box 10.

15. Letter, Loren Johnston to E. J. Lincourt, July 8, 1942, GB.

16. Invitation from Loren Johnston, July 10, 1942, GB.

17. Letter, Loren Johnston to Heads of Departments, July 6, 1942, GB.

18. Sibold, "Report of the Axis Diplomats," 5.

19. Conte, *History of the Greenbrier*, 136.

20. "The White Passes," *Cumberland (MD) News*, August 27, 1942, 4.

21. Laurence Leonard, "Hospital at Resort Is a 'Shangri-La for Soldiers,'" *Richmond Times-Dispatch*, February 17, 1946, 49.

22. Memo, E. J. Lincourt to Mr. W. F. Kelly, September 1, 1942, NARA, RG85, box 2412.

23. Spencer D. Irwin, "Behind the Foreign News," *Cleveland Plain Dealer*, January 10, 1943, 22.

24. Kato, *Lost War*, 148.

25. Winston Churchill, BBC Home Service Broadcast, November 10, 1942.

22. VICHYSWAP

1. Helen Lombard, "Strained U.S.-Vichy Relations End French Embassy Parties," *Evening Star*, May 26, 1942, 10.

2. Hope Ridings Miller, "In the Capital Spotlight," *Washington Post*, October 22, 1942, B7.

3. Memo, William Bullitt, November 14, 1942, NACP, RG59, box 1842.

4. Memo, Breckinridge Long, November 15, 1942, LOC, BLP, box 206.

5. Lisbeth Solling, "Henry-Haye and Staff Leave Washington to Begin Internment," *Evening Star*, November 17, 1942, 1.

6. Tony Smith, "French May Stay at Hershey Hotel," *Evening Bulletin* (Philadelphia), November 13, 1942, 3.

7. Letter, Antonio Arrivabene to the Minister of Switzerland, Washington DC, March 10, 1943, NACP, SWPD, box 103.

8. Advertisement, *Evening Star*, May 14, 1933, 31.

9. Letter, Edwin Plitt to Breckinridge Long, December 21, 1942, LOC, BLP, box 206.

10. Letter, Charles Brousse to Cordell Hull, January 5, 1943, NACP, RG50, box 1846.

11. Memo, J. Edgar Hoover to Adolf Berle Jr., November 24, 1942, NACP, RG59, box 1842.

12. Theodore Draper, "Pro-Nazi Vichy 'Diplomats' Paid through Secret Funds," *PM Daily*, August 16, 1942, 3.

13. Memo, George Brandt to Breckinridge Long, November 16, 1942, NACP, RG59, box 1842.

14. Willard Wiener, "U.S. Frees All but 12 Interned Vichyites," *PM Daily*, March 12, 1943, 1.

15. Walter Winchell, "On Broadway," *Richmond Times-Dispatch*, October 15, 1943, 26.

16. Letter, Dorothy Thompson to Walter Winchell, November 3, 1946, Port Washington Public Library, http://www.pwpl.org/collections/sinclairlewis/association-letters.

17. Frank Whelan, "Vichy French Had War-Time Sojourn at Hotel Hershey," *Morning Call*, March 3, 1993, 15.

18. Abner Schreiber, interview with Paul F. Clark, March 19, 1979, Oral History Program, Japanese American Project, California State University, Fullerton, 1980, 32.

19. Letter, Dr. Constantine P. Faller to Dr. Wayne D. Stettler, January 22, 1943, NACP, RG59, box 1842.

20. Memo, R. L. Bannerman to Thomas Fitch, June 11, 1943, NACP, RG59, SWPD, box 122.

21. Letter, Edgar Innes to Thomas Fitch, February 25, 1943, NACP, RG59, SWPD, box 166.

22. Letter, Mrs. Rene Tanquerey to Julia, June 8, 1943, NACP, RG59, SWPD, box 122.

23. Memo, Breckinridge Long, June 22, 1943, LOC, BLP, box 206.

24. Memo, Edgar Innes to Thomas Fitch, March 10, 1943, NACP, RG59, SWPD, box 103.

25. Letter, Ned to R. L. Bannerman, March 2, 1943, NACP, RG59, SWPD, box 122.

26. Memo, Breckinridge Long, June 22, 1943, LOC, BLP, box 207.

27. Lovell, *Cast No Shadow*, 266.

28. Memo, Breckinridge Long, September 16, 1943, LOC, BLP, box 206.

29. Memo, Edwin Plitt, September 21, 1943, NACP, RG59, SWPD, box 122.

30. Memo, Edwin Plitt, October 16, 1943, NACP, RG59, SWPD, box 122.

31. Memo, Breckinridge Long, n.d., LOC, BLP, box 205.

32. Memo, Mr. Brandt to Breckinridge Long, December 13, 1943, LOC, BLP, box 205.

33. Memo, Albert E. Clattenburg Jr. to Mr. Long, November 17, 1943, LOC, BLP, box 205.

34. Memo, Edwin Plitt, February 8, 1944, NACP, RG59, SWPD, box 122.

35. "U.S. Diplomat Curt to Vichy Ex-Envoy," *New York Times*, March 10, 1944, 4.

## 23. LAST GRASP

1. "Jap Diplomats Held as Blue Chips of War," *Omaha World-Herald*, July 20, 1945, 18.

2. George Horne, "34,355 More Troops Back, Record for a Day in Port," *New York Times*, July 12, 1945, 3.

3. Letter, Commander James L. Gatins to Richard B. Russell, June 29, 1945, NACP, RG59, SWPD, box 3974.

4. Letter, U.S. Representative Harve Tibbott to Dean Acheson, July 10, 1945, NACP, RG59, SWPD, box 3974.

5. "Protests Use of Deluxe Hotel for Nippon Envoys," *Jersey Journal*, June 29, 1945, 18.

6. Letter, Effie Wertz, *Johnstown Tribune*, June 29, 1945.

7. Letter, Mrs. H. Haas, *Johnstown Tribune*, July 3, 1945.

8. Letter, J. D. Stevenson to VFW Post, July 23, 1945, NACP, RG59, SWPD, box 3974.

9. "Aren't We Being Too Nice?" *Johnstown Tribune*, July 27, 1945, RG59, SWPD, box 3974.

10. "Frankly, We Think They Are Nuts," *Johnstown Observer*, July 5, 1945, 1.

11. "State Dept. Men Call Meeting at Bedford Springs," *Bedford Gazette*, July 20, 1945, 1.

12. "Japs to Be Housed at Springs Called Blue Chips of War," *Bedford Gazette*, July 27, 1945, 1.

13. "For Americans' Sake," *Charleston Evening Post*, July 25, 1945, 4.

14. "Bedford Fair to Open Tuesday," *Bedford Gazette*, August 3, 1945, 1.

15. "Oshima and Aides Mum as Internees," *New York Times*, August 10, 1945, 16.

16. "Japs at Springs Remain Impassive at Surrender," *Bedford Gazette*, August 17, 1945, 1.

17. "The War Criminal Trials," *New York Times*, August 9, 1945, 20.

18. Charles Fenyvesi, "Japan's Unwitting D-Day Spy; Berlin Envoy's Intercepted Cables Provided Crucial Intelligence," *Washington Post*, May 26, 1997, A10.

19. Letter, Albert Clattenburg to Miss Ruckh, September 27, 1945, NACP, RG59, SWPD, box 3974.

20. Memo, Albert Clattenburg, September 11, 1945, NACP, RG59, SWPD, box 3974.

21. Jeremy Arnold, "Behind the Rising Sun," Turner Classic Movies, http://www.tcm.com/this-month/article/93529%7C0/Behind-the-Rising-Sun.html.

22. James Young, "Jap War Figures Loll Here in Ease," *Detroit Sunday Times*, September 9, 1945, 53.

23. Memo, Albert Clattenburg, October 9, 1945, NACP, RG59, SWPD, box 3974.

24. "Inside Story of Jap Hypocrisy Described," *Bedford Gazette*, December 21, 1945, 1.

25. "German Trial Set for Nov. 20 as Indictments Are Served," *New York Times*, October 20, 1945, 1.

26. "Sgt. Murphy, Jap Prisoner 3 Years, Here," *Bedford Gazette*, November 21, 1945, 1.

# BIBLIOGRAPHY

ARCHIVES AND MANUSCRIPT MATERIALS

Bath County Historical Society, Warm Springs, Virginia

Catholic University

    History Research Center and University Archives

District of Columbia Public Library

    Washingtoniana Collection

Franklin D. Roosevelt Presidential Library, Hyde Park, New York

    Adolph A. Berle, Jr. Papers

    Francis Biddle Papers

    Franklin D. Roosevelt Papers

    Frank A. Schuler, Jr. Papers

Georgetown University Library Archives

    Alfred M. Beck Collection

Greenbrier Hotel, White Sulphur Springs, West Virginia

    Historical Collection

Historical Society of Washington DC

    Clarence Hewes Scrapbook Collection

Library of Congress, Washington DC

    Cordell Hull Papers

    Breckinridge Long Papers

    Archibald MacLeish Papers

    Hope Ridings Miller Papers

National Archives and Records Administration, Washington DC

    Record Group 21, Records of the District Court for the District of Columbia

    Record Group 60, Department of Justice

    Record Group 85, Department of Naturalization and Immigration

National Archives and Records Administration, College Park, Maryland

    Record Group 59, State Department

    Record Group 131, Office of Alien Property

    Record Group 208, Office of War Information

    Record Group 226, Office of Strategic Services

Private Collection
    Charlie Spruks Papers
Syracuse University
    Dorothy Thompson Papers
University of Virginia
    Albert and Shirley Small Special Collections Library
    School of Law Library
        Roy L. Morgan Papers
Unpublished Memoirs
    Ingalls, Fay. *A Journal of the Sojourn of the Axis Diplomats at the Homestead.*
    Stocker, Frederick. *An Eye Surgeon Turns Diplomat.*
    von Boetticher, Hildegard. *Waiting for Letters.*
    von Gienanth, Ulrich. *Wedding and Internment.*


PERIODICALS

*American Foreign Service Journal*
Department of State Bulletin
*New York Times*
*Washington Post*
*Washington Evening and Sunday Star*


PUBLISHED WORKS

Abell, George, and Evelyn Gordon. *Let Them Eat Caviar.* New York: Dodge Publishing, 1936.

Acheson, Dean. *Present at the Creation: My Years at the State Department.* New York: Norton and Norton, 1969.

Argall, Phyllis. *My Life with the Enemy.* New York: Macmillan, 1944.

Arnecke, Else. *Mein Traum-Amerika.* Bremerhaven, Germany: German Emigration Center, 2002.

Baxa, Paul. "Capturing the Fascist Moment: Hitler's Visit to Italy in 1938 and the Radicalization of Fascist Italy." *Journal of Contemporary History* 42, no. 4 (April 2007): 227–42.

Beale, Betty. *Hello I'm Betty Beal.* Washington DC: Regnery Gateway, 1993.

———. *Power at Play.* Washington DC: Regnery Gateway, 1993.

Beasley, Maurine. *First Ladies and the Press: The Unfinished Partnership of the Media Age.* Evanston IL: Northwestern University Press, 2005.

———. *Women of the Washington Press: Politics, Prejudice, and Persistence.* Evanston IL: Northwestern University Press, 2012.

Beck, Alfred. *Hitler's Ambivalent Attaché: Friedrich von Boetticher.* Washington DC: Potomac Books, 2005.

Berle, Beatrice Bishop, and Travis Beal Jacobs, eds. *Navigating the Rapids, 1918–1971: From the Papers of Adolf A. Berle.* New York: Harcourt Brace Jovanovich, 1973.

Berridge, G. R. *Embassies in Armed Conflict.* New York: Bloomsbury Continuum, 2012.

*Bicentennial History of Bath County, Virginia.* Marceline MO: Heritage House Publishing, Bath County Historical Society, 1991.

Biddle, Francis. *In Brief Authority.* Garden City, New York: Doubleday, 1962.

Bliss, Edward, Jr. *Now the News: The Story of Broadcast Journalism.* New York: Columbia University, 1991.

Bloom, Vera. *There's No Place Like Washington.* New York: G. P. Putnam's Sons, 1944.

Bosworth, Allan R. *America's Concentration Camps.* New York: W. W. Norton, 1967.

Boveri, Margret. *Verzweigungen: Eine Autobiographie.* Munich, Zurich: R. Piper, 1977.

———. *Wir lügen alle: eine Hauptstadtzeitung unter Hitler.* Olten: Walter-Verlag, 1965.

Boyd, Carl. *Hitler's Japanese Confidant.* Lawrence: University Press of Kansas, 1993.

Briggs, Carol, ed. *Taken in Hong Kong: December 8, 1941.* Baltimore: Publish America, 2006.

Brinkley, David. *Washington Goes to War.* New York: Knopf, 1988.

Brown, Anthony Cave. *The Last Hero.* New York: Vintage Books, 1982.

Burdick, Charles. *An American Island in Hitler's Reich: The Bad Nauheim Internment.* Menlo Park CA: Markgraf, 1987.

Cameron, Norman, and R. H. Stevens, trans. *Hitler's Table Talk, 1941–44: His Private Conversations.* London: Weidenfeld and Nicolson, 1973.

Chapman, Michael E. *Arguing Americanism: Franco Lobbyists, Roosevelt's Foreign Policy, and the Spanish Civil War.* Kent OH: Kent State University Press, 2011.

Childs, Marquis W. *I Write from Washington.* New York: Harper and Brothers, 1942.

Clark, Delbert. *Washington Dateline.* New York: Frederick Stokes, 1941.

Clifford, J. Garry, and Masako Okura, eds. *The Desperate Diplomat: Saburo Kurusu's Memoir of the Weeks before Pearl Harbor.* Columbia: University of Missouri Press, 2016.

Compton, James V. *The Swastika and the Eagle.* Boston: Houghton Mifflin, 1967.

Conant, Jennet. *The Irregulars: Roald Dahl and the British Spy Ring in Wartime Washington.* New York: Simon and Schuster, 2008.

Concadi, Peter. *Hitler's Piano Player.* New York: Carroll and Graf, 2004.

Connell, Thomas. *America's Japanese Hostages.* Westport CT, London: Praeger, 2002.

Conner, Catherine. *From My Old Kentucky Home to the White House.* Lexington: University Press of Kentucky, 1999.

Contag, Kimberly, and James Grabowska. *Where the Clouds Meet the Water.* Portland: Inkwater Press, 2004.

Conte, Robert S. *The History of the Greenbrier.* White Sulphur Springs: The Greenbrier, 1998.

Cooke, Alistair. *The American Home Front, 1941–1942.* New York: Atlantic Monthly Press, 2006.

Corbett, P. Scott. *Quiet Passages.* Kent OH: Kent State University Press, 1987.

Daniels, Jonathan. *Frontier on the Potomac.* New York: Macmillan, 1946.

Dashiell, Samuel. *Victory through Africa.* New York: Smith and Durrell, 1943.

Davis, Kenneth S. *FDR: Into the Storm, 1937–1940.* New York: Random House, 1993.

*Documents on German Foreign Policy, 1918–1945.* Series D, 1937–1945, Vol. I–XIII, Washington DC, Government Printing Office.

Dodd, Martha. *Through Embassy Eyes.* New York: Garden City, 1940.

Doherty, William H. "Hawaii Looks Ahead." *American Foreign Service Journal* 17, no. 12 (December 1940): 661–65.

Downes, Donald. *The Scarlet Thread.* New York: British Book Centre, 1953.

Dunlop, Richard. *Donovan: America's Master Spy.* Chicago: Rand McNally, 1982.

Dunn, Susan. *1940: FDR, Wilkie, Lindbergh, Hitler—the Election amid the Storm.* New Haven: Yale University Press, 2013.

"Editor's Column." *American Foreign Service Journal* 17, no. 8 (August 1940): 438.

Elleman, Bruce. *Japanese-American Civilian Prisoner Exchanges and Detention Camps, 1941–45.* London: Routledge, 2006.

Eppinga, Jane. "Pearl Harbor, Japanese Espionage and Arizona's Triangle Ranch." *Prologue* 29 (Spring 1997): 43–50.

Farago, Ladislas. *The Game of the Foxes.* New York: David McKay, 1971.

Fischer, Klaus. *Hitler and America.* Philadelphia: University of Pennsylvania Press, 2011.

Friedman, Max Paul. *Nazis and Good Neighbors.* Cambridge: Cambridge University Press, 2003.

Fromm, Bella. *Blood and Banquets: A Berlin Social Diary.* London: Geoffrey Bles, 1943.

Gentry, Curt. *J. Edgar Hoover: The Man and the Secrets.* New York, Norton, 1991.

Gies, Joseph. *The Colonel of Chicago.* New York: E. P. Dutton, 1979.

Goldstein, Donald M., and Katherine Dillon. *The Pacific War Papers: Japanese Documents of World War II.* Washington DC: Potomac Books, 2004.

Görtemaker, Heike B. *Ein deutscher Leben: Die Geschichte der Margret Boveri, 1900–1975.* Munich: C. H. Beck Verlag, 2005.

Graham, Katherine. *Katherine Graham's Washington.* New York: Alfred A. Knopf, 2002.

Guthrie-Shimizu, Sayuri. *Transpacific Field of Dreams: How Baseball Linked the United States and Japan in Peace and War.* Chapel Hill: University of North Carolina Press, 2012.

Hagner, Helen Ray, ed. *The Social List of Washington.* Washington DC: Lewis Printing, 1938.

Haldane, R. A. *The Hidden War.* New York: St. Martin's Press, 1978.

Harmon, Dudley. "Diplomatic Dilemma." *American Foreign Service Journal* 17, no. 10 (October 1940): 566–67, 591.

Harris, Ruth. "The 'Magic' Leak of 1941 and Japanese-American Relations." *Pacific Historical Review* 50, no. 1 (February 1981): 77–96.

Hart, Scott. *Washington at War, 1941–1945.* Englewood Cliffs NJ: Prentice Hall, 1970.

Hastedt, Glenn P., ed. *Spies, Wiretaps, and Secret Operations: An Encyclopedia of American Espionage.* Santa Barbara: ABC-CLIO, 2011.

Herzstein, Robert. *Henry R. Luce*. New York: Charles Scribner's Sons, 1994.

Hill, Henrietta McCormick. *A Senator's Wife Remembers: From the Great Depression to the Great Society*. Montgomery: New South Books, 2010.

Hill, Max. *Exchange Ship*. New York: Farrar and Rinehart, 1942.

Hindley, Meredith. *Destination Casablanca* New York: PublicAffairs, 2017.

*History of the Bureau of Diplomatic Security of the U.S. Department of State*. Global Publishing Solutions, October 2011.

Hixson, Walter, ed. *The American Experience in World War II: Pearl Harbor in History and Memory*, vol. 4. New York: Routledge, 2003.

Hoge, Alice. *Cissy Patterson*. New York: Random House, 1966.

Hotta, Eri. *Japan 1941: Countdown to Infamy*. New York: Alfred Knopf, 2003.

Hull, Cordell. *The Memoirs of Cordell Hull*. New York: Macmillan, 1948.

Hyde, H. Montgomery. *Room 3603*. New York, Dell Publishing, 1962.

Ingalls, Fay. *The Valley Road*. Cleveland: World Publishing, 1949.

Israel, Fred, ed. *The War Diary of Breckinridge Long: Selections from the Years 1939–1944*. Lincoln: University of Nebraska Press, 1966.

Jeans, Roger. *Terasaki Hidenari, Pearl Harbor and Occupied Japan: A Bridge to Reality*. Lanham MD: Lexington Books, 2009.

Jeffreys, Diarmuid. *Hell's Cartel: IG Farben and the Making of Hitler's War Machine*. New York: Metropolitan Books, 2008.

Kashima, Tetsuden. *Judgment without Trial: Japanese American Imprisonment during World War II*. Seattle: University of Washington Press, 2003.

Kato, Masuo. *The Lost War: A Japanese Reporter's Inside Story*. New York: Knopf, 1946.

Keefer, Louis E. *Shangri-la for Wounded Soldiers*. Reston VA: Cotu, 1995.

Kennan, George. "Report, the Internment and Repatriation of the American Official Group in Germany—1941–1942." *American Foreign Service Journal* (September 1942): 473–77, 502–7.

Keyes, Frances Parkinson. *Capital Kaleidoscope*. Washington DC: Harper and Brothers, 1937.

Kiplinger, W. M. *Washington Is Like That*. New York: Harper and Brothers, 1942.

Klurfeld, Herman. *Behind the Lines: The World of Drew Pearson*. Englewood Cliffs NJ: Prentice Hall, 1968.

Kurth, Peter. *American Cassandra: The Life of Dorothy Thompson*. Boston: Little, Brown, 1990.

Kurusu, Saburo. *Treacherous America: Ambassador Kurusu's Address on Nov. 26, 1942 and Excerpts From The Roberts Report*. Tokyo: Japan Times, 1944.

Laing, Francis S. *Father Felix M. Kirsch, O.F.M. Cap.: A Sketch of His Life and Activities*. Pittsburgh: Catholic Home Journal, 1952.

Littell, Norman M. *My Roosevelt Years*. Seattle: University of Washington Press, 1987.

Lochery, Neill. *Lisbon: War in the Shadows of the City of Light, 1939–1945*. New York: PublicAffairs, 2011.

Lochner, Louis P., ed. *The Goebbels Diaries*. New York: Doubleday, 1948.

Lombard, Helen. *Washington Waltz*. New York: Alfred A. Knopf, 1941.

———. *While They Fought*. New York: Charles Scribner's Sons, 1947.

Lovell, Mary S. *Cast No Shadow*. New York: Pantheon Books, 1992.

Manning, Martin. *Historical Dictionary of American Propaganda*. Westport CT: Greenwood Press, 2004.

Martin, Ralph G. *Cissy: The Extraordinary Life of Eleanor Medill Patterson*. New York: Simon and Schuster, 1979.

———. *Henry and Clare: An Intimate Portrait of the Luces*. New York: G. P. Putnam's Sons, 1991.

Masterson, Daniel. *The Japanese in Latin America*. Champaign: University of Illinois Press, 2003.

Mauch, Christof. *The Shadow War against Hitler*. New York: Columbia University Press, 2003.

Mauch, Peter. *Sailor Diplomat: Nomura Kichisaburo and the Japanese-American War*. Cambridge MA: Harvard University Press, 2011.

Mayers, David. *FDR's Ambassadors and Diplomacy of Crisis*. New York: Cambridge University Press, 2013.

Melosi, Martin. *The Shadow of Pearl Harbor: Political Controversy over the Surprise Attack, 1941–1946*. College Station: Texas A&M University Press, 2000.

Miller, Edward. *Bankrupting the Enemy: The U.S. Financial Siege of Japan before Pearl Harbor*. Annapolis MD: U.S. Naval Institute Press, 2007.

Miller, Hope Ridings. *Embassy Row: The Life and Times of Diplomatic Washington*. New York: Holt, Rinehart and Winston, 1969.

Miller, James Edward. "Sforza in America: The Dilemmas of Exile Politics, 1940–43," *Journal of Modern Italian Studies* 15, no. 5 (November 2010): 678–92.

Olson, Lynne. *Those Angry Days*. New York: Random House, 2013.

*The Overseas Targets: War Report of the OSS*, vol. 2. New York: Walker, 1976.

Parmet, Herbert, and Marie Hecht. *Never Again: A President Runs for a Third Term*. New York: Macmillan, 1968.

Persico, Joseph E. *Edward R. Murrow: An American Original*. New York: McGraw-Hill, 1988.

———. *Roosevelt's Secret War: FDR and World War II Espionage*. New York: Random House, 2001.

Pogue, Forrest C. *George C. Marshall: Ordeal and Hope, 1939–1942*. New York: Viking Press, 1966.

Prange, Gordon W. *Dec. 7 1941: The Day the Japanese Attacked Pearl Harbor*. New York: McGraw-Hill, 1988.

Reed, Donald A. *Admiral Leahy at Vichy France*. Chicago: Adams Press, 1948.

Regnery, Henry. "At the Eye of the Storm: A Remembrance of Paul Scheffer." *Modern Age* 20, no. 1 (Winter 1976): 24.

Reiss, Curt. *The Nazis Go Underground.* Garden City NY: Doubleday, Doran 1944.

———. *Total Espionage.* New York,: G. P. Putnam's Sons, 1941.

Reynolds, David. *Lord Lothian and Anglo-American Relations, 1939–40.* New York: American Philosophical Society, 1983.

Ritchie, Donald. *Reporting from Washington.* Oxford: Oxford University Press, 2005.

Rogge, O. John. *The Official German Report: Nazi Penetration, 1924–1942.* New York: A. S. Barnes, 1961.

Russell, William. *Berlin Embassy.* New York: E. P. Dutton, 1940.

Ryback, Timothy W. *Hitler's First Victims.* New York: Alfred A. Knopf, 2014.

Sanders, Marion K. *Dorothy Thompson: A Legend in Her Time.* Boston: Houghton Mifflin, 1973.

Sayers, Michael, and Albert E. Kahn. *Sabotage! The Secret War against America.* New York: Harper and Brothers, 1942.

Scheffer, Paul. *Seven Years in Soviet Russia.* Westport CT: Hyperion Press, 1973.

———. *USA 1940: Roosevelt-America im entscheidungsjahr.* Berlin: Im Deutschen verlag, 1940.

Schwarz, Jordan A. *Liberal: Adolf A. Berle and the Vision of an American Era.* New York: The Free Press, 1987.

Seabury, Paul. *The Wilhelmstrasse: A Study of German Diplomats under the Nazi Regime.* Berkeley: University of California Press, 1954.

Simonds, James. "The Mechanized Force in Warfare." *American Foreign Service Journal* 18, no. 6 (June 1941): 305–8, 337.

"Slide, Togo, Slide." *Far Eastern Trade* 2, no. 3 (Fall 1940): 50–52.

Sperber, A. M. *Murrow: His Life and Times.* New York: Freundlich Books, 1986.

Stevenson, William. *A Man Called Intrepid.* New York: Harcourt Brace Jovanovich, 1976.

Sweeney, Michael S. *Secrets of Victory.* Chapel Hill: University of North Carolina Press, 2001.

Takeo, Iguchi. *Demystifying Pearl Harbor: A New Perspective from Japan.* Tokyo: International House of Japan, 2010.

Terasaki, Gwen. *Bridge to the Sun.* Chapel Hill: University of North Carolina Press, 1957.

Thompson, Laurence. *1940: Year of Legend, Year of History.* London: Collins, 1966.

Tolischus, Otto D. *Tokyo Record.* London: Manish Hamilton, 1943.

Trefousse, Hans L. "Failure of German Intelligence in the United States, 1935–1945." *Mississippi Valley Historical Review* 42, no. 1 (June 1955): 84–100.

Troy, Thomas F. *Wild Bill and Intrepid.* New Haven CT: Yale University Press, 1996.

Tully, Grace. *F.D.R., My Boss.* New York: C. Scribner's Sons, 1949.

Vining, Elizabeth Gray. *Quiet Pilgrimage.* Philadelphia: Lippincott, 1970.

Von Klemperer, Klemens. *German Resistance against Hitler.* Oxford: Clarendon Press, 1992.

Wallace, Max. *The American Axis.* New York: St. Martin's Griffin, 2003.

*War Comes to the U.S.—Dec. 7, 1941, The First 30 Hours.* As reported to the Time-Life-Fortune News Bureau from the U.S. and Abroad, 1942.

*War Report of the OSS.* New York: Walker, 1976.

*Washington City and Capital.* Washington DC: Works Progress Administration Federal Writers' Project, 1937.

*Washington Social Register.* New York, Social Register Association, 1941.

Weintraub, Stanley. *Pearl Harbor Christmas.* New York: Da Capo Press, 2011.

Winks, Robin. *Cloak and Gown: Scholars in the Secret War, 1939–1961.* New York: Quill William Morrow, 1987.

Ybarra, T. R. *Young Man of the World.* New York: Ives Washburn, 1942.

Yellin, Emily. *Our Mothers' War: American Women at Home and at the Front during World War II.* New York: Free Press, 2004.

# INDEX